Mies Reconsidered

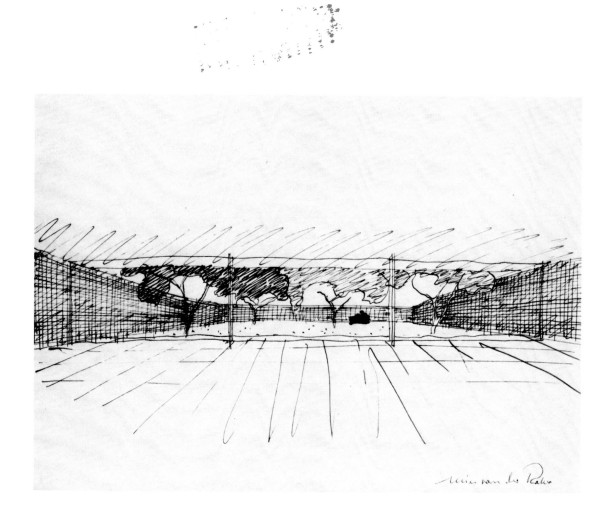

Mies Reconsidered: His Career, Legacy, and Disciples

Organized by John Zukowsky

With essays by
Francesco Dal Co, Peter Eisenman, Kenneth Frampton,
Christian F. Otto, David Spaeth, and Stanley Tigerman

Published by The Art Institute of Chicago
in association with Rizzoli International Publications, Inc.

This book and the exhibition it accompanies were made possible through the generous support of the Paul and Gabriella Rosenbaum Foundation. Additional support was provided by the John D. and Catherine T. MacArthur Foundation Special Exhibitions Grant.

The exhibition "The Unknown Mies van der Rohe and His Disciples of Modernism" was held at The Art Institute of Chicago from August 22 to October 5, 1986.

Published in the United States of America in 1986 by The Art Institute of Chicago and Rizzoli International Publications, Inc., 597 Fifth Avenue, New York, New York 10017

Library of Congress Cataloging in Publication Data
Mies reconsidered.
    Catalog of an exhibition.
    1. Mies van der Rohe, Ludwig, 1886-1969 – Exhibitions.   2. Mies van der Rohe, Ludwig, 1886-1969 – Criticism and interpretation.
3. Mies van der Rohe, Ludwig, 1886-1969 – Influence – Exhibitions.   I. Mies van der Rohe, Ludwig, 1886-1969.   II. Zukowsky, John, 1948-   .   III. Dal Co, Francesco, 1945-   .
NA2707.M5A4   1986a   720'.92'4   86-17303
ISBN 0-8478-0771-1 (Rizzoli)

Executive Director of Publications, The Art Institute of Chicago: Susan F. Rossen
Edited by Robert V. Sharp, Associate Editor
Designed by Michael Glass Design, Chicago
Typeset in Walbaum by AnzoGraphics Computer Typographers, Chicago
Printed by Eastern Press, New Haven, Connecticut

Cover illustration: Robert Damora, Autographed portrait photograph of Ludwig Mies van der Rohe, c. 1947 (see cat. no. 1).

Frontispiece: Ludwig Mies van der Rohe, Perspective sketch of a court house with garden sculpture, c. 1931-38 (see cat. no. 64).

Contents

1. Philip Johnson with Mies van der Rohe at the 1947 retrospective exhibition, The Museum of Modern Art, New York

2. Exhibition of Mies van der Rohe's work at The Art Institute of Chicago, 1968, installation designed by A. James Speyer

Foreword

The Art Institute of Chicago is pleased to publish this volume documenting an exhibition on Ludwig Mies van der Rohe and his disciples in the centennial year of Mies's birth, especially in view of our long association with this great architect and his enormous contribution to architecture in Chicago. When Mies van der Rohe first visited Chicago in 1937, he stopped at the Art Institute, then the home of the Architecture School of Armour Institute of Technology, to see drawings by Louis Sullivan in the collection of the Burnham Library of Architecture. When Mies was appointed the director of Armour's Architecture School, the Art Institute organized a month-long exhibition on Mies that opened on December 15, 1938. Although Mies had been included in the seminal exhibition on international architecture organized by Philip Johnson and Henry-Russell Hitchcock at the Museum of Modern Art, New York, in 1932, the Art Institute exhibition was his first one-man show in the United States. The installation consisted of drawings, twenty large photomurals, and four models, including one of the Tugendhat House, which was touted in the Institute's publications as Mies's most famous work. The exhibition was accompanied by a brief catalogue by John Barney Rodgers, the young American architect who had studied at the Berlin Bauhaus and joined Mies on the faculty at the Illinois Institute of Technology.

Since the 1930s, Mies has been the subject of many exhibitions, including the 1947 retrospective at the Museum of Modern Art in New York (fig. 1) and another large exhibition at the Art Institute in 1968 (fig. 2). In that year, A. James Speyer, the Art Institute's curator of twentieth-century art and one of Mies's former students, organized an international traveling exhibition of his mentor's work – a show that opened a bit more than a year before Mies's death on August 17, 1969. Art Institute staff member Katharine Kuh asked Mies to design a permanent gallery space in the museum for her "Gallery of Art Interpretation," a unique experimental approach to museum education. The first installation in this space was the interpretative exhibition "Who is Posada," which complemented the traveling show "Posada – Printmaker to the Mexican People," shown at the Art Institute in the spring of 1944. In addition, the Department of Prints and Drawings at the Art Institute acquired a number of Edvard Munch prints from Mies's collection, and the Institute's Department of Architecture has amassed a large number of Mies's architectural studies and sketches, principally through the generosity of Mr. Speyer. Other students and colleagues have been extremely generous in donating their own related drawings to our permanent collection. Together, the items on loan from private collections and those selected from our own holdings bring to light certain materials that might previously have been thought to be lost or destroyed, objects not represented in the archive Mies van der Rohe established at the Museum of Modern Art.

The essays in this book represent a variety of critical approaches to architecture, from the biographical and analytical treatments by David Spaeth, Kenneth Frampton, and Christian F. Otto, to the speculative and more metaphysical expositions by Francesco Dal Co, Peter Eisenman, and Stanley Tigerman. We hope that this volume, and the exhibition it accompanies, will be an important contribution to architectural scholarship in a way that serves as a fitting tribute to Mies van der Rohe and his colleagues, whose impact on urban environments here and throughout America is of undeniable importance. Finally, I wish to express our gratitude for the generous support received from the Paul and Gabriella Rosenbaum Foundation for both this catalogue and the exhibition.

James N. Wood, *Director*
The Art Institute of Chicago

Lenders to the Exhibition

The Arts Club of Chicago
Dr. h.c. Berthold Beitz, President of the
Alfred Krupp von Bohlen and Halbach
Foundation
Mr. Peter Carter
The Chicago Historical Society
Mr. George Danforth
Mr. Charles B. Genther
Mrs. Herbert S. Greenwald
Mr. David Haid
Hedrich-Blessing Photographers
Krefelder Kunstmuseen
Mr. Reginald Malcolmson
Metropolitan Structures
Mr. Peter Palumbo
The School of Social Service
Administration of the University of
Chicago
Mr. A. James Speyer
Staatliche Hochbauverwaltung,
Bundesrepublik Deutschland
Städtische Kunsthalle, Mannheim
Mr. Martin Werwigk, Architect of the
Landesbank, Stuttgart

Acknowledgments

The idea for an exhibition on Mies van der Rohe and his colleagues and disciples was one that grew over the past few years into this book and the show it represents. We are especially grateful to the Paul and Gabriella Rosenbaum Foundation for the funding given toward this undertaking. In this regard, Director James N. Wood was particulary supportive of our proposal to the foundation. Gabriella Rosenbaum and her daughter Edith Leonian were especially positive forces in the realization of this project. A. James Speyer, George Danforth, and other students and colleagues of Mies van der Rohe have been very generous in giving and lending objects to this exhibition.

In order to organize the exhibition of these items and to publish this catalogue, a number of people aided us as well, and I greatly appreciate their advice and assistance. The Art Institute's Committee on Architecture – David C. Hilliard (chairman), James N. Alexander, J. Paul Beitler, Edwin J. DeCosta, Stanley M. Freehling, Bruce J. Graham, Neil Harris, Carter H. Manny, Jr., Peter Palumbo, Mrs. J. A. Pritzker, and Stanley Tigerman – was eager to see the project reach a successful conclusion. Ines Dresel located and thoroughly researched the German items included in the show. Others who helped her are: Wolfgang Mayer of the Landesdenkmalant, Stuttgart; Wilfried Beck-Erlang; Brigitte Riedmüller and Wolfgang Riemann of Strähle Luftbild; Hermann Nägele, Staatliche Hochbauamt III, Stuttgart; Martin Werwigk of the Landesbank, Stuttgart; Albrecht Schatter of City-Fotolabor, Stuttgart; Dr. Manfred Fath, Director of the Kunsthalle, Mannheim; Liselotte Homering and Wilhelm Hermann, both of the Städtisches Reissmuseum; Drs. Julian Heynen and Gerhard Storck, both of the Museum Haus Lange – Museum Haus Esters, Krefeld; Drs. Berthold Beitz, Dominik Freiherr van König, and Renate Köhne-Lindenlaub, all from Krupp; Dr. Christian Wolsdorff of the Bauhaus-Archiv, Berlin; Christine Mengin, Paris; and Hansjörg Koch, Marianne Spathelf, Thomas and Jacqueline Dresel, and Erika Podday, all of whom lent additional assistance. Ines Dresel and Ariane Nowak, along with Robert V. Sharp of the museum's Publications Department, provided much of the translation for the project.

In America and England, the following people were most helpful in providing access to objects, information on the exhibited materials, photographs, and advice on the project: Claire Rose and Joseph Fujikawa of Fujikawa Johnson and Associates; Edward Duckett; George Danforth; David Haid; Dirk Lohan; Reginald Malcolmson; H. P. Davis Rockwell; A. James Speyer; Jerry Singer; Deborah Slayton; Patricia Scheidt, Director of the Arts Club of Chicago; Jack O. Hedrich of Hedrich-Blessing Photographers; Wim De Wit, Curator for the Architectural Collections, The Chicago Historical Society; Kevin Harrington and Rolf Achilles of the Illinois Institute of Technology; Mrs. Herbert S. Greenwald; William Pollak, Associate Dean, School of Social Service Administration of the University of Chicago; Bernard Weissbourd, Gerald Flegel, and Joseph Shure, all of Metropolitan Structures; Peter Carter and Dennis Mannina; Colin Morris of Presentation Unit, Ltd. Along with the staff of Presentation Unit, who came to Chicago to install the Mansion House Square models, we are grateful to Richard Tickner, who restored the model of the Arts Club, and to Pablo Diaz, who conserved and matted most of the drawings on exhibit. Further acknowledgment is owed to Suzette Morton Davidson and Phyllis Lambert, who, through the Sterling Morton Charitable Trust and the Canadian Centre for Architecture, respectively, underwrote the expenses of the oral history of Mies's students.

At the Art Institute, many staff members who participated in this project deserve special thanks: Pauline Saliga, the Assistant Curator of Architecture, Angela Licup, the department's secretary, and Luigi Mumford, our technical assistant; Betty Blum, Coordinator of the Oral History Project, Department of Architecture; Susan Godlewski, Associate Librarian, who selected Hilberseimer manuscripts and memorabilia for display in the Chicago installation; Mary Woolever, Architectural Archivist; Alan Newman, Executive Director of Photographic Services, and his staff; Douglas Severson of the Department of Photography, who conserved the Damora portrait of Mies, and who with David Travis, Curator of Photography, assisted in securing frames for the exhibit; Reynold Bailey, Coordinator of Art Installation; George Preston and Ron Pushka of the Physical Plant Department; Kathy Stover of Museum Archives; Ann Wassmann Gross, Graphic Designer, Marketing Services; and Mary Solt of the Registrar's Office.

Special mention should be made of those responsible for this catalogue. Robert V. Sharp, Associate Editor of Publications, devoted months to the editing and compiling of the material for this book. He and Sarah Mollman, Publications Intern, worked with great dedication and enthusiasm gathering photographic materials and supervising the book's production. Stanley Tigerman advised in the selection of authors, to all of whom we are especially grateful for their contributions. The book's handsome design is the work of Michael Glass Design, Chicago. Expert manuscript typing was provided by Cris Ligenza and Holly Stec Dankert of the Publications Department. Publications Intern Tom Fredrickson also provided assistance.

Finally, I would like to thank the following people for their efforts to make ours an international traveling exhibition and multilingual catalogue: Heinrich Klotz and Hans Peter Schwarz of the Deutsches Architekturmuseum, Frankfurt, who will exhibit this show and publish a German edition, and Alain Guiheux and Claude Evenou of the Centre Georges Pompidou, who will produce a French edition of this book.

John Zukowsky, *Curator of Architecture*
The Art Institute of Chicago

Mies van der Rohe in an apartment at 860 Lake Shore Drive, c. 1952

10

Ludwig Mies van der Rohe: A Biographical Essay

by David Spaeth

Mystification is simple; clarity is the hardest thing of all.
– Julian Barnes, *Flaubert's Parrot*

Thus far, I suppose, the reason for my research has been self-ish: I have wanted to understand Mies van der Rohe's life and his work for myself. This essay, drawing as it does directly from my previously published works,[1] offered me an opportunity to examine Mies's work with a more specific focus than a general work affords, for an audience already predisposed to understand more about him and his architecture. Over the years that I have studied Mies's work, re-examining it on numerous occasions, I have come to hold it in ever greater respect because it is concerned with eternal values, with eternal verities: 1) that technology is the most significant force animating this or any other age; it is the spirit of the times, the *Zeitgeist;* 2) that an architecture worthy of the name is an expression of this force; 3) that a clear structure, both physical structure as well as intellectual and spiritual structure, is the only means by which architectural space can be realized; and 4) that space exists as a continuum, rather than as something finite, of which architecture is, then, simply a more defined part (or phenomenon).

For the reader's benefit, I feel it useful (and necessary) to explain my background relative to Mies and to clarify my bias for his work. From 1959 to 1966, I studied architecture in the program Mies inaugurated in 1938 at what is now the Illinois Institute of Technology. Many of Mies's early students were my teachers; a few became close friends. I worked briefly in his office as a draftsman, making presentation drawings in ink on illustration board. In addition to going to school on a campus he designed, for a time I lived in one of his apartment buildings.

What follows is as much a part of what I have done, a record of my experiences, as it is an example of the understanding I am in the process of coming to. Like Julian Barnes, I would find it easier to mystify my subject than to make it clear. For me, however, the intention as well as the result of writing is clarity – to find essential order in what appears to be disor-der, to separate what is important from what is merely interesting, and to make all this accessible to a larger audience in the clearest manner possible. Clarity implies the "why" as well as the "how," and so biographical information has been woven into a narrative that also includes descriptions and explanations of Mies's work. Of necessity I have been selective; I trust that my selections illustrate the important achievements of Mies's life.

The Industrial Revolution had already reached a "critical mass" when a son, Maria Ludwig Michael, was born to Michael and Amalie (née Rohè) Mies on March 27, 1886, in Aachen (Aix-la-Chapelle), Germany. Their youngest child grew up in the modest circumstances one might expect from a family headed by a master mason. Michael Mies owned a small stone-cutting shop that produced essentially funeral monuments and carved fireplace mantelpieces. The family's humble origins and modest material means precluded an extensive education for any of their four children who survived early childhood.

Ludwig Mies (or simply Mies as he was almost universally known during his professional life) described his education as follows:

> I had no conventional architectural education. I worked under a few good architects; I read a few good books – and that's about it.[2]

While this may be true for his architectural education, such a laconic statement creates the impression that Mies had little formal education. Actually, he attended Aachen's *Domschule* (cathedral school) from age six to thirteen. After school and during holidays, he acquired a more pragmatic education working for his father and alongside his older brother, Ewald, in the family business. Here he learned firsthand the physical properties of stone and the value of fine materials and crafts-manship.

Michael Mies was an authoritarian figure very much in the tradition of the time. His relationship with his sons was not close, predicated as it was on discipline and hard work. Mies was closer to his older brother. Of his mother, little is known. We do know that because of her efforts and persistence, Mies attended mass daily, serving as a choir boy in the chapel built by the Emperor Charlemagne. In spite of his mother's obvious concern for his spiritual well-being, Mies was less interested in the celebration of the mass than he was in the space in which the celebration took place, the manner in which stones and mortar had been transformed into the chapel's structure. During mass he counted stones and traced mortar joints with his eyes. In his attempt to "read" and "see" the structure was the beginning of the idea which would later manifest itself in his architecture: that architecture is a language with a vocabulary and syntax in which the parts clearly relate to and grow out of the whole, a complete morphology.

In the ninth century, through Charlemagne's patronage, Aachen was endowed with a number of substantial buildings, which, in addition to the chapel, included a palace and a royal school. Further, the prosperity Aachen enjoyed in the mid- to late nineteenth century enhanced both the city's architectural fabric and its urban presence. The Carolingian structures, those from the Middle Ages, and the later ones survived until World War I, when many were destroyed. Years after his departure from Aachen Mies recalled them with deep feeling:

> I remember seeing many old buildings in my hometown when I was young. Few of them were important buildings. They were mostly very simple, but very clear. I was impressed by the strength of these buildings because they did not belong to any epoch. They had been there for over a thousand years and were still impressive, and nothing could change that. All the great styles passed, but . . . they were still as good as on the day they were built. They were medieval buildings, not with any special character, but they were really *built*.[3]

The origin of Mies's interest first in structure, later in architecture, was the result of native curiosity and ability combined with the influence of his parents and the impact of the built environment in which he was born and raised.

In 1899 at thirteen, Mies left the cathedral school to attend the *Spenrathschule,* a local trade school, for two years on a scholarship arranged by his father. During this time he was also apprenticed as a brick mason to a local builder. Like other apprentices, Mies was unpaid for his labors; however, since he and his family were in need of money, at fifteen he went to work for Max Fischer, whose firm specialized in stucco decorations for building interiors. Here Mies developed his emerging talent in freehand drawing. Years later he liked to recall with obvious relish but with mock horror how mornings in the firm were spent making full-size cartoons for elaborate Louis XIV plaster ornaments; afternoons were spent drawing the more restrained details of the Renaissance. Soon he was able to draw even the most difficult cartouches while looking in the opposite direction, a feat he performed to the delight and dismay of his fellow employees.[4]

With the obvious exception of drawing, designing stucco decorations developed neither Mies's intellect nor his other abilities. But the experience in Fischer's firm had given him an opportunity to see the work of local architects and to work closely with a few of them. After three years with Fischer, Mies took a job as a draftsman in an architect's office, and he began to learn those skills expected of an architect. One of the two firms by whom Mies was employed in Aachen (first by Goebbels [first name unknown], later by Albert Schneider) was doing work in association with a firm from Berlin. Through this association, Mies met Dülow (first name unknown), an architect from Königsberg, whose background, experience, and interests were broader and more sophisticated than Mies's. It was Dülow who encouraged Mies to take a job in Berlin, an event which, like an earlier one in Schneider's office, would make a profound and lasting impression. As Mies described it:

> On the day I was assigned a drawing table at Schneider's, I was cleaning it out when I came across a copy of *Die Zukunft* [The Future], a journal published by Maximilian Harden, plus an essay on one of Laplace's theories. I read both of them and both of them went quite over my head. But I couldn't help being interested. So every week thereafter, I got hold of *Die Zukunft* and read it as carefully as I could. That's when I think I started paying attention to spiritual things. Philosophy. And culture.[5]

What reading *Die Zukunft* did for his mind, Berlin did for his career. Within two years of his arrival and after being employed in the office of Bruno Paul, an architect/designer known for his appreciation of wood and his sensitive use of this material, Mies received his first independent commission, the Riehl House (fig. 1), Berlin-Neubabelsberg (1907). Its design, in the neighborhood's prevailing tradition of domestic architecture, was a simple mass with a pitched roof. What distinguished it from adjacent residences was the way Mies sited the house, taking advantage of the slope, as well as his evident concern for proportion and detail. One critic wrote shortly after the house was completed: "The work is so faultless that no one would guess it is the first independent work of a young architect."[6]

A frequent guest in the Riehl home was Adele Auguste Bruhn (1885-1951), daughter of a well-to-do industrialist. During one of many social events at the Riehls', she and Mies were

1. Riehl House, Berlin-Neubabelsberg, 1907

introduced. After a two-year courtship, they were married on April 10, 1913, taking up residence in Lichterfelde, an upper-middle-class suburb of Berlin. Sometime later, Mies attached a variation of his mother's maiden name, Rohè, to his surname, becoming Ludwig Mies van der Rohe. In German "mies" means "out of sorts, poor, bad, or wretched." It would not do for Mies to have his professional accomplishments linked to or, for that matter, hindered by a surname which carried with it the connotation of wretchedness. Despite this somewhat pretentious gesture, he was always known as Mies to friends and associates, as well as to students. Outside the members of his immediate family, no one called him Ludwig; and he was addressed as Ludwig Mies van der Rohe only on the most formal occasions and then by people who did not know him well. When the quality of his work was universally recognized, "Miesian," ironically enough, came to be accepted as a synonym for precision, refinement, and elegance.

At various times between 1908 and 1911, Mies was employed in Peter Behrens's office, first working under Behrens's assistant, Walter Gropius, and later with Behrens directly. Early in this century, Behrens was Europe's most influential architect and a leading member of the *Schinkelschule,* followers or students of Karl Friedrich Schinkel, Germany's leading neoclassical architect of the nineteenth century, whose influence persisted well into the twentieth. Just prior to Mies's arrival in the office, Behrens had been appointed "artistic advisor" to the AEG (Allgemeine Elektricitäts-Gesellschaft, the German equivalent of the General Electric Company). In that capacity, Behrens designed everything from the company's logo, its letterhead, and the light fixtures it manufactured, to the factories in which the products were made.

The aesthetic breadth of Behrens's work is represented by two of the buildings on which Mies worked during his tenure there: the AEG Turbine Factory (1909), Berlin, a building clearly a product of the Industrial Revolution, and the German Embassy (1911-12), St. Petersburg, Russia, a building as sober in its neoclassicism as anything by Schinkel. For the embassy, Mies served as project manager, making frequent trips to the site to inspect the work. It was in this capacity that he incurred Behrens's wrath on two occasions, signaling the tension resulting directly from Mies's emerging need for personal as well as artistic freedom. As project manager, Mies negotiated substantially lower bids from local contractors than Behrens had been able to do. Mies further angered Behrens by allowing a conversation on the embassy's interiors to be overheard by a journalist who then published the descriptions without formal governmental approval.[7] Their professional relationship, however, was terminated by an event of more relative

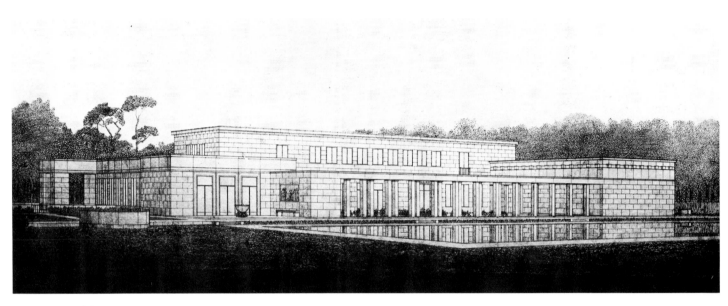

2. Kröller-Müller House project, Wassenaar, The Netherlands, 1912, perspective drawing

importance than lower building costs or an unauthorized news story: it was terminated by a commission.

In 1911, Mr. and Mrs. A.G. Kröller of the Netherlands contacted Behrens regarding a house they wished him to design. Although Mies was already occupied with the embassy, Behrens appointed him his chief assistant on the Kröller house. The building Behrens proposed to the client was neoclassical in spirit as well as detail. It was, however, an ungainly structure, awkward in its massing. Mrs. Kröller (née Müller) was uneasy about Behrens's design. To allay her concerns, Mr. Kröller had a full-size model of the proposed design constructed from wood covered with canvas on the actual site. Mrs. Kröller remained unconvinced. Nonetheless, she had been impressed with Mies and invited him to The Hague to prepare a second design for the residence, which was to be something of a museum because of their extensive collection of paintings. Mies's proposal (fig. 2) for the Kröller House (or Kröller-Müller House as it is often called) was also constructed full-size on the site; like Behrens's design, his too was rejected. Yet, Mies's solution was simpler and more elegant than Behrens's, manifesting the strength and clarity of Schinkel's work through assimilation rather than imitation.

Returning to Berlin, Mies re-established an independent architectural practice, designing a number of quite competent houses for upper-middle-class families. While these clearly demonstrated Mies's understanding and appreciation of Schinkel's principles, they presaged his later rejection of neoclassicism's forms and details: to continue working in the neoclassical idiom meant rejecting what he had learned in Behrens's office about an architecture appropriate to and expressive of an industrial-technological age. Mies was unable to do this. Furthermore, there were two other individuals whose work influenced Mies to make the break with neoclassicism: Frank Lloyd Wright and Hendrik Petrus Berlage.

A major exhibition of Wright's work was mounted in Berlin in 1910. This exhibition coincided with Wasmuth's publication of a portfolio of Wright's drawings and early works. Thirty years after the exhibition, Mies described the impact Wright's work had on European architects (including himself) in 1910:

The work of this great master presented an architectural world of unexpected force, clarity of language and disconcerting richness of form. Here, finally, was a master-builder drawing upon the veritable fountainhead of architecture; who with true originality lifted his creations into the light. Here again, at long last, genuine architecture flowered. The more we were absorbed in the study of these creations, the greater became our admiration for his incomparable talent, the boldness of his conceptions and the independence of his thought and action. The dynamic impulse emanating from his work invigorated a whole generation. His influence was strongly felt even when it was not actually visible.[8]

During his stay in the Netherlands, Mies saw a number of Berlage's buildings. One in particular, the Amsterdam Stock Exchange (1909), was especially important. During an interview a year before his death, Mies described the impact of Berlage's work:

> Berlage's Exchange had impressed me enormously [in 1911]. Behrens was of the opinion that it was all passé, but I said to him: "Well, if you aren't badly mistaken." He was furious; he looked as if he wanted to hit me. What interested me most in Berlage was his careful construction, honest to the bones. And his spiritual attitude had nothing to do with classicism; nothing with historic styles altogether. After Berlage, I had to fight with myself to get away from the classicism of Schinkel.[9]

In a sense, it was a fight Mies never really won. He could not unlearn the lessons, the greater truths, of Schinkel's work; and like Schinkel's mature work, Mies's is characterized by a profound concern for detail and craftsmanship *at all levels.* Mies's buildings, like Schinkel's, sit their sites well; and there is about their work the quality of being timeless, of belonging to no particular epoch. Yet their buildings are the very expression, the embodiment and reflection, of their respective eras. This is the quality that makes them so great.

Mies's independent work prior to and immediately following the end of World War I clearly demonstrates the combined influences of Behrens and Schinkel. It took longer for Mies to assimilate or synthesize the lessons of Berlage's and Wright's work. It is not until the early 1920s that the strength of Berlage's ideas about structure and the spatial openness of Wright's architecture manifest themselves in five seminal projects by Mies. Of Behrens, Berlage, Schinkel, and Wright, it can be said that their collective influence awakened in Mies an idea about architecture appropriate to an industrial-technological age, one that Mies clearly articulated in his work and which none of his "mentors" had achieved individually.[10]

These five seminal projects, two Glass Skyscrapers (1921-22), the Concrete Office Building (1922-23), the Concrete Country House (1923), and the Brick Country House (1923-24), were unique in conception, definition, and expression. In their originality and sensitivity to line, value, and tex-

ture, Mies's drawings of them are like the buildings they represent: no disparity between *idea* and *technique* exists. The architectural philosophy which unifies them derives from the thesis that is fundamental to understanding Mies's architecture: technology is the most significant force animating architecture and society in the twentieth century. Mies expressed this in his "Address to Illinois Institute of Technology" (1950): "Wherever technology reaches its real fulfillment, it transcends into architecture."[11] But as early as 1924, Mies had postulated the relationship between architecture and its place in time:

> Greek temples, Roman basilicas and medieval cathedrals are significant to us as creations of a whole epoch rather than as works of individual architects. Who asks the names of these builders? Of what significance are the fortuitous personalities of their creators? Such buildings are impersonal by their very nature. They are pure expressions of their time. Their true meaning is that they are symbols of their epoch.

> Architecture is the will of the epoch translated into space. Until this simple truth is clearly recognized, the new architecture will be uncertain and tentative. Until then it must remain a chaos of undirected forces. The question as to the nature of architecture is of decisive importance. It must be understood that all architecture is bound up with its own time, that it can only be manifested in living tasks and in the medium of its epoch. In no age has it been otherwise.[12]

It is this transcendent, almost metaphysical attitude toward technology which sets Mies's work apart from that of his contemporaries. This quality, this attitude, was only suggested in his houses dating from the mid- to late 1920s, i.e., the Wolf House, Guben, Germany (1925-27); and the Esters and Hermann Lange houses, Krefeld, Germany (1927-30). While technology began to reveal itself in his 1927 Apartment Building at the Weissenhofsiedlung (figs. 3, 4), Stuttgart, where the choice of a steel skeleton structure allowed apartment plans to be changed by individual residents, it is not present in his earlier Municipal Housing Development on Berlin's Afrikanischestrasse (1926-27), a solid brick-bearing wall structure. It was in his German Pavilion for the Barcelona International Exposition of 1929 that Mies was first able to achieve in three dimensions the transcendent quality of technology.

Except to accommodate a reception for the King and Queen of Spain during the fair's opening ceremonies, the Barcelona Pavilion (fig. 5), as the German Pavilion is more commonly known, had no real building program. In its precision and refinement, however, the pavilion was an apotheosis of German craftsmanship and industry, a metaphor for technology in the twentieth century. It represents two important de-

3. Weissenhofsiedlung, Stuttgart, September 21, 1927 (cat. no. 13)

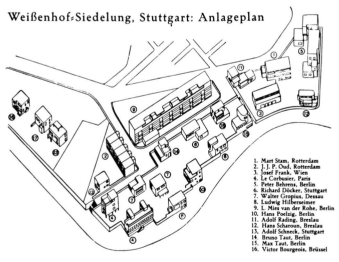

Weißenhof=Siedelung, Stuttgart: Anlageplan

1. Mart Stam, Rotterdam
2. J. J. P. Oud, Rotterdam
3. Josef Frank, Wien
4. Le Corbusier, Paris
5. Peter Behrens, Berlin
6. Richard Döcker, Stuttgart
7. Walter Gropius, Dessau
8. Ludwig Hilberseimer
9. L. Mies van der Rohe, Berlin
10. Hans Poelzig, Berlin
11. Adolf Rading, Breslau
12. Hans Scharoun, Breslau
13. Adolf Schneck, Stuttgart
14. Bruno Taut, Berlin
15. Max Taut, Berlin
16. Victor Bourgeois, Brüssel

4. Weissenhofsiedlung, plan of buildings and their architects

velopments in Mies's work: the "free plan" and the concept of a spatial continuum. In the free plan, walls are liberated from their load-bearing function, becoming light screens or planes in space. As Mies described it, "One evening as I was working late on [the pavilion] I made a sketch of a free-standing wall, and I got a shock. I knew that it was a new principle."[13] The other idea that Mies articulated in the Barcelona Pavilion is that space exists as a continuum. It has the characteristic of a Möbius strip in that as one moved through the pavilion, what was at first perceived as inside was, in actuality, outside. Floor, roof, and wall planes do not contain the space but define it, clarifying and articulating its existence. As a result, the pavilion exhibits profound structural clarity; simultaneously, it is spatially ambiguous. As if to further exploit this ambiguity, Mies had the pavilion's two pairs of doors – those traditional architectural elements that separate inside from outside – removed for the official photographs. Only the surface-mounted hinges in the floor and ceiling betrayed their existence (fig. 6).

Critics of the exposition's architecture were confused by Mies's use of traditional and rich materials (Roman travertine, Tinian and vert antique marbles, and tawny onyx) in a "modern" building. Only one contemporary critic, Helen Appleton Read, understood Mies's intent. Writing for an American audience, Read commented, "Of nations represented, Germany alone symbolized her industrial and cultural status in a modern gesture." On Mies's work specifically, she wrote:

Radical rationalist that he is, his designs are governed by a passion for beautiful architecture. He is one of the very few modern architects who has carried its theories beyond a barren functional formula into the plastically beautiful. Material and space disposition are the ingredients with which he gets his effect of elegant serenity. Evincing in his work a love for beautiful materials and textures he emphasizes this predilection.[14]

The chair Mies designed for use by the visiting royalty, the now famous Barcelona chair (see cat. no. 125), became a twentieth-century icon. Like his earlier designs for tubular metal furniture, the MR chairs (see cat. nos. 49, 50), it exploited the principle of the cantilever. Other architects and designers had tried to accomplish this, but Mies was the first one to do so successfully. Mies's professional associate, Lilly Reich, is credited with suggesting the use of caning in the MR chair (fig. 7) and roll-and-pleat cushions for the MR lounge chair.[15]

Mies's application of his ideas about space and structure was first made in a pragmatic and utilitarian manner, albeit a poetic one, in the Tugendhat House (1928-30). The lower level of this two-story residence – the major living space – was treated as one large "room." The space was subdivided by a freestanding onyx plane and a curved wall of ebony, further articulated as to function by furniture designed by Mies, the

5. Barcelona Pavilion, 1929

6. Barcelona Pavilion, interior with doors in position

7. MR Chair, 1927

ment of products (e.g., utilitarian goods, furniture, wall coverings, fabrics, jewelry, etc.) appropriate to an industrialized society. After Mies's appointment, the changing political climate exacerbated the problems that had beset the school from its founding. Mies was forced to close the Dessau Bauhaus in 1932, reopening it a few months later in Berlin as a private academy. In August 1933, the school was again forced to close; this time, however, it was a decision of the faculty. The conditions the National Socialists demanded for reopening would have ended the school's pedagogic freedom, its ideological integrity.

For the next few years, Mies built very little. He survived on the royalties from the sale of his furniture and a few commissions, while occupying himself with a series of projects. Of particular interest are the numerous studies he made for one-story houses with walled courtyards (see cat. nos. 39, 41). These not only indicate a genuine interest in this building type, but also suggest his gradual and unconscious retreat and isolation from life in the Third Reich. As the National Socialists moved to control all aspects of life in Germany, clients were discouraged or openly prevented from retaining architects and designers identified with the modern movement, Mies included. At the official level, Mies's work was judged incompatible with the goals and values of the Third Reich. According to one account, Mies's 1934 proposal for the German Pavilion for the 1935 International Exposition, Brussels, was rejected by Hitler himself.[17] Another competition entry, this one in 1933 for the Reichsbank headquarters building, Berlin, suffered a similar fate, despite the fact that Mies's solution was among the six finalists.

Gradually, Mies was forced to accept the fact that to preserve his artistic freedom, to say nothing of his life, he would have to leave Germany.[18] Several possibilities arose. First, in 1936, Dean Joseph Hudnut of Harvard interviewed him in Berlin for the professorship of design at the university's College of Architecture. (Gropius was also under consideration and was ultimately appointed.) Then, at Philip Johnson's suggestion, Mies was invited to the United States in 1937 by Mr. and Mrs. Stanley Resor. The Resors wished to have Mies design a guest house on property they owned near Jackson Hole, Wyoming. During Mies's visit to the States, John A. Holabird, a prominent Chicago architect and chairman of the search committee for a director of architecture at the Armour Institute of Technology, invited Mies to Chicago to discuss his possible appointment. The directorship was offered; Mies accepted. He returned to Germany, quickly settled his affairs, and sailed for the United States early in 1938.

It would appear predestined that Mies should move to Chicago. In Chicago he found a tradition of building, of architectural expression, similar to his own. Although he would not directly admit to it, he was clearly aware that "the Chicago School" emerged from the same technological roots and con-

placement of which assumed an architectural significance. In the Tugendhat house, traditional definitions of "room" and "function" lost their meaning. "Space" and "functional" took on new meaning. As critics attempted to evaluate Mies's work, the limitations of their traditional criteria and definitions became clear. In answer to the question, "Can one live in the Tugendhat House?" even the idea of living changed, and took on new meaning. The architect and critic Ludwig Hilberseimer, who would become Mies's associate at the Bauhaus and later at IIT, understood Mies's work with great insight. For him, the importance of this residence was not that it was a specific solution to a specific set of programmatic requirements. Rather, the importance of the house lay in the "manner [the architectural means] in which the specific solution had been achieved [realized]."[16] It was its general, rather than its specific, nature that appealed to Hilberseimer.

In 1930, at the height of his European career, Mies was appointed the third and, as it turned out, the last director of the Bauhaus in Dessau, which had been founded in 1919 by Walter Gropius. The philosophy of education at the Bauhaus was predicated on two important and interrelated concepts: artists are craftsmen to whom the responsibility for fulfilling specific aesthetic and functional needs has been given; and the machine, the primary tool for production, when combined with techniques for mass production, is to be used in the develop-

cerns for structural clarity and expression as did his own work. When asked if the Chicago School had been a direct influence on his architecture, he remarked somewhat dryly:

> I really don't know the Chicago School. You see, I never walk. I always take taxis back and forth to work. I rarely see the city.[19]

When pressed by another interviewer about the work of Frank Lloyd Wright and Louis Sullivan, Mies responded:

> We would not do what Sullivan did. We see with different eyes, because it is a different time. Sullivan still believed in the façade. It was still the old architecture. He did not consider that just the structure could be enough. Now we would go on for our own time – and we would make architecture with structure only. Likewise with Wright. He was different from Sullivan, and we for equal reasons are different from Wright.[20]

At Armour, Mies was given a free hand to develop a new curriculum for architectural education. As the curriculum evolved over the next two decades during which he served as director, it became clear that Mies's and the faculty's approach to education was not a transplanted version of Gropius's Bauhaus. Chicago was not Weimar, Dessau, or Berlin; the new situation demanded a different approach.[21]

Within two years of Mies's arrival in Chicago, Armour merged with Lewis College, another of Chicago's educational institutions, to form the Illinois Institute of Technology (IIT). Dr. Henry Heald, first president of IIT, asked Mies to prepare a master plan for the new campus and to undertake the design of all the new facilities. It was an almost unprecedented opportunity. Not since the University of Virginia had one architect been permitted to design an entire campus. In some ways, Mies's task was more complicated than Thomas Jefferson's. Unlike the virgin Charlottesville site, the IIT campus had to be painstakingly inserted into an already existing neighborhood on Chicago's South Side (see fig. 8). By 1940 this once fashionable residential neighborhood had become a slum. Seeing the new campus as a means whereby the neighborhood might be revitalized, Heald urged IIT's trustees to begin the acquisition of land for the new campus adjacent to Armour's existing facilities. Over 3,000 individual parcels were to be assembled. Because acquisition would be a long, slow process, Mies had to think in terms of decades, not years, for the realization of his campus plan.

8. IIT Campus, Chicago, 1941, photomontage of final plan

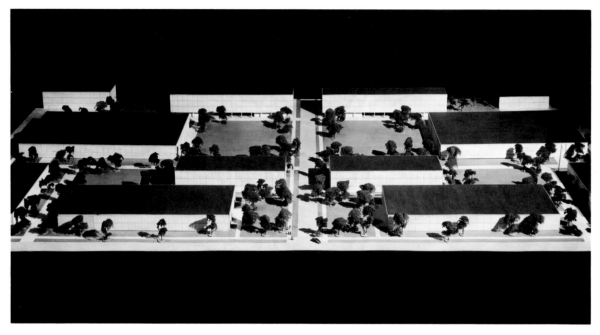

9. IIT Campus, 1939-41, early model

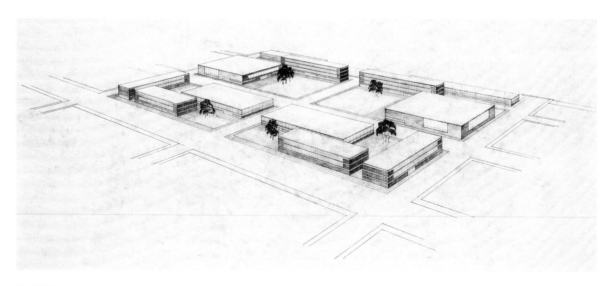

10. IIT Campus, c. 1939, preliminary design

Mies's analysis of the problem suggested the use of a module or ordering device that would be flexible enough to accommodate classrooms, laboratories, and offices; such a repetitive module could be both economical and efficient in terms of construction. Together, these conditions suggested the use of skeleton construction because of the resultant flexibility and economy; but only rarely had such a structure been clearly expressed. For Mies, "Only a clear expression of the structure could give us a solution that would last."[22] When challenged that the earlier buildings for the campus might become outmoded, Mies responded:

> I was not afraid of that. The concept would not become outmoded for two reasons. It is radical and conservative at once. It is radical in accepting the scientific and technological driving and sustaining forces of our time. It has a scientific character, but it is not scientific. It uses technological means, but it is not technology. It is conservative as it is not only concerned with a purpose but also with a meaning, as it is not only concerned with a function but also with an expression. It is conservative as it is based on the eternal laws of architecture: Order, Space, Proportion.[23]

It was a characteristic of his preliminary master plans for the campus, as well as the final one, that the principal buildings were arranged symmetrically about an axis which runs across the site's least dimension (see figs. 9, 10). Individual buildings, however, relate asymmetrically to each other. In the IIT plan there is never that sense of enclosure or containment so characteristic of the collegiate quadrangle. There is always the feeling of the existence of a spatial continuum, "the greater whole," to use Mies's term. Buildings, open spaces, and the existing street pattern are treated as a unified idea, not disparate parts.

The first of the new structures constructed on the campus, the Minerals and Metals Research Building (1942–43), demonstrated the appropriateness of Mies's vision for the campus, his mastery of architecture, as well as his understanding of a larger order. The laboratory has an exposed skeletal structure of painted steel, infilled, both inside and out, with either factory glazing or brick. Shortly after the building was completed, one writer said that the building was "of special interest to those who have followed modern architecture, for it is the first executed work of Mies van der Rohe in this country. Like his earlier buildings in Europe, the laboratory is distinguished by the utmost simplicity in the handling of structure and materials."[24]

Within the discipline he had accepted for the campus buildings, Mies refined a new grammar whose vocabulary consisted of rolled angles, channels, I-beams, and H-columns. In doing so, he made a new language for architecture from the means which society had placed at his disposal. As Philip

Johnson commented on Mies's proposed Library and Administration Building (1944), "Steel is joined to steel or steel to glass or brick with all the taste and skill that formerly went into the chiseling of a stone capital or the painting of a fresco."[25]

As World War II ended, Mies emerged as a figure whose work would shape the course of American and world architecture for the next two decades. An exhibition of Mies's work mounted in 1947 at the Museum of Modern Art in New York firmly established his reputation. Yet, one senses from a contemporary review of the exhibition that Mies's architecture was not universal in its appeal:

> Mies appeals to an almost rarified type of intellect.... There is something quite terrifying in [his] work, a clarity and decisiveness of vision that brushes aside everything that is not brutally honest, and ends up with a monumental simplicity.[26]

11. Mies van der Rohe with Farnsworth House model at the 1947 Museum of Modern Art exhibition

Similar criticism leveled against Mies's Farnsworth House in Plano, Illinois, has not stood the test of time. Elizabeth Gordon, editor of *House Beautiful* magazine, interviewed the owner of the house, Dr. Edith Farnsworth, a member of the faculty of Northwestern University Medical School. Gordon reported that she had "talked with a highly intelligent, now disillusioned, woman who spent more than $70,000 building a one-room house that is nothing but a glass cage on stilts."[27] Dr. Farnsworth, unhappy about the costs, sued Mies for breach of contract – and lost. She chose to vent her disappointment in a

12. Left to right: Lora Marx, Waltraut Mies van der Rohe, and Bruno Conterato on the terrace of the Farnsworth House, Plano, Illinois, 1951

public forum, and Gordon used her article to compose a diatribe against modern architecture.

With the Farnsworth House (1946-51), Mies radically changed the nature, the idea, of domestic architecture. The house consists of roof and floor planes supported on eight exposed steel H-columns (fig. 11); a glass-enclosed living space contains only two fixed elements. The larger of the two, the service core, contains the kitchen, two bathrooms, mechanical equipment room, and the fireplace. By its asymmetrical placement in the enclosed space, this core defines areas for living, dining, and sleeping. The other element, the wardrobe unit, screens the living from the sleeping area and vice versa. Because this site is periodically subject to flooding, Mies elevated the floor of the house five feet three inches above grade (figs. 12, 13). The prosaic result of this is protection of the living volume from inundation; the poetic effect is a lightness and sense of space only suggested in his earlier work. And to further heighten our awareness of the existence of architectural space, Mies cantilevered roof and floor planes beyond the columns at either end of the structure (fig. 14). The finishes are simple, muted, and understated throughout. Everywhere the sensitive and discerning eye of a master craftsman has seen that no detail distracts from an appreciation of the house as an artifact integral with its environment. As architect Craig Ellwood, a member of the jury of the American Institute of Architects, said when the Farnsworth House was awarded the AIA's prestigious "25-Year Award" in 1981, "All we need to do is compare the Farnsworth House with the nonsense we now call architecture. The truth about truth is it *is*."[28]

Sometime in 1946, during the early stages of the Farnsworth commission, Mies met Herbert S. Greenwald (fig. 15). This meeting and their subsequent friendship had a profound and lasting impact on American urban architecture. Despite the thirty-year difference in their ages, the two men shared a deep interest in philosophy, which Greenwald had studied at the University of Chicago. In their respective ways, Mies and Greenwald were idealists: Mies wanted to raise architecture to the realm of art; Greenwald wanted to build the finest architecture within the framework of twentieth-century technology and the economic realities of construction and land development costs. When Greenwald was killed in an airplane crash in 1959, Mies commented, "Herbert Greenwald began with an idea of the social consequences of his work; along the way he also discovered that he was a very good business man."[29]

13. Farnsworth House in flood conditions, 1950-51

14. Farnsworth House

15. Herbert S. Greenwald, c. 1954, with model of 900-910 Lake Shore Drive Apartments

16. 860-880 Lake Shore Drive Apartments, Chicago, 1948-51

17. Opposite page: Lafayette Park, Detroit, 1963

After their initial endeavor, the Promontory Apartments, Chicago (1946-49), Mies began work on two other highrise apartment buildings at 860 and 880 Lake Shore Drive, Chicago (1948-1951). These were the first highrise apartments in the world constructed almost solely in glass and steel (fig. 16). They ushered in a new age of architecture and established with their level of finishes a new standard of excellence for the apartment building. Surprisingly, on a per-square-foot basis, they cost between five and ten percent less than more conventional apartments being constructed in Chicago at the same time.[30]

While building other apartments together (900-910 Lake Shore Drive, the Esplanade Apartments [1953-56], among the many), Mies and Greenwald, along with Mies's friend and IIT teaching colleague, Ludwig Hilberseimer, began work on two important urban renewal projects: Lafayette Park (1955-63), Detroit, also known as the Gratiot Park Development, and the Hyde Park Plan (1956), Chicago. Although only the Lafayette Park project was realized, both plans posited ways in which the quality of life might be improved and enhanced through the re-formation of the urban fabric. For Lafayette Park this meant constructing new one- and two-story row houses and highrise apartment buildings adjacent to a green space running the length of the development (fig. 17). Automobiles were confined to the perimeter, thereby maintaining a pedestrian precinct free from intrusion by the automobile. With its open spaces and extensive landscaping, Lafayette Park offers the best of suburban living in proximity to the center of Detroit. The plan for Hyde Park differs from that for Lafayette Park in terms of application rather than principle. Habitable housing was to remain, and the gridiron pattern of streets was to be modified, routing automobile traffic around, rather than through, residential areas. Buildings beyond rehabilitation were to be replaced with new construction consisting of row houses and tall apartment buildings, thereby freeing land for development as parks and green space.

Two-dimensionally, the arrangement of interconnecting green spaces in Lafayette Park recalls Mies's earlier plan for the IIT campus, where buildings define but do not enclose exterior spaces. The inclusion of tall apartment buildings with the lower row houses creates a vertical spatial richness not found at IIT. From a distance, Alfred Caldwell's landscaping gives the impression that tall buildings exist amid a verdant, naturalistic landscape. While the history of urban renewal in the United States is littered with failures, Lafayette Park is not one of them. It is a model for future urbanization; it is a new structure predicated on human values, accommodating but not dominated by the automobile.

Lafayette Park and the plan for Hyde Park clearly reveal Mies's application of the idea of a spatial continuum to planning problems. But it was not until completion of S.R. Crown Hall (1950-56) on the IIT campus that Mies was able to articu-

18. Crown Hall, IIT, Chicago, 1950-56, under construction

19. Crown Hall

late a similar idea, the "universal" space, in a large, clear-span building (figs. 18, 19). His earlier proposal for the German Pavilion for the International Exposition in Brussels, suggested, through its sheer size, that he was already considering the architectural implications of large-span buildings as early as 1934. The Concert Hall project of 1942 is another example. The pavilion for Brussels was to be a large, columned hall; the Concert Hall had a two-way steel structure of heroic proportions. Crown Hall's span of 120 feet is more modest; it is large enough to suggest the possibilities for a universal space, one which might accommodate a variety of activities or functions while giving physical form to the existence of a spatial continuum. The culmination of his development of long-span structures would have been the Chicago Convention Hall (1953-54). As proposed, this colossal structure was 720 feet square (fig. 20). A series of steel Pratt-type trusses, 30 feet deep and spaced 30 feet apart, spanned the 500,000 square foot column-free space. With the Convention Hall project, Mies's spatial typology was complete; but realization of a universal space approaching the Convention Hall's scale was only achieved with completion of the New National Gallery, Berlin, West Germany (1962-67).

The museum's program called for a large space for temporary exhibition of paintings and sculpture, as well as smaller galleries for display of the permanent collection. These galleries are located in a base or plinth containing offices, storage and work spaces, and service facilities. Upon this the major glass-walled exhibition space is located (fig. 21). As a result, the New National Gallery stands apart, isolated from the other buildings in West Berlin's Kemperplatz culture center. It is very special in its isolation: a temple to art on a man-made acropolis. Of all Mies's buildings, the New National Gallery is his most classical in feeling and his most timeless.

With the New National Gallery, Mies culminated his exploration and refinement of the idea of a universal space. In a similar manner, the Seagram Building (1954-58) in New York is his summary statement concerning the tall office building. The search for the quintessential expression of this building type began, for Mies, in 1921, with the first of two projects for glass skyscrapers. Writing in 1922, he described the problems associated with this building type:

> Skyscrapers reveal their bold structural pattern during construction. Only then does the gigantic steel web seem impressive. When the outer walls are put in place, the structural system, which is the basis of all artistic design, is hidden by a chaos of meaningless and trivial forms. When finished these buildings are impressive only because of their size; yet they could surely be more than mere examples of our technical ability. Instead of trying to solve the new problems with old forms, we should develop the new forms from the very nature of the new problems.[31]

20. Convention Hall project, Chicago, 1953-54, photomontage

21. New National Gallery, Berlin, 1962-67

Critic and historian Lewis Mumford likened the Seagram Building (fig. 22) to a "pyramid – a building that exhausts every resource of art and engineering to create an imposing visible effect out of all proportion to its human significance."[32] Arguably, the contribution to the quality of urban life the Seagram Building and its plaza make to New York City is more important than its symbolic value. By setting the building back from Park Avenue and preserving nearly half the site as open space, Mies avoided the numerous setbacks required by the building code. The resulting plaza appears more spacious than it is because Mies incorporated streets and sidewalks beyond the property lines into the overall composition. Neither the benches paralleling Fifty-second and Fifty-third streets, nor the low steps along Park Avenue are visually strong enough or tall enough to contain the plaza's space. Only the tightly packed buildings on the other sides of the streets do that.

Although the Seagram Building is a monument to an idea first and to a corporation second, it makes a gesture to the quality of urban life in an age not given to such gestures. As a cab driver said, looking first at Lever House across the street and then at the Seagram Building: "The copy doesn't usually get built before the original, does it?"[33] And the plaza, a magnanimous, costly, and wonderfully humane gesture, became one of the city's most successful open spaces. In 1984, the AIA bestowed its "25-Year Award" on the Seagram Building, formally recognizing Mies's contributions to architecture and urban design. In their remarks, the jury commented that "25 years after its completion, it fully retains its enduring vitality and quiet beauty, and still holds a special place in the hearts and imaginations of all who see it, work in it, and admire its brilliant solution to the still-vexing problems of urban design."[34] For Mies, though, the Seagram Building was not essentially different from his other work:

> My approach to the Seagram Building was no different from that of any other building that I might build. My idea, or better "direction," in which I go is toward a clear structure and construction – this applies not to any one problem but to all architectural problems which I approach. I am, in fact, completely opposed to the idea that a specific building should have an individual character. Rather, I believe that it should express a universal character which has been determined by the total problem which architecture must strive to solve.
>
> On the Seagram Building, since it was to be built in New York and since it was to be the first major office building which I was to build, I asked for two types of advice for the development of the plans. One, the best real estate advice as to the types of desirable rental space and, two, professional advice regarding the New York Building

Code. With my direction established and, with these advisers, it was then only a matter of hard work.[35]

Mies's career reached its zenith with the completion of the Seagram Building. Among the many honors accorded him (fig. 23) Mies, in 1960, was awarded the AIA's Gold Medal for distinguished service to the profession. A year earlier the Royal Institute of British Architects awarded him its highest award, also a gold medal. As much for his contributions to American architecture as for his work on the Federal Center

23. Right to left: Mies van der Rohe with Henry Heald, president of IIT, and Raymond J. Spaeth, vice-president for business affairs, at the presentation of an Honorary Doctor of Engineering Degree from the *Technische Hochschule*, Karlsruhe, Germany, at the Ambassador East Hotel, Chicago, 1951

(1959-73), in Chicago, President John F. Kennedy selected Mies as a recipient of the Presidential Medal of Freedom in 1963. This last award was an especially fitting tribute from a man who valued achievement and excellence to one whose work came to symbolize the best of postwar architecture in the United States. Mies was deeply moved by this; it indicated appreciation of his work by an audience not limited to his fellow professionals.

22. Opposite page: Seagram Building, New York, 1954-58

In 1958 at the height of his professional career (fig. 24), Mies resigned as director of IIT's School of Architecture. Fully expecting to be retained as architect for the campus, Mies wanted to be relieved of his administrative responsibilities to devote all his energies to his practice. IIT took this opportunity to sever its relationship with Mies completely. Despite protest from the architectural community – including Le Corbusier – another firm of architects was retained to continue work on the campus. Privately angered and disappointed by this action, publicly Mies was philosophical: he would have to be satisfied with an incomplete work, an unfinished idea.

With a patience that by now had become legendary, Mies pursued his vision of architecture, heedless of critics and fashion. His work became the standard against which the work of other architects was measured, but many architects found Mies's standards too exacting. Chicago architect Harry Weese noted, "Mies continues to be our conscience, but who listens to his conscience these days."[36] Aware of this attitude but, at the same time, perplexed by it, Mies observed: "I get up. I sit on the bed. I think, 'What the hell went wrong? We showed them what to do.'"[37] As Mies aged, critical reaction to his work became increasingly more negative. Shortly before his death, Mies addressed this attitude towards his work:

> I have tried to make an architecture for a technological society. . . . I have wanted to keep everything reasonable and clear – to have an architecture that anybody can do. . . . Some people say that what I do is "cold." That is ridiculous. You can say that a glass of milk is warm or cold. But not architecture. You can be bored with architecture, however. I am bored by this stuff I see around me. It has no logic or reason.[38]

That Mies valued logic and reason should surprise no one. Together with technology they played major roles in the determination and articulation of his work. Logic and reason are aspects of order, as he stated almost fifty years ago in his inaugural address as director of architecture at Armour Institute of Technology:

> Every decision leads to a special kind of order.
>
> Therefore we must make clear what principles of order are possible and clarify them.
>
> Let us recognize that the mechanistic principle of order overemphasizes the materialistic and functionalistic factors in life, since it fails to satisfy our feeling that means must be subsidiary to ends and our desire for dignity and value.
>
> The idealistic principle of order, however, with its overemphasis on the ideal and the formal, satisfies neither our interest in simple reality nor our practical sense.

24. Mies van der Rohe at the opening of Cullinan Hall, Museum of Fine Arts, Houston, October 1958

We shall emphasize the organic principle of order as a means of achieving the successful relationship of the parts to each other and to the whole.

And here we shall take our stand.

The long path from material through function to creative work has only a single goal: to create order out of the desperate confusion of our time.

We must have order, allocating to each thing its proper place and giving to each thing its due according to its nature.

We would do this so perfectly that the world of our creations will blossom from within.

We want no more; we can do no more.

Nothing can express the aim and meaning of our work better than the profound words of St. Augustine: "Beauty is the splendor of truth."[39]

Mies died in Chicago on August 17, 1969. With dignity and little ceremony, he was buried in Graceland Cemetery, the final resting place of many of Chicago's architectural leaders, including Louis Sullivan. On October 25, 1969, relatives and friends, associates and former students, gathered in Crown Hall on the IIT campus for a memorial service. Those present did not mourn his death as much as they expressed their sense of loss his death precipitated. Three years earlier in a ceremony at which Mies received the Gold Medal from the Chicago Chapter of the American Institute of Architects, John Entenza, then director of the Graham Foundation for Advanced Studies in the Fine Arts and a long-time friend of Mies's, delivered a moving tribute to Mies that could well serve as a eulogy:

> Under any other circumstances, and with any other man, one would approach this kind of thing with the recitation of a long list of accomplishments. But, after all, we are, hopefully, professionals, and I assume knowledgeable concerning the backgrounds of our great men. And besides, a recitation of victories, not only professional, but moral, might only shame those of us who had done so little.
>
> It is all very well to honor a great man for the things he has accomplished, but it is also very important to be aware of the victories that were not entirely won: to know of the moments of despair when he must have been borne down by the small, incomprehensible stupidities of those who possess power without mind, vanity without substance, and greediness without honest appetite. . . .
>
> Mies van der Rohe has accomplished so much so quietly that one wonders why other men have had to be so

> noisy. In my experience, I have never known silence to become so overwhelmingly monumental and charged with meaning.
>
> In a day tending toward conformity, he remains a most singularly literate man, with an uncompromising rationale, who is too often embarrassingly too close to the truth. He has never asked to be forgiven anything. And he has shown an Olympian indifference to anyone who would presume to make excuses for him.
>
> He has refused to speak when in his judgment there was nothing to say, and has permitted very little to be put down by way of characterizing material. I am sure, however, that there have been wonderful evenings of great unrecorded conversations, awash in a river of double Gibsons, and lost forever.
>
> More than any major figure that I have known or heard of, he demands to be judged by his work alone. There are no ill-conceived judgments or personal furies, no public tantrums, little evidence of tension and doubt with which to mark out the geography of this great man.
>
> Certainly there have been several of his contemporaries who have made great thunders as shakers and movers, in order to get the best out of their moment in time and place, but none of them have done all that he has done with his very special kind of surprisingly illuminating light; with a logic at the highest level of meaningful truth, with an intellect making its points so precisely that it develops a most exciting progression from fact to the inevitabilities of reason, and on to the exquisite balance of poetry.
>
> And so, if I were a native of Chicago, I would want him to know how grateful my city is for his having lived here, and for being not only a man fulfilling its greatest tradition, but also for being its architectural conscience.[40]

It was characteristic of Mies's approach to architecture to reduce every building problem to its clearest, most elemental form or state. These same qualities of economy and visual integrity, however, offer the greatest impediment to understanding and appreciating his work, because he wrote little, and made fewer public statements to illuminate his work. We are, therefore, compelled to look at the work itself, to see its inner structure, and to seek those ideas and values that characterize the work and embody the times. As a result, interest in Mies's work will continue beyond that generated by the celebration of the centennial of his birth – beyond the last speech, the last exhibition, the last review. Because he was so personally exacting, his work so uncompromising, he continues to be the architectural conscience of the age. This alone makes him worthy of our continued attention.

Notes

1. David Spaeth, *Ludwig Mies van der Rohe: An Annotated Bibliography and Chronology* (New York, 1979), and *Mies van der Rohe* (New York, 1985).

2. Katherine Kuh, "Mies van der Rohe: Modern Classicist," *Saturday Review* 48 (January 23, 1965), p. 61.

3. Peter Carter, "Mies van der Rohe, An Appreciation on the Occasion, This Month, of His 75th Birthday," *Architectural Design* 31 (March 1961), p. 97.

4. "Mies Speaks. 'I Do Not Design Buildings, I Develop Buildings,'" *Architectural Review* 144 (December 1968), p. 451.

5. Excerpt from a documentary film, *Mies van der Rohe,* directed by Mies's daughter, Georgia van der Rohe, sponsored by Knoll International and Zweites Deutsches Fernschen, Mainz, and produced by IFAGE Filmproduktion, Wiesbaden. English version, 1979. (German version, 1980.)

6. "Architekt Ludwig Mies: Ville Des . . . Prof. Dr. Riehl in Neubabelsberg," *Moderne Bauformen* 9 (1910), pp. 42-48.

7. Franz Schulze, *Mies van der Rohe: A Critical Biography* (Chicago, 1985), p. 58.

8. Philip Johnson, *Mies van der Rohe* (New York, 1953), p. 201.

9. "Mies Speaks" (note 4), p. 451.

10. As André Gide observed: "Influence creates nothing. It awakens."

11. The text of this address is included in Johnson (note 8), p. 203.

12. Ludwig Mies van der Rohe, "Baukunst and Zeitwille," *Der Querschnitt* 4 (1924), pp. 31-32.

13. "6 Students talk with Mies," *North Carolina University State College of Agriculture and Engineering, School of Design Student Publication* 2 (Spring 1952), p. 28.

14. Helen Appleton Read, "Germany at the Barcelona World's Fair," *Arts* 16 (October 1929), pp. 112-113.

15. Mies's relationship with Reich was complex. She was the only woman with whom he had a professional, working relationship. Evidence suggests that sometime shortly after he separated from his wife, he and Reich became lovers, late in 1927 or early in 1928. Her influence on his work is limited to encouraging Mies's use of color and texture in his interiors and on his furniture. Prior to the start of their relationship, Mies was an established architect and he had essentially articulated his architectural principles. Reich's influence was less in the realm of ideas than in the application of those ideas which, prior to 1927, Mies was only beginning to address – color, texture, and furniture.

16. "Die Bewohner des Hauses Tugendhat äussern sich," *Die Form* (November 15, 1931): 439.

17. Sergius Ruegenberg, "Ludwig Mies van der Rohe (1886-1969)," *Deutsche Bauzeitung* 103 (September 1, 1969), p. 660.

18. According to Howard Dearstyne, one of Mies's Bauhaus students, Mies's arrest was imminent (in 1937). For a discussion of the problems that beset the Bauhaus, see Howard Dearstyne, *Inside the Bauhaus* (New York, 1986).

19. Kuh (note 2), p. 61.

20. Carter (note 3), p. 115.

21. Ludwig Mies van der Rohe, [Address to the 37th Association of Collegiate Schools of Architecture Annual Convention], *Journal of Architectural Education* 7 (Summer 1951), pp. 13-15.

22. Carter (note 3), p. 105.

23. Ibid.

24. "Metals and Minerals Research Building, Illinois Institute of Technology," *Architectural Forum* 79 (November 1943), p. 88.

25. Johnson (note 8), p. 138.

26. Peter Blake, "Ludwig Mies van der Rohe," *Architectural Forum* 87 (November 1947), p. 132.

27. Elizabeth Gordon, "The Threat to the Next America," *House Beautiful* 95 (April 1953), p. 129.

28. "Mies' Farnsworth House Wins 25 Yr. Award," *American Institute of Architects Journal* 70 (March 1981), p. 9.

29. Peter Carter, *Mies van der Rohe at Work* (New York, 1973), p. 177.

30. "Apartments . . . ," *Architectural Forum* 92 (January 1950), p. 70.

31. Ludwig Mies van der Rohe, "Hochhausprojekt für Bahnhof Friedrichstrasse in Berlin," *Frühlicht* 1 (1922), p. 122.

32. Lewis Mumford, "Skyline: The Lesson of The Master," *New Yorker* 34 (September 13, 1958), p. 148.

33. From a classroom discussion (1966) with Myron Goldsmith, then Adjunct Professor of Architecture at IIT.

34. "The Seagram Building Wins AIA's 25-Year Award," *American Institute of Architects Journal* 74 (April 1984), p. 15.

35. Carter (note 29), pp. 61-62.

36. "Affirming the Absolutes," *Time* 87 (February 11, 1966), p. 58.

37. Quoted in Arthur Drexler, *Transformations in Modern Architecture* (New York, 1979), p. 4.

38. "Affirming the Absolutes" (note 36), p. 61.

39. Johnson (note 8), pp. 199-200.

40. John Entenza, "The Presentation of the Gold Medal, Chicago Chapter, American Institute of Architects" (Graham Foundation for Advanced Studies in the Fine Arts, 1966), pp. 1-4.

Modernism and Tradition in the Work of Mies van der Rohe, 1920-1968

by Kenneth Frampton

Adolf Loos once said that an architect is a mason who has learned a little Latin. Like Loos, whose father was a stonemason and who trained as a mason himself before studying architecture, Mies van der Rohe had a traditional craft background, serving a three-year apprenticeship with his stonemason father from the age of fourteen onwards. It was surely in his father's yard in Aachen that he first acquired the profound respect for masonry which was to remain with him throughout his life. Mies also worked briefly as a stucco designer before leaving Aachen for Berlin in 1905 at the age of nineteen, and these apprenticeships were to set the pattern for those he would subsequently serve in Berlin, first with an architect specializing in timber construction, and then with the famous designer Bruno Paul.

In his pursuit of the various crafts, from masonry to plasterwork, from carpentry to cabinetwork, Mies established himself early on as an architect-builder with an emphasis on the intrinsic sensibility of craftwork, rather than on aesthetic speculation. From this training Mies developed a bias that artistic expression should arise directly from the exercise of craft. His initial attitude was thus patently antithetical to that which the Viennese historian-theorist Alois Riegl had referred to as *Kunstwollen* or "will to form."[1] Mies's expressive reserve was already evident in his first independent work, the pseudo-Arts and Crafts Riehl House, built in Berlin-Neubabelsberg when he was twenty-one years old. This restraint characterized his work until the outbreak of World War I, as is demonstrated by the simplified, neoclassical projects and commissions he designed and carried out between 1912 and 1914, including the seminal Kröller-Müller House project of 1912.

One may argue that apart from his stint with Bruno Paul, who was ultimately a traditional craft-designer, Mies was not to come in contact with the practice of artistic will or *Kunstwollen* until he started to work for Peter Behrens in 1908. Mies, up to this date, had patently received a traditional rather than a Jugendstil design orientation. Only when he entered Behrens's office did he finally come into contact with artistic voli-

tion *in se*. In this case, it was grounded in the sobrieties of romantic classicism as exemplified by the work of Karl Friedrich Schinkel, whose architecture profoundly influenced Behrens.

From this point of view, Mies's role as assistant and site architect for Behrens's German Embassy in St. Petersburg of 1912 must have been both a decisive and an ambiguous experience. While the finest workmanship and highest craft values were maintained throughout, and the spirit and even the letter of Schinkel were perennial references, the overall work was nonetheless willful in the extreme. It was, in many ways, an exercise in *atectonic* form, as the bonded Ashlar columns of the peristylar stone façade announce all too clearly. While something of Behrens's heavy Schinkelschüler manner is evident in Mies's Bismarck Memorial design of 1910, and even in the more delicate profiles of the Kröller-Müller House, Mies seems to have distanced himself from the more willful side of Behrens's artistic personality. Despite their compositional picturesqueness, these early Miesian works are classical down to the last reduced cornice and simplified stylobate.

This, then, was Mies van der Rohe in 1914: a tyro architect of romantic classical persuasion. But he was to emerge from the crucible of World War I with a very different artistic and emotional outlook. Although his initial classical formation was to remain, the discipline of tectonic form on the one hand and the modern "will-to-form" on the other would henceforth provide the characteristic tension in his work. This schism began in the decisive four or five years of Mies's activity following the end of World War I. Mies resorted to classical metaphor throughout his life, all the while playing with the bourgeois associations that accompany the use of rich and handcrafted material, yet he did not engage again in the specific syntax of Western classicism. It was as though the reality of modernization and the traumatic experience of the first industrialized war had decisively transformed the members of his generation. While something often remained in his domestic work of the organic plan-form of the Arts and Crafts house,

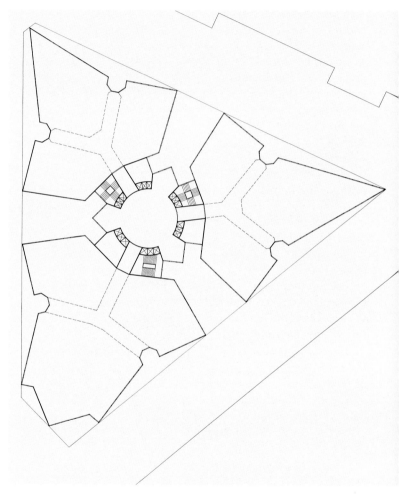

1. Friedrichstrasse Office Building project, Berlin, 1921, perspective drawing

2. Friedrichstrasse Office Building project, plan

particularly in his brick *Landhäuser* of the 1920s, Mies immersed himself immediately in the postwar avant-gardist climate, focusing, above all, on the "otherness" of modern material, as though the emerging radicalism of the epoch stemmed as much from the facts of technical and material transformation as from the promise of political and cultural revolution.

The ultimate modern building material, in this regard, was mass-produced high-quality glass. It had already been celebrated as a millenial material prior to the war by those who participated in the so-called utopian correspondence of the Glass Chain, particularly in the writings of Paul Scheerbart and the visionary works of Bruno Taut and his quasi-expressionist associates of *Die Gläserne Kette*.[2] The two canonical works in this volatile development were Scheerbart's utopian prose-poem *Glasarchitektur* and Taut's Glass Pavilion realized for the Deutscher Werkbund exhibition mounted in Cologne during the first year of the war. As Scheerbart wrote in his proto-Dadaist, aphoristic style: "Building in brick only does us harm. Colored glass destroys hatred. . . . We feel sorry for brick culture. Without a glass palace life becomes a burden."[3] This vision of a world made pure and whole again through the unprecedented construction of an entirely glass environment that could achieve both apparent *and* actual dematerialization was the expression of a new spirituality. This, one may argue, linked the mystical, part secular, part religious cult of *Die Gläserne Kette* to the redemptive visions of romantic classicism in its prime. Scheerbart's statement evokes the landscape paintings of Caspar David Friedrich: his spires, crosses, and mizzenmasts rising like auspicious mirages from the heights of the forest, or suspended like ominous ghosts on the wastes of a hostile sea.

Mies's Glass Skyscraper models of the 1920s were certainly spectral, given the medieval Golem-like background against which they were invariably photographed. This dematerialized, ominous, "almost nothing" (*beinahe nichts*) quality could be found in his 1921 competition entry for the Friedrichstrasse Office Building (fig. 1). Mies's large wax-crayon perspective of this building presents us, like glass itself, with the paradox of a *materialized demateriality* or a *dematerialized materiality*, depending, quite literally, on the point of view. The case can be made that, from this point onwards, the evident tension in Mies's work between classicism (or tradition) and modernism was partially balanced and possibly resolved in this paradox. An almost featureless high-rise structure faced entirely in glass was completely radical sixty years ago, as was Mies's perception of the material as a substance in a phenomenological sense. He regarded glass as a new material which had to be approached through an inversion of the traditional modes of architectural conception and perception. This, no doubt, accounts for the unusual terms in which he chose to describe the prismatic plan (fig. 2) of his Friedrichstrasse proposal:

> I placed the glass walls at slight angles to each other to avoid the monotony of over-large glass surfaces.
>
> I discovered by working with actual glass models that the important thing is the play of reflections and not the effect of light and shadow as in ordinary buildings.
>
> The results of these experiments can be seen in the . . . scheme [for the Glass Skyscraper project (figs. 3, 4)]. . . . At first glance the curved outline of the plan seems arbitrary. These curves, however, were determined by three factors: sufficient illumination of the interior, the massing of the building viewed from the street, and lastly the play of reflections.[4]

A similarly subtle intention is surely present in Mies's Seagram Building, New York, realized in 1958. Brown-tinted glass is now used in conjunction with bronze fenestration in such a way as to suggest that it is of the same opaque and fractious nature as stone. Mies's intention is perhaps clearer in the all-metal maquette of the building, made during the penultimate design phase, where the curtain-wall glazing is represented by metal sheets as though it were of the same material order as the metal mullions and spandrels. Here stone, glass, and metal are rendered as a sublime equivalence.

There was an almost imperceptible yet significant shift in Mies's sensibility during the following year, when, having made contact with the editors of the magazine *G: Material zur elementaren Gestaltung* – namely, with El Lissitzky, Hans Richter, and Werner Graeff – he moved closer to a Dadaist-Constructivist view of the modern world, where all that remained of culture and life was the radical artistic "otherness" of modern technology and material form.

This cold assertion of the almost abrasive facticity of modern industrial building methods, and the alienated conditions of metropolitan life which they dispassionately serve to accommodate and even to engender, is all too evident in Mies's Concrete Office Building proposal of 1922 (fig. 5), first published in the inaugural issue of *G* in the following year. The text that accompanied this publication, with its rhetorical and typographic stress on the words *Beton, Eisen,* and *Glas* (concrete, iron, and glass) expressed the laconic objectivity of Mies's incipient materialism. Once again, as in the earlier glass skyscrapers, it was the material-technique and not the form or the function which carried the essential architectural statement. Aside from the slight widening of the end structural bay in order to introduce a subtle classical "coda" in an otherwise uninflected intercolumnar grid, composition, as such, was given little import in the design. The same must be said of

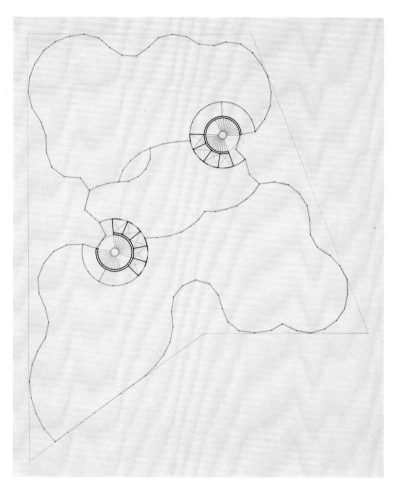

3. Glass Skyscraper project, 1922, model

4. Glass Skyscraper project, plan

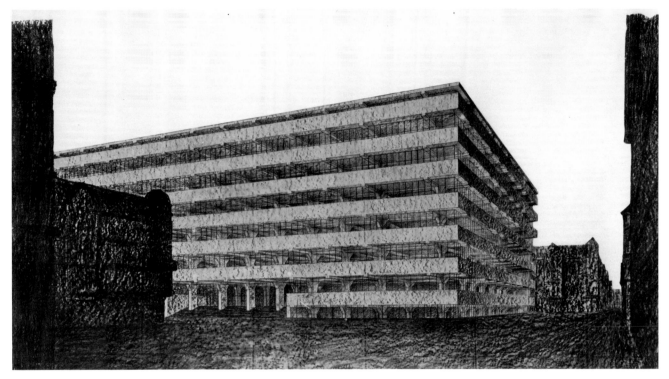

5. Concrete Office Building project, 1922-23, perspective drawing

the supposedly functional criteria employed, particularly when one realizes that the occupants of the building would not have been able to see out. That the form was to stand as a polemical representation of the obduracy and power of cantilevered concrete construction is evident from the text which accompanied its initial publication.

> The materials: concrete, steel, glass.
>
> Reinforced concrete structures are skeletons by nature. No gingerbread. No fortress. Columns and girders eliminate bearing walls. This is skin and bone construction.
>
> Functional division of the workspace determines the width of the building: 16 meters. The most economic system was found to be two rows of columns spanning 8 meters with 4 meters cantilevered on either side. The girders are spaced 5 meters apart. These girders carry the floor slabs, which at the end of the cantilevers are turned up perpendicularly to form the outer skin of the building. Cabinets are placed against these walls in order to permit free visibility in the center of the rooms. Above the cabinets, which are 2 meters high, runs a continuous band of windows.[5]

Two things are evident from this publication. The first is that the implied transcendental immateriality of glass has been largely replaced by the obdurate materiality of concrete; the wax-crayon rendering used to represent translucence in the Glass Skyscraper projects is used here to represent textured opacity. The second is that the work as a whole accords a polemical priority to *building* as opposed to *architecture*; a priority which Mies later rejected as being among the more narrow-minded dogmas perpetuated by the architects of the *Neue Sachlichkeit* ("the new objectivity").

The closeness of Mies's sensibility to both the functionalism of the *Neue Sachlichkeit* and the estranging effect of the Dadaist "displaced" object, as seen in the constructions of Vladimir Tatlin and Kurt Schwitters, indicates his affinity for the theories of the Berlin avant-garde. Despite this affinity, the building was to assert itself primarily as a tectonic procedure, rather than as an aesthetic manipulation. The following text, which appeared in 1923 in the second issue of *G*, makes this patently clear.

> We refuse to recognize problems of form, but only problems of building.
>
> Form is not the aim of our work, but only the result.

6. Wolf House, Guben, 1925-27

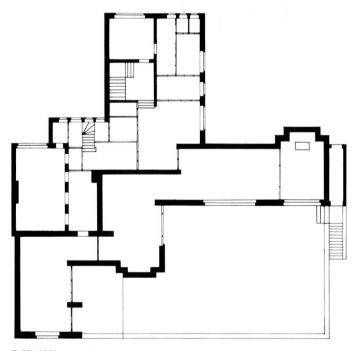

7. Wolf House, plan

Form, by itself, does not exist.

Form as an aim is formalism; and that we reject. . . .

Essentially our task is to free the practice of building from the control of the aesthetic speculators and restore it to what it should exclusively be: building.[6]

Apart from the typical *G* group attack on aestheticism that this text constitutes, Mies seemed to be searching here for some substantial paradigm from which to develop a convenient and technically pragmatic format for the *modern* house. In opting for a pseudo-Italianate, flat-roofed assembly in brick for the Wolf House of 1925-27 (fig. 6), Mies temporarily settled the conflict between modernism and traditionalism in favor of tradition. In so doing, Mies returned from his exploration of the polemical extremes of structures projected exclusively in glass or concrete, to embrace the craft tradition of precisely bonded, load-bearing brickwork that he had learned from his father. Mies's realized *Landhäuser* of the 1920s are solid, bourgeois, bonded-brick structures of the highest possible quality.

Thus, for all the picturesque asymmetry of its composition and the polemical use of a dramatically cantilevered concrete roof, the basic plan of the Wolf House (fig. 7) is largely cellular and conventional; that is to say, it is not in any respect a *free plan*. The principal rooms of the Wolf House interconnect along a diagonal line. The same is true of the Lange and Esters houses, built in Krefeld between 1927 and 1930. This visual continuity, which cuts across the ground floor of each house, is interrupted by steel-framed, plate-glass double doors that separate the staggered volumes of the smoking, living, and dining rooms. At the same time, as Werner Blaser demonstrated in his reconstruction of the brick bonding pattern used in the Brick Country House project of 1924, the treatment of the exposed brickwork was basically the same in each case: all the dimensions and proportions were worked out in *accordance* with the basic brick module. These three works, the Wolf, Lange, and Esters houses, together with the Ulrich Lange and Hubbe house projects of the 1930s, are particularly relevant to a re-evaluation of Mies today. They impart a much more complex intentionality to his early German career than we commonly recognize; one which was as much dedicated to traditional tectonic values as it was influenced by modernist aspirations.

While there is nothing remotely classical about these brick villas, the presence of exposed, load-bearing brickwork brings them within the rubric of traditional building culture, even if the walls and openings are occasionally manipulated as though they were made out of a continuous plastic substance such as concrete. Although there is little here of the structural rationalism of the Dutch master H.P. Berlage, whom Mies greatly admired, the way in which these houses are detailed and built establishes them as tectonically disciplined

8. Barcelona Pavilion, 1929

works. As Philip Johnson informs us, Mies went so far as not only to calculate all dimensions in brick sizes, but also to separate the underfired long bricks from the overfired short ones and to combine them in such a way as to compensate for this discrepancy.[7] As Mies, himself, was to remark at a later stage in his career:

> Architecture begins when two bricks are put carefully together. Architecture is a language having the discipline of a grammar. Language can be used for normal day-to-day purposes as prose. And if you are really good, you can be a poet.[8]

The climax of Mies's early career came with the three diminutive master works that he realized between 1929 and 1931: the German Pavilion built for the Barcelona International Exhibition of 1929 (recently reconstructed), the Tugendhat House realized at Brno, Czechoslovakia, in 1930, and an exhibition house erected for the Berlin Building Exposition of 1931. In all these works, a pin-wheeling spatial arrangement comprised of freestanding columns and planes announced that the free plan had suddenly entered Mies's architectural repertoire. Mies's peculiarly horizontal interpretation of this *plan libre* (so called here because it was derived from Le Corbusier) was never to have a more pure and didactic rendering than in the Barcelona Pavilion.

An analysis of the Barcelona Pavilion (fig. 8; for plan, see Eisenman, fig. 8) must always commence with the eight freestanding columns, which, together with the freestanding asymmetrical planes, constitute the most active spatial elements of the composition. Already we can see how certain classical and vernacular metaphors are latent in what is normally regarded as a quintessentially modern work. The eight columns, regularly spaced on a square grid and symmetrical with regard to the flat slab they support, may be read as a metaphor for a classical belvedere, while the spatial figure implied by the asymmetrical freestanding walls and glass screens may be read as a reference to the compressed and elongated Arts and Crafts house, as exemplified by Frank Lloyd Wright's Robie House (fig. 9), built in 1908 in Chicago, with which Mies was certainly familiar. (See Mies's personal appreciation of Frank Lloyd Wright written in 1940).[9]

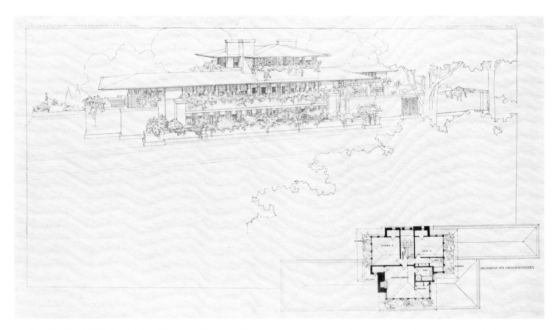

9. Frank Lloyd Wright, Robie House, Chicago, 1908, perspective and plan from the Wasmuth portfolio, 1910

10. Barcelona Pavilion

A referential complexity of this order demands that such generalized categories as *modernism* and *traditionalism* be broken down into their specific syntactic and semantic referents if we are to arrive at a more precise understanding of Mies's unique sensibility. In this light, it is possible to regard the Barcelona Pavilion as a proliferation of a number of complementary opposites: columnar versus planar, tectonic versus atectonic, opaque versus translucent, still versus agitated, open versus closed, and, even, architecture versus building. The first opposition is largely formal and virtually self-evident. The fourth and fifth are best described by the nature of the water's surface, ruffled where open and absolutely flat where enclosed. The last opposition may be said to derive from the fact that the "classical" cruciform columns imply *architecture*, whereas the pin-wheeling, planar space-form implies *building*, by recalling the organic nature of the vernacular.[10]

A detailed analysis of the cruciform steel column of the Barcelona Pavilion indicates that the modernist/traditionalist opposition manifests itself in Mies's work as much at the level of detail as in the constitution of the whole. Cruciform in plan and clad in chromium, this dematerialized column could hardly be more modernist, particularly when compared to Le Corbusier's cylindrical white *piloti* of the same date, a form of column which Mies employed, presumably as a demonstration of a more normative architecture, for the 1931 Berlin Building Exposition. While Mies's Barcelona column is, like any column, essentially a point support, it is also, by virtue of its cruciform section, paradoxically planar.

Nothing could be more modernist than this dematerialized, partially planar column clad in a shimmering, reflective surface (fig. 10); yet, at the level of cultural memory, what do these serried vertical highlights of varying width remind us of, if not the perceptually varying flute-widths of classical columns? What is mnemonic in the case of the columns is equally so in the case of the freestanding space dividers, faced here in polished onyx and marble. Again, nothing could be more abstract and avant-garde than these mysteriously suspended wall planes; but they once again recall classical form in the nature of the associations aroused by their stone-veneered surfaces. What is true of the columns and walls is also true, in a different way, of the planes of the raised floor and the ceiling: where the former is a travertine podium and, hence, by definition classical, its planar counterpart, the continuous white plastered ceiling, could hardly be more modernist and abstract. And yet the fact that the chromium columns lack any kind of conceptual fixity in relation to the floor and the ceiling (there is not even a vestigial capital or base) establishes a strange state of equivalence between those two parallel layers, despite their superficial differences. The volume contained between them becomes a seemingly unlimited expanse of abstract, universal space. This modernist space field is at once checked and terminated by traditional elements: marble-clad walls, a reflecting pool, and a figurative sculpture by Georg Kolbe. In the floor and ceiling of the Barcelona Pavilion, we can see how the poles of the *modernist/traditionalist* opposition gravitate, in expressive terms, to fundamentally different architectural elements: to the ceiling in the first instance and to the floor in the second.

A similar opposition is also expressed in the Tugendhat House, only now the split is not between the white linoleum floor and the white plastered ceiling, since they are both obviously equally abstract, but rather between the traditionally

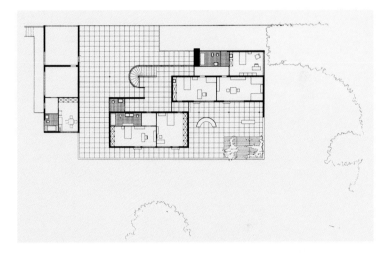

11. Tugendhat House, Brno, 1928-30, plan of upper floor

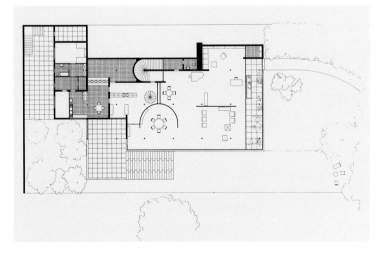

12. Tugendhat House, plan of ground floor

13. Tugendhat House, living room

14. Tugendhat House, library and living room

planned, cellular volumes of the bedrooms on the upper level, and the open, modernist space of the living volumes beneath (figs. 11, 12). It is, moreover, a poetic irony that this *plan libre*, regularly modulated by a grid of equidistant columns, can be converted into a space which is reminiscent of a classical belvedere once the entire plate-glass wall on its southern face is lowered into the basement with the aid of electrical gears. The provision of a single flat-bar, chromium guard rail inside the glass multiplies the dialogical references still further: monumental podium versus nautical taffrail; antique loggia versus *machine à habiter* (fig. 13).

If one adds to this the full range of associations evoked by the various finishes employed throughout the living volume of the house, then we must concede that the Tugendhat House is just as much the apotheosis of Mies's German career as the more celebrated Barcelona Pavilion. In fact it may well be the more complex of the two works, for apart from the *modernist/traditionalist* spatial differences already alluded to, other dyads are introduced which raise the work to a higher level of semantic complexity. The exotic conservatory which flanks the shorter side of the living volume seems to operate at this level since the shallow glass house containing tropical vegetation appears to posit itself as a third term; one which is capable of mediating between the crystallized structure of the freestanding onyx plane on the interior and the natural vegetation of the garden-landscape beyond (fig. 14). The decorative here appears as nature herself, rather than artistic invention. At another level, the rectangular space-divider separating the living room from the library evokes the worldly discourse which attends its presence on either side, through the refined formality of its onyx revetment. Similarly, the warmer Macassar ebony veneer of the semicircular dining alcove evokes the earth-bound social ritual that it serves both to contain and support (see Eisenman, fig. 12). It is nothing less than masterly that all of this should take place behind a dematerializable glass façade that, apart from being disarmingly simple, is also supremely functional, since it is paralleled by chromium-plated heating tubes at floor level and by curtain tracks and concealed roller blinds under the continuous lintel above. Where the first compensates for the heat loss of the glass, and the second provides for intimacy at night, the last, when lowered as a projected awning, serves to protect the interior from exposure to the sun.

Traditional form also plays a mediatory role in the canonical furniture pieces which Mies designed during this period. Once again, a hierarchical shift occurs as one passes from, say, the more formal Schinkelesque profiles of the Barcelona chair, with its tufted leather cushions, to the anthropomorphic modernism of the cantilevered springy frame of the Tugendhat chair, with its softer leather upholstery in pale green cowhide. Even these contrasting pieces, with their

different connotations, fail to do justice to the full range of occasional furniture designed by Mies during this period.

Subject in the late 1920s to the strong influence of the interior architect Lilly Reich, Mies possessed an astonishing capacity during this period to make very delicate allusions at the level of finishes and furnishings. As never before or after, he was able to express subtle nuances of character as he passed, say, from pleated to tufted leather, or from transparent to translucent glass. For all his later denial that the Russian avant-garde had any influence on his work ("I was very strongly opposed, even to Malevich," he was to tell Peter Blake in 1962),[11] there was an uncanny affinity between his work of the late 1920s and the visionary projects of the neo-Suprematist architect Ivan Leonidov. Aside from the play with tinted, transparent, and etched glass in the Barcelona Pavilion, and the somewhat Russian color scheme of black, red, orange, and lemon-yellow used in the Silk and Velvet Cafe (fig. 15) at the 1927 Exposition de la Mode in Berlin, designed with Lilly Reich, a number of other exhibitions designed by Mies at this time show the influence of the Russian avant-garde; above all, the Glass Room in the 1927 Industry and Craft Exhibition in

15. Mies van der Rohe with Lilly Reich, Silk and Velvet Cafe, Exposition de la Mode, Berlin, 1927

Stuttgart, mounted on the occasion of the Werkbund Ausstellung. For this last, we need only read Philip Johnson's description of the materials and colors employed by Mies to sense that his concept of *beinahe nichts* (almost nothing) was not so far removed from Malevich's famous *Suprematist Composition: White on White* of 1928: " . . . chairs, white chamois and black cowhide; table, rosewood; floor, black and white linoleum; walls, etched, clear and gray opaque glass."[12]

All of this progressively and irrevocably changed as Mies moved away from the domestic milieu and began to take on industrial work or large-scale urban structures, as in the case of the Verseidag Administration Building project of 1937 or the Reichsbank competition entry of 1933 (fig. 16). In each instance, the idea of building, *Bauen*, as opposed to architecture seems to re-emerge as a fundamental value; as something that has been rediscovered rather than invented. In the Reichsbank project in particular, the articulation of tradition versus modernity seems to divide rather schematically along the lines of architecture versus building. While the bowed front is symmetrical and classically modulated with its monumental, double-height, curtain-walled *piano nobile*, and its internal "peristyle," the back wings of the block are rendered as a normative industrial building. Here we are reminded of the steel office building "un-artistically" considered, rendered in similar terms as the laconic Concrete and Glass Office Building projects of the early 1920s.

As the historian Ludwig Glaeser has pointed out, Mies's model for the curtain wall of the Reichsbank, comprising continuous runs of square-gridded industrial sash with horizontal brick spandrels, was almost certainly derived from the German industrial vernacular, in which exposed steel framing was invariably combined with brick and glass infill. This vernacular, derived from the traditional, timber-framed *Fachwerkbauten*, was a common model for inexpensive factory structures from the late nineteenth century onwards, and numerous examples of such industrial buildings can be found throughout continental Europe, particularly in Germany and France.[13] As it so happens, the Reichsbank project, like the initial scheme for the Illinois Institute of Technology of 1939, features a continuous curtain wall rather than a frame and infill system, although there is no doubt that it is this last which Mies would utilize most in his American career. Perhaps no one has written more perceptively of the consequences of this new emphasis on the frame than Colin Rowe.

Mies's characteristic German column was circular or cruciform; but his new column became H-shaped, became that I-beam which is now almost a personal signature. Typically, his German column had been clearly distinguished from walls and windows, isolated from them in space; and, typically, his new column became an element integral with the envelope of the building where it came to function as a kind of mullion or residue of wall. Thus the column section was not without some drastic effects on the entire space of the building.

The circular or cruciform section had tended to push partitions away from the column. The new section tended to drag them towards it. The old column had offered a minimum of obstruction to a horizontal movement of space; but the new column presents a distinctly more substantial stop. . . .

As an International Style element, the column put in its last appearance in the museum project of 1942; while in the Library and Administration Building project of 1944, the effects of the H-shaped column are already apparent and are clearly exhibited in the published drawings of its plans. From these drawings it is evident that the columns are no longer to be allowed to be ambiguously beneath a slab. It is now – apparently for the first time – tied to a network of beams, and these beams have appointed definite positions for the screens, and for the most part the screens have already leapt into these positions – in fact only the extra-thick walls around the lavatories seem to have been able to resist the new attraction.[14]

As Rowe indicates, this change is of an epistemic nature, not only because the integration of the structural frame with the outer membrane and with the internal partitions serves to transform the ontological character of the space, but also because the drive to reveal the structural joint between columns and beams (only fully achieved in Mies's Minerals and Metals Research Building at IIT) returns us to a primary tectonic category. The conceptual focus now shifts from universal modernist space to the traditional primacy of the frame and its joint. This change is fundamental, for the tension between modernity and tradition can now no longer be mediated, as it was in the Tugendhat House, by provoking subtle semiotic exchanges in the literal "gap" which separates the order of freestanding supports from the system of spatial enclosure. At the same time, the cellular homogeneity of traditional masonry is rejected as an alternative. As a result, the plastic energy of Mies's later work (irrespective of the specific program) tends to gravitate toward the perimeter of the building, as is evident in the published designs of the unbuilt IIT Library and Administration Building of 1944. From now on there is an emphasis on certain honorific elements, such as the entry foyer, the large public internal volume, the courtyard, and, last but not least, the exposed megastructural form. Apart from such prominent articulations as these, and the provision of openloft space whenever it is deemed appropriate, the body of any structure is largely filled with the bureaucratic and operational banalities of everyday life, a discrimination that no doubt prompted Louis Kahn to distinguish, in his own work, between *servant* and *served* space. This distinction is an effec-

16. Opposite page: Reichsbank project, Berlin, 1933, perspective drawing

tive tool for examining the postwar work of Mies van der Rohe, for evidently certain programmatic and tectonic elements were seen as meriting an articulation which duly belonged to the realm of *architecture,* while others, relegated to the status of repetitive cellular space, were seen as belonging only to the category of *building,* irrespective of the scale at which they occur. As Mies put it later, "Every building has its position in the stratum – every building is not a cathedral."

While Mies more or less relinquished the liberative, utopian program of the prewar avant-garde at the beginning of his American career, he replaced it with the *deus ex machina* of universal technology. Under this new aegis, traditional cultural references could only be sustained where they could be made to coincide with the technological imperatives of the epoch. Thus, apart from simple single or two-story industrial structures, such as the Boiler House which Mies realized on the IIT campus in 1950, not even the traditional tectonic of the steel frame could be made manifest and sustained where the technical demands of fireproofing and mechanical services enforced the encasement of its essential substance and the use of suspended ceilings. Nonetheless, it was as though Mies sensed that the technological imperative was the only discipline left with which to prevent the world from degenerating into kitsch. This vision of technology as the demiurge of the age, latent in his thought from the beginning, was finally expressed in his 1950 address to the Illinois Institute of Technology.

> Technology is rooted in the past.
> It dominates the present and tends into the future.
> It is a real historical movement –
> one of the great movements which shape and
> represent their epoch.
> It can be compared only with the Classical
> discovery of man as a person,
> the Roman will to power,
> and the religious movement of the Middle Ages.
> Technology is far more than a method,
> it is a world in itself.
> As a method it is superior in almost every respect.
> But only where it is left to itself as in
> gigantic structures of engineering, there
> technology reveals its true nature.
> There it is evident that it is not only a useful means,
> that it is something, something in itself,
> something that has meaning and a powerful form –
> so powerful in fact, that it is not easy to name it.
> Is that still technology or is it architecture?
> And that may be the reason why some people
> are convinced that architecture will be outmoded
> and replaced by technology.
> Such a conviction is not based on clear thinking.

> The opposite happens.
> Wherever technology reaches its real fulfillment,
> it transcends into architecture. . . . [15]

Here, twelve years after he first assumed the didactic leadership of the architecture department at IIT, technology was set forth as the means with which to continue the culture of architecture. This perception, articulated in a familiar mixture of romanticism and realism, may go some way toward accounting for the "value-free" universal grid of Mies's IIT campus plan, imposed upon the available site in 1940. Here a 24-foot by 24-foot by 12-foot module prevailed throughout, extending to the limits of the site as though this grid could be infinitely prolonged. In part symmetrical, in part asymmetrical, but always regular, save for an inexplicable half-modular inflection here and there, the final plan gives little indication that one part of the campus may be of greater symbolic import than another. Like Behrens before him, who had already conceived of industry as the dominant force of the epoch,[16] Mies strove from the early 1940s to bring the office building under the rubric of the factory and vice versa, as though Louis Mumford's neotechnics, like the electricity that was its motivating force, was becoming manifest as a universal, invisible grid, reaching the most remote corners of our lives and stamping our very being with its mark.

No building type or institution could claim any special immunity from the imprint of this universal matrix that ruthlessly determined the late modern world for Mies; be it a church, a house, a theatre, a block of apartments, or an academic institution. It was as though information itself, as evidenced by the rise of the service industry in the postwar economy, had already transformed every conceivable system and institution into a semibureaucratized domain. This "one-dimensional" perception of the modern world as a vast, seamless technological web echoes, in an uncanny way, Walter Benjamin's observation that "around the middle of the nineteenth century, the center of gravity of reality shifted from the home to the office."[17]

The paradoxical problem that Mies faced throughout the rest of his career was how to achieve a subtle yet adequate form of hierarchic inflection within the restrictions of his own, self-imposed, architectural syntax. He wished to distinguish, as it were, between architecture and building, without compromising the probity of the structural frame or logic of its necessary infill. The specific scope of the problem is evident when one compares the IIT Minerals and Metals Research Building of 1942-43 (fig. 17; see Otto, fig. 9) to Alumni Memorial Hall (fig. 18; see Otto, fig. 13), realized three years later. In the first instance, the German factory vernacular is directly applied in all its technical and tectonic purity, without any manipulation; in the second, the frame is not only encased in concrete for the purposes of fire protection, but the "represen-

17. Minerals and Metals Research Building, IIT, Chicago, 1942-43

18. Alumni Memorial Hall, IIT, Chicago, 1945-46

tation" of its hidden presence, in terms of classically profiled steel facings and fenestration mouldings, emerges here as the essential tectonic theme of Mies's American style. One need only to compare the brick, steel-framed, sides of the two buildings to observe the shift that has taken place, for where the framing components of the former are rather freely disposed according to constructional necessity, the frame of the latter is rigidly symmetrical. Apart from the different legal and technical constraints operating in each case, it is clear that Alumni Memorial Hall is the more monumental of the two, and was apparently considered to be an appropriate vehicle for *architecture* or rather for that level of expression which Mies preferred to call *Baukunst* – building art. The Minerals and Metals Research Building, on the other hand, is nothing more than a laboratory, and thus is worthy of no additional level of tectonic elaboration than that required by the process of *building* or *Bauen*. In the first, then, there is an attempt at symbolic representation, evident in the steel column facings which do not touch the ground and thereby declare their non-load-

bearing status. In the second, there is simply the elegant refinement of a given set of technical components.

The syntax employed by Mies in most of the structures he built on the IIT campus in the 1940s falls somewhere between that used in these two buildings. In one building after another, the treatment of end walls and the recession of entrances occurs almost indifferently within the discipline of the exposed steel frame and the limits of the campus grid. Even so, the necessity for fireproofing assured that, in the main, what one saw was a representational simulation of the frame rather than the frame itself.

From the mid-1940s onwards, Mies tried to escape the limitations imposed by his German factory aesthetic without relinquishing his commitment to technology as the only remaining collective ethos of the epoch. In this endeavor he looked both forwards and backwards: forwards to a series of wide-span structures, which, of necessity, would be capable of creating great symbolic spaces and which, like large engineering works such as bridges, would manifest themselves as technological forms having a transcendental and monumental character, and backwards, to the twin-benighted moments of the German Enlightenment; first, to the short-lived triumph of the European avant-garde prior to the apocalypse of the Third Reich and World War II, and second, to the even more remote golden age of Schinkelschüler classicism. Indeed, the remaining twenty-five years of his output can be seen as a constant oscillation between these *prospective* and *retrospective* references; between the indifferent but inevitable megatechnology of an unforeseeable future, and an impossible nostalgia for the threads of the lost utopia of the beginning of the nineteenth century.

Two projects dating from the mid-1940s seem to establish these polarities in his work in terms of building types; the unrealized twin-truss, long-span, drive-in restaurant designed for Joseph Cantor in 1945-46 (fig. 19), and the Farnsworth House (1946-51), in Plano, Illinois. Where the Cantor Drive-In gives rise to the design of a number of long-span structures with exposed trusses, including Crown Hall (fig. 20), designed for the IIT campus, and the 1952-53 competition project for the National Theatre in Mannheim (cat. nos. 130-138); the Farnsworth House returns us, at least in part, to Mies's high avant-garde period of the late 1920s. Here, however, the abstract space field implied by the floating floor and roof planes is balanced by the picturesque composition of the work as a whole, which contains both Schinkelschüler and Italianate elements. At the same time, Mies attempted to reduce the tectonic system of the Farnsworth House to a sublimely minimalist statement, thereby evoking both Suprematism and romantic classicism. This is evident in the open-jointed paving of the exterior terraces, where square stone slabs are laid on an absolutely flat structural bed of square, shallow, gravel-filled drain pans, which are inverted pyramids of welded steel. A similar minimalism is manifest in the face mounting of the H-section columns to the shallow trimming channels of the suspended floor and roof slabs. The tectonic purity of this joint (formally minimal but hardly expressive from the point of view of constructional logic) is achieved by grinding the welds flat, and by finishing the steelwork in white throughout.

At this point, Mies began to achieve a kind of consummate synthesis in his work, wherein the same minimal components are open to double "readings," so that the *six* symmetrically placed column supports for the lower terrace of the Farnsworth House turn out (because of the overlapping of the terrace and the house) to be *four* stub columns, which also carry in part the floor and roof planes of the house. In a similar way, of the *eight* columns carrying the house itself, only *six* engage on their flanges with the plate glass membrane which encloses the volume. These inconsistencies arise out of the complex overlapping of terrace and house, and thereby serve to express this condition as an asymmetrical topology, which resists any form of mono-semantic resolution.

19. Cantor Drive-In Restaurant, Indianapolis, 1945-46, model

20. Crown Hall, IIT, Chicago, 1950-56, signed photopanel (cat. no. 105)

A comparable syntactic fusion of two separate propositions can be found in the twin towers realized for Herbert S. Greenwald in 1951: the 860-880 Lake Shore Drive Apartments (figs. 21, 22) of which Peter Carter has made the following remarkable analysis:

> Mies's introduction of projecting steel mullions at the quarterpoints of each bay and on the column surfaces engenders a new and unexpected quality from the separate identities of the elements involved. The structural frame and its glass infill become architecturally fused, each losing part of its particular identity in establishing the new architectural reality. The mullion has acted as a kind of catalyst for this change.
>
> The columns and mullion dimensions determine window widths. The two central windows are, therefore, wider than those adjacent to the column. These variants produce visual cadences of expanding and contracting intervals.... Before Mies' "860" solution, there were two clear basic possibilities for the enclosure of skeleton frame buildings. Either the skin acted as an infill between the structure or it hung in front of it.... While acceptable on their own pragmatic terms, these solutions have, with the exception of the Seagram Building, rarely been touched by the magic of great architecture. At "860" the solution has come directly out of the problem of finding a single architectural expression which would embrace both skin and structure. At "860" the structure and skin retain much of their individual identities but the application of the mullion has caused a philosophical transformation from a pluralistic to a monotheistic character.[18]

Mies's canonical long-span, exposed lattice-truss structure, which first appeared with the Cantor Drive-In Restaurant, is paralleled in the early 1950s by his use of a megastructural space-frame. With regard to this last, he developed two different types of structures for the support of the square, two-way span roof. In the first of these, the Chicago Convention Hall project of 1953-54, in which the 720-foot clear span has civil engineering or bridge-like dimensions, the steel-framed roof transmits its load to the ground via steel trusses. These continuous trussed walls rest on stub concrete columns, which equipped with "hinged" column heads, are deployed around the perimeter at 120-foot intervals with 60-foot cantilevers at the corners. In the second, the 50 by 50 House project of 1950-51 (fig. 23), a 50-foot-square space-frame is carried on four mid-span column supports, yielding 25-foot cantilevers at the corners (although Mies also considered the use of overhead plate girders [fig. 24]). While the Convention Hall is the more structurally ambitious of the two works, Mies was to synthesize these two prototypes in his pro-

21. 860-880 Lake Shore Drive Apartments, Chicago, 1948-51, under construction

22. 860-880 Lake Shore Drive Apartments, under construction

23. 50 by 50 House project, 1950-51, model in landscape setting by Phil Hart and others for "Advanced Architecture I" at IIT

24. 50 by 50 House project, model of preliminary design in landscape setting by Phil Hart and others for "Advanced Architecture I" at IIT

25. New National Gallery, Berlin, 1962-67

ject for the Bacardi Office Building in Santiago, Cuba, in 1957. This square, space-frame type, with eight columns distributed around the perimeter, is returned to in the Schaefer Museum project of 1960-61 and in the New National Gallery in Berlin, which was finally completed in 1967, two years before his death.

The representational space-frame pavilion which dominates the podium base of the New National Gallery (fig. 25) was Mies's final homecoming in more ways than one, for it enabled him to reconcile the polarities of his work: on the one hand, the modernist, planar space-field; on the other, the articulate constructional logic of the Western tectonic tradition. As Rowe suggests, these two values were perhaps never more at variance than in Crown Hall, IIT, where, internally at least, the uninterrupted suspended ceiling tends to repudiate the tectonic probity of the perimeter structure. This dilemma of the suspended ceiling, which occurred in various forms throughout Mies's American career, is finally resolved in the New National Gallery. Here, the synthesis of the space-frame with its columnar-hinged support depends upon the dual nature of the upper and lower chords that make up the welded steel-plate roof structure. Thus, while the roof as a whole may be read as an infinite floating plane, it also asserts its tectonic presence through its evident structural substance. In a similar way, the cruciform steel megacolumns that carry the roof are able to convey their pragmatic and mythical character in terms of both technology and classicism. This expressive synthesis attains its apotheosis in the hinged, roller-bearing joint separating the space-frame from the column head (see Dal Co, fig. 9). Clearly this hinged-joint is both a bridge-bearing and a metaphorical capital. As the latter, it appears to invert the technologically symbolic role of the steel hinged-joint as it first appeared in a significant architectural context, with Behrens's Schinkelschüler Turbinenfabrik of 1909. The flanges of the chords in Mies's space-frame at the New National Gallery, painted matte black, depend for their internal legibility upon the play of reflected light as it penetrates the depths of the totally black egg-crate frame (see Spaeth, fig. 21). Here Mies's black-on-black aesthetic returns us to the tradition of the modernist avant-garde. Thus, in his last realized work, Mies van der Rohe achieved a highly accomplished architectonic integration of two primary aspects within the Western building tradition: structural rationalism on the one hand, and romantic classicism on the other. He was to combine this synthesis with a reassertion of the sublimity of the avant-garde, as it appears in the paintings of Ad Reinhardt or in Malevich's Suprematist White-on-White paintings of the late teens.

Notes

1. Alois Riegl, *Spatrömische Kunstindustrie* (Vienna, 1901).

2. It should be noted that Mies was not part of this circle.

3. These translated excerpts appear in Dennis Sharp's *Modern Architecture and Expressionism* (New York, 1966). The complete text by Paul Scheerbart is entitled *Glasarchitektur* (Berlin, 1914).

4. The full translation of Mies's remarks on the Glass Skyscrapers that originally appeared in *Frühlicht* 1 (1922), pp. 122-24, is given in Philip Johnson, *Mies van der Rohe* (New York, 1947), p. 187.

5. Here again, the complete translation from *G* 1 (1922), p. 1, is given in Johnson (note 4), p. 188.

6. The original text from *G* 2 (1923) is translated in Johnson (note 4), p. 189.

7. Johnson (note 4), p. 35.

8. Walter F. Wagner, Jr., "Ludwig Mies van der Rohe: 1886-1969," *Architectural Record* 146 (September 1969), p. 9.

9. Frank Lloyd Wright's Robie House of 1908 can be seen as a version of the typical "head and tail" Arts and Crafts house plan, where the head and tail have both been elongated and placed side by side. Mies had surely seen Wright's work in 1910 when a major exhibition was mounted in Berlin, and the Wasmuth publishing house issued a portfolio of Wright's drawings. As Mies wrote in 1940 for an unpublished catalogue of an exhibition at the Museum of Modern Art, "At this moment [1910], so critical for us, the exhibition of the work of Frank Lloyd Wright came to Berlin. This comprehensive display and the exhaustive publication of his works enabled us to become really acquainted with the achievements of this architect." The full text appears in Johnson (note 4), pp. 200-201.

10. Most Arts and Crafts houses were typologically related to the English yeoman farmhouse, which grew organically in a pin-wheeling U- or L-formation, with the great hall at the head and the farm sheds and outhouses at the tail. This was, of course, a vernacular form.

11. See Peter Blake, *The Master Builders: Le Corbusier, Mies van der Rohe, Frank Lloyd Wright* (New York, 1960). See also *Four Great Makers of Modern Architecture: Gropius, Le Corbusier, Mies van der Rohe, Wright* (New York, 1963), a verbatim record of a symposium held at the School of Architecture, Columbia University, 1961.

12. Johnson (note 4), p. 51.

13. For a discussion of Mies's choice of the German vernacular and its relation to the traditional *Fachwerkbauten*, see "Epilogue: Thirty Years After" in Johnson (note 4), pp. 205-211.

14. Colin Rowe, "Neoclassicism and Modern Architecture," *Oppositions* 1 (Sept. 1973), p. 18.

15. Mies van der Rohe, "Address to Illinois Institute of Technology." A full transcript of this address is given in Johnson (note 4), pp. 203-204.

16. See Behrens's 1908 essay "What is Monumental Art."

17. Walter Benjamin, "Paris, Haupstadt des XIX Jahrhunderts," in *Illuminationen* (Frankfurt, n.d.).

18. Peter Carter, "Mies van der Rohe: An Appreciation on the Occasion, This Month, of His 75th Birthday," *Architectural Design* 31 (March 1961), p. 108.

Mies and the Highrise – Recent Correspondence on History, Ideology, and Succession

Edited by Christian F. Otto

This correspondence, though between an amateur and one of the formidable authorities on architectural history and theory, appears sufficiently interesting to warrant reproduction. Editor

16 June 1986

Professor Colin Rowe
Architecture/Sibley
Cornell University
Ithaca, NY 14853

Dear Professor Rowe:

You are probably the most influential voice of the last quarter century to speak to the issue of history in the making of a contemporary architecture. It is difficult to locate an architect in the United States or Europe who does not profess familiarity with you or your writings. That you were presented with AIA "Institute Honors" in 1982 and the next year made an honorary fellow of the Royal Institute of British Architects (RIBA) appears to be institutional confirmation of this influence.

I am an aficionado of architecture, and have spent what friends consider exorbitant amounts of time and hard cash traveling to see and experience it, then in reading what I can about those buildings and their architects (and surely you agree that the cost of books and periodicals has become unconscionable, which makes your work all the more valuable to me; it has appeared at dignified intervals and rewards sustained contemplation, so that Rowe provides an ample return on investment).

But to the reason for this letter. I am especially intrigued by the architecture that Mies van der Rohe designed during the Weimar Republic and later in America. I am intrigued by the relation between these two "careers," by the inordinate impact that his work appears to have had, and why this should have been so. If Mies's architecture in the United States does indeed derive from ideas that evolved during the 1920s, and if

we agree with a recent commentator that his American work is of an "aesthetic excellence" and "sublime order," why were his imitators not able to push beyond the "uniformly neat," why did they produce only "the dumbness and . . . redundancy of glass-box city centres . . . the slick, alienated environment of 'Alphaville'"?[1]

You have addressed just these questions in ways that I find to be brilliantly illuminating, providing me with a point of entry into Mies's architecture. Recent research that I've undertaken on Mies, however, has led me into unanticipated regions. Since you (obviously without being aware of it) are my historical geographer, I would feel very much more comfortable having some sense of your response to this new terrain. Would you have the time, and the willingness, to read a few pages on this material? I will keep them as short and clear as I am able.

Cordially,
Hyrcanian Woods

27 June 1986

Mr. Hyrcanian Woods
1100 Pennsylvania Ave., NW
Washington, DC 20506

Dear Mr. Woods:

I am eternally confounded that Waspish types – which I presume you to be on the basis of your name and tenor of your letter, simultaneously demanding and obsequious – insist on being agitated about most any matter at hand. I do find it enervating.

But what am I to do with your letter, which leaves me in an intolerable predicament. I cannot be rude to your gentle request, yet I find myself disposed to having you purge yourself of your argument with me, whatever it may be, by publishing your thoughts somewhere – anywhere at all. Then you could mail me an offprint and we'd meet over wine as the best of adversaries without my having to suffer the excruciating boredom of commenting on something that I once wrote and perhaps now only half believe. Woof! woof! woof! If you must have me read about myself, I can, I suppose, manage it.

Colin Rowe

4 July 1986

Professor Colin Rowe
Architecture/Sibley
Cornell University
Ithaca, NY 14853

Dear Professor Rowe:

I appreciate your willingness at least to read this through. To the best of my ability, I will studiously attempt to avoid agitation in what I have to say. Be forewarned, however, that my presentation may become pedantic. For many years I have been an employee in the Bureau of Standards and the prose of governmental reports at times informs even my most casual letters.

For me, the hallmarks of your writing are wonderfully compelling observations about architecture combined with presentations of ideas from the past that offer striking corollaries with present concerns – suggesting, I would presume, persuasive design rationales for architects today. To observe a continuity between past and present provides current ideas with authority; to shift these ideas back into historical situations brings them alive with persuasive immediacy. There is, presumably, a liability here as well: as another author observes, wandering in and out of history "teaches you how the past animates the present, but it also makes everything slightly hallucinatory."[2] Meaning, as I understand it, that one may unconsciously manipulate the past for present purposes.

But I am specifically concerned with Mies. You have published trenchant comments on his architecture in relationship to sixteenth-century Italian Mannerism, nineteenth-century architectural composition, and the Chicago frame; in longer discourse you have considered transactions among Mies, neoclassicism, and modern architecture.[3] Because I am especially interested in the discourse about the highrise and the significance of the structural frame, both for modern architecture and for architects following in the Miesian wake, your observations were of particular pertinence to me. You observed that Mies devised an "idealistic principle of order" that imbued his architecture with inordinate authority. You noted that his architectural position was "pure," that it was "a statement magnificent in its single-mindedness," and that in this way it became a "demand." You then suggested that "the incentive for change" was inherent in the very nature of this situation. Because his architecture was a demand, it stimulated "those anti-Miesian . . . gestures in which disciples of Mies have lately been indulging."

With this, you seemed to embrace all of Mies. You characterized his achievement as it evolved during the twenties and thirties; you explained why his work appeared so urgent, inevitable, and persuasive, producing disciples of Miesian modernism in America; and you proposed reasons for the strong reaction to it.

I not only found this large-scale assessment compelling, but some of the detail in it spoke to my particular interests. You distinguished between the structural frame in the tall building as used in late nineteenth-century America and later by European modernists. "In Chicago," you wrote, "it might be said that the frame was convincing as fact rather than as idea, whereas in considering the European innovators of the twenties one cannot suppress the supposition that the frame to them was much more often an essential idea before it was an altogether reasonable fact."[4] You characterized Mies's glass tower project of 1922 as an "advertisement for a cause . . . a

1. Park Avenue, New York, looking south

2. Opposite page: Friedrichstrasse Office Building project, Berlin, 1921, perspective drawing

highly charged symbolic statement . . . an implicit social criticism," and you wrote that it implied "an altruistic order of society," and also that it engaged "both the moral and the aesthetic interests of our Utopian sentiment." Mies, in short, presented the tall building "primarily as a symbol rather than as any object for use. It was a symbol of a technically oriented future society."[5]

I found these observations to be heady stuff, not only in their juxtaposition of fact and idea, and not only because they assumed that a building does convey meaning (I am committed to the proposition that visual thought is as powerful an instrument as verbal thought), but also and especially because they suggested why for decades after World War II Americans packed versions of the Miesian highrise into their cities (fig. 1), whether in the staid Northeast, raw Houston, icy Chicago, or balmy California: buildings like these were not merely practical to build, but they also broadcast a message about a brilliant present. In this way, Professor Rowe, your deliberations lent shape to an amorphous query that had been much on my mind about the general enthusiasm for the glazed skyscraper and proposed an explanation of it.

Having been provided with this orientation, I began a closer study of Mies's architecture, beginning at that moment when he made a conscious commitment to the "Neues Bauen,"[6] namely his participation in the Friedrichstrasse highrise competition announced in December 1921 (fig. 2).[7] Here I was immediately confronted with an unexpected contradiction. Writing about his Friedrichstrasse glass tower and its companion project of 1922, Mies lauded the constructional nature of the steel frame for its aesthetic potential: the "structural pattern" of skyscrapers was to be found in their "gigantic steel web," which was the "basis of all artistic design." Shortly thereafter, he specifically renounced all efforts at formal design:

> We reject all esthetic speculation, all doctrine, all formalism.
>
> Architecture is the will of an epoch realized as space; living, changing, new.[8]

Yet the projects themselves were formal configurations that displayed sheets of glass shaped into architecture – idealized, abstract designs presented without any consideration of structure. Mies never indicated how these tall buildings were to be constructed or what structural system would permit them to stand.[9] His written and visual positions appeared to pass by one another: form was not derived from structure, as the written statement demanded, and his stated assertion about structure was not realized in the formal presentation.

Another disjuncture informed his 1922-23 project for a reinforced concrete office building (fig. 3). Mies emphasized that the "reinforced concrete beam construction" was crucial

3. Concrete Office Building project, 1922-23, perspective drawing

to the undertaking, a structural system based on a regular arrangement of reinforced concrete posts and beams carrying reinforced concrete slabs as floors, ceilings, and roofs,[10] or "skin and bones construction" as he characterized it. This striking phrase, which has become a shibboleth for the curtain wall highrise, was more dramatic than the building material and technology employed in the project, both of which had been well established by the early 1920s. Moreover, the details of this structural system were scant in Mies's dramatic renderings of the building. Nor did he employ a continuous glass "skin," since the exterior consisted of horizontal strips of concrete (the slabs were bent up along the edges as parapets) alternating with recessed strip windows; each floor projected out over the one below it, emphasizing the impression of stacked, horizontal trays. More important to Mies, both as a design and in what he wrote about it, was that here he addressed a basic architectural task of the time, the nature of modern office space, and revealed how it could be made flexible, workable, efficient, and pleasant. Reinforced concrete in the service of this purpose was made architectural,[11] verbal and visual statements about structurally determined form remained dichotomous.

In his Weissenhof Apartment Building (fig. 4), designed in 1926, Mies began to resolve this opposition between structure and form by means of the steel frame, the first time that he actually employed one in either project or realized structure. The exterior walls of the three-story apartment block consisted of masonry infill covered by a smooth stucco, large

windows, and glass doors; floors and roof were hollow block between joists.[12] The steel frame was crucial to Mies's architectural vision in this project. He referred to the frame as "the most appropriate system of construction. It can be produced rationally and permits every freedom for the division of spaces inside."[13] It enabled him to limit the use of solid walls to separations between apartments, to introduce moveable partition walls, and to extensively open the façades with glass. It was the means by which he could mediate between the traditional plan that he employed here, which was a standard arrangement for row houses and apartments that had been in use since the mid-nineteenth century,[14] and the decisive, modern elevation with its flat, unadorned surface and long, horizontal windows.

The major east and west façades were composed with larger symmetries and local asymmetries, but in them Mies assiduously acknowledged the frame even though it was literally hidden beneath a layer of stucco.[15] Within the long horizontal bands of windows, thin vertical strips of stucco regularly marked the location of steel columns; the steel beams established the level of window lintels; and the width of the frame determined the close placement of windows to the corners of the building (fig. 5). In this way, the frame grid controlled the organization of the elevations, an invisible presence behind flat surfaces.

At Weissenhof, then, the steel frame as built fact replaced the frame as a proposition reflected upon in written theory; Mies discussed the frame in this building in terms of

4. Apartment Building, Weissenhofsiedlung, Stuttgart, 1925-27, detail of west façade

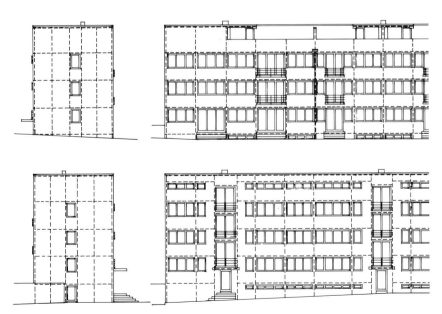

5. Apartment Building, Weissenhofsiedlung, indication of steel frame superimposed on elevation

59

its practical advantages rather than, as earlier, according to its formal purposes. Even so, the frame had become a mediator between plan and façade, each realized independently yet in consonance with the other.

In the decade after Weissenhof and before his departure for the United States, Mies worked with the steel frame in house designs, the Barcelona Pavilion, and the proposed Krefeld Golf Club, all one- or two-story buildings. He also undertook several projects, however, that addressed the multistory, steel-framed, glass-sheathed building, three of them already in 1928. The Adam Store in Berlin and the Stuttgart Bank were intended to be built, the Alexanderplatz competition was didactic in character, but all of these buildings (including fourteen proposed for Alexanderplatz!) were rectangular, glass-sheathed slabs with steel frames revealed at ground level.[16]

The glass curtain wall employed for both the Adam Store (fig. 6) and the Stuttgart Bank Building (see cat. no. 25) consisted of large sheets of glass held in place by a frame of slender verticals and wider horizontals that formed an uninterrupted grid. Rounded corners emphasized the flat, continuous character of the wall, giving the impression of a thin sheet drawn tautly around the structure. The rectangular piers of the structural frame were revealed at ground level, since the wall was not drawn down to this floor. Otherwise, the structure was hidden behind the glass sheathing, which Mies depicted as opaque rather than transparent, almost as if he were still handling the stucco surface of Weissenhof: it was not possible to see the structure of piers and floor slabs that stood immediately behind the glass, nor did the composition of the wall acknowledge the structure supporting it.[17] Neither structure nor skin was detailed in these projects, although each was recognized separately, one superimposed over the other.

Mies's only opportunity to build a multi-story, steel-framed building during this decade was the four-story block of the Krefeld Industry Dye Works of 1931-35.[18] Here, and for the later four-story Administration Building designed in 1937 but never built, he proceeded as at Weissenhof, encasing the structures with a flat stucco and glass sheathing.[19] Then with his move to Chicago and the start of work on the IIT campus and buildings, he turned fully to the frame/sheathing investigation, pursuing it to a resolution by 1946.

The 1939 preliminary scheme for the IIT campus (fig. 7)[20] contained several buildings derived from the 1928 Berlin and Stuttgart projects, in that the grid of structural piers was revealed at ground level, with the reticulated sheathing of glass and frames drawn thinly and tautly around the upper floors. For the four long buildings that marked the periphery of the campus, however, Mies introduced new considerations. The short flanks were treated as contrasting horizontal bands (fig. 8), and stair towers projected from one of the long sides of

6. Adam Department Store project, Berlin, 1928, perspective collage

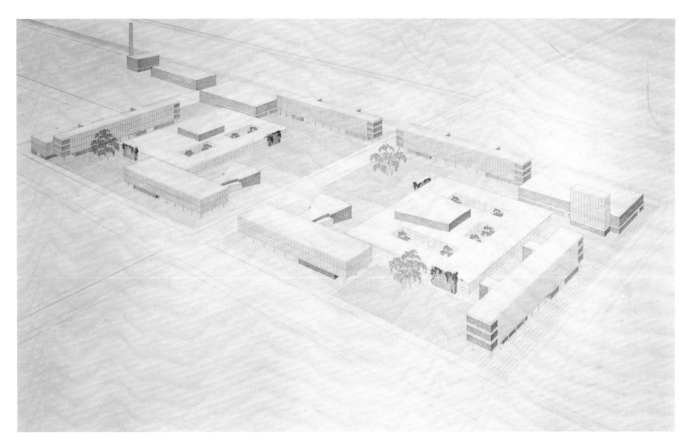

7. IIT Campus, Chicago, 1939, preliminary plan

8. IIT Campus, c. 1939, preliminary design for a classroom building

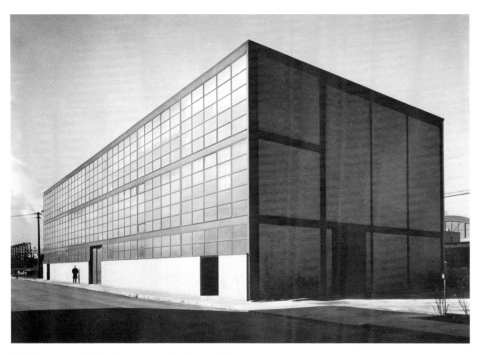

9. Minerals and Metals Research Building, IIT, Chicago, 1942-43

each building. In these ways, the composition of the buildings was changed from that of continuously wrapped slabs, to slabs with distinct fronts, backs, and sides. Within a few years, Mies would capitalize on this differentiation to help resolve his investigation, but it is several IIT buildings of the early 1940s that establish an intermediate stage in this effort.

In the first of the new IIT structures, the Minerals and Metals Research Building of 1942-43 (figs. 9, 10), Mies employed the ubiquitous American structural element, the I-beam, to erect a structural frame that he filled with windows and bricks. This was the Weissenhof and Krefeld system, except that now both frame and infill were visible at one and the same time. The façade with extensive windows was distinguished from the brick flanks, capitalizing on the suggestion of the peripheral buildings in the 1939 scheme. Since neither frame nor masonry infill was covered over with stucco, both had to be as precisely detailed as only the window frames had been in the earlier projects. On the other hand, the lack of a continuous surface, whether of stucco or glass, meant that Mies had sacrificed the continuity of wall for the gain of permitting both structure and infill to signify architecturally.

His contemporary but unrealized project for the Library and Administration Building (figs. 11, 12) grappled with the issue differently. Although it was two stories high, Mies treated the building as a single space, a scheme that permitted him, according to building codes of the time, to use structural supports that were not encased for fireproofing. Using free-

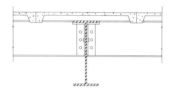

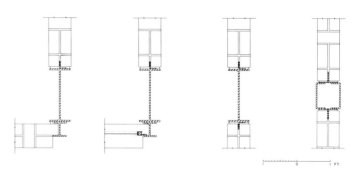

10. Minerals and Metals Research Building, section details

11. Library and Administration Building project, IIT, Chicago, 1944, perspective drawing

standing, I-section columns, as he had employed cruciform columns for Barcelona, Tugendhat, and other projects into the thirties, he established a wide-span structural grid wrapped by large glass plates and brick walls. Externally, the I-section columns registered only on the shorter ends of the building. The result was a variation on the Adam Store and Stuttgart Bank, in that structure was revealed at certain points, though sheathing mostly dominated the exterior.

Alumni Memorial Hall (figs. 13, 14) followed, built in 1945-46. The I-shaped columns of this two-story building had to be encased in concrete fireproofing. Mies now made a decisive architectural response to this pragmatic requirement. As in the Library and Administration project, he put the glass and brick wrapper around the structure, but he also chose to represent the structure symbolically on the external surface. He developed a system of smaller I- and T-shaped steel pieces as a frame for the brick and glass, which visually conferred a structural grid to the exterior. At the corners, the system permitted part of the column (though encased in concrete and dressed with metal) to emerge, again establishing a symbolic presence of the structure.[21] The smaller I-shaped frame held the wall in place and organized it visually, in form and function a variation on the I-shaped column employed as the major structural element of the building. The I-shaped frames were not actually revealed as such on the exterior, however, so that the architectural interaction between the two systems was but partially demonstrated.

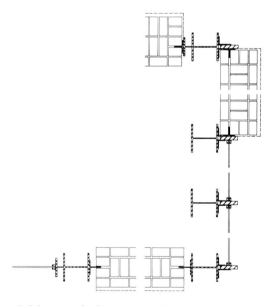

12. Library and Administration Building project, section details

13. Alumni Memorial Hall, IIT, Chicago, 1945-46

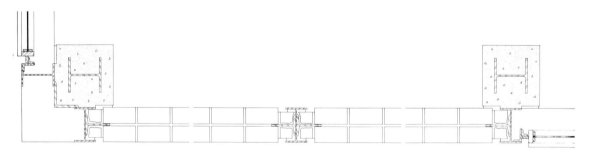

14. Alumni Memorial Hall, section details

These investigations of the early 1940s were brought to bear on Mies's design of Promontory Apartments in 1946, where he established new ground in the dialectic between structure and sheathing.[22] For the steel version of Promontory (fig. 15; the built structure employed a concrete frame and a design strategy similar to the IIT projects), the tall slab had a distinct front, back, and flanks, rather than being uniformly encased by the wall; here Mies drew on the implications of the 1939 IIT project. The encased columns of the frame were revealed at ground level, as in earlier projects, but in addition the post and beam was visible on the flanks. The metal and glass wall was attached only to the façade and was more complex in composition than heretofore. Projecting mullions with an I-shaped section, like the piers of the frame and set four to a bay as established by the frame, were emphatically separated visually from the flat spandrels and plates of glass. In this way, Mies presented a structural frame with infill on the flanks, and a highly articulated curtain wall for the façade, each fully part of the total design. The curtain wall was a transformation of the structural frame, and the structure with infill a variation of the sheathing. The sheathing represented the structure on the façade, and structure assumed characteristics of the sheathing on the flanks.[23]

In the early twenties, Mies had perceived an opposition between structure and sheathing in the tall building. Time and again, he returned to this seemingly irreconcilable disjuncture, and eventually at Promontory created an architectural synthesis of extraordinary power and authority. Having achieved this resolution, he would then draw on it to realize such elegant performances as the 860-880 Lake Shore Drive Apartments (figs. 16, 17) and the Seagram Building.

I apologize, Professor Rowe, for having been excessively longwinded – even if I am concerned that I've given the material shorter shrift than is responsible. On the other hand, I hope that I have been able to demonstrate what has occupied me in considering Mies and the structural frame of the highrise. It was this consideration, stimulated by your discussion, that led me to perceive a discrepancy between your more abstract, large-scale assessment of the frame and my more detailed, particular one. In our different enterprises, we appear to have arrived at different understandings of architectural meaning and significance. You generalize about a Miesian product as part of a process leading to observations on contemporary architecture,[24] whereas I examine a specific process with the end result of explaining the Miesian product. This is the new historical territory about which I initially wrote to you, and I would appreciate knowing of your response to it.

Cordially,
Hyrcanian Woods

15 July 1986

Mr. Hyrcanian Woods
1100 Pennsylvania Ave., NW
Washington, DC 20506

Dear Mr. Woods:

Contemplating your frenetic activity in sorting through all those Miesian words and projects and buildings makes me sweat quite profusely. I am, however, happy for you to do this as long as you do not imply that I am obliged to engage in a similar ritual. Somewhere I do observe, more or less, that "generalizations will scarcely respect the thickness of texture" present even in the most elementary historical situation, but that "if they are understood to be no more than implements they might still do some rough justice to the facts."[25] And I do make appropriate noises about questions "so pressing that one may be justified in proceeding with speculation," and I do offer disclaimers such as "one might surmise" and "one might believe." Which is to say that in dredging the Miesian sediment you appear quite to overlook familiar oppositions such as between fact and reflection, evidence and interpretation, which presumably would account for the manner in which you conduct your enterprise and the manner in which I, differently, conduct mine.

Insouciantly,
Colin Rowe

15. Promontory Apartments, Chicago, 1946-49, perspective drawing of preliminary steel version

16. 860-880 Lake Shore Drive Apartments, Chicago, 1948-51, under construction

17. Opposite page: 860-880 and 900-910 Lake Shore Drive Apartments, Chicago

19 July 1986

Professor Colin Rowe
Architecture/Sibley
Cornell University
Ithaca, NY 14853

Dear Professor Rowe:

I had no intention of bypassing analysis, which I know full well cannot be done; but the realization that began to develop as I explored Mies's work was that understanding depends on acknowledging the complexities of a particular situation. I saw that statements become vulnerable when they are removed from the context within which they were originally made. Used in isolation, they are rendered meaningless – or, what amounts to the same thing, can be declared to contain any meaning a user wishes them to possess.

The Seagram Building is a highly articulate and complex statement. If it is taken as a product isolated in the present, the most curious observations may result. A recent telling instance would be that "the very façade is itself a kind of ornament, for the vertical I-beams of bronze that are attached to the façade serve no real structural purpose – they are really a form of modernist decoration."[26] This suggests that the writer has granted Seagram only a cursory glance, since the I-beams are not attached to the façade but constitute a major part of it; however, another aspect of the assertion concerns me. If the building had been located in its historical context and some effort made to consider the process that led up to it (as I attempted to do in my letter of 4 July), it would be clear that this statement bypasses Mies's architecture entirely. As an observation apparently derived from another agenda, perhaps the impulse to justify ornament in architecture, and retroactively applied to the Seagram Building, it obfuscates the past in equal measure to its disservice to the present.

Persistently,
Hyrcanian W

31 July 1986

Mr. Hyrcanian Woods
1100 Pennsylvania Ave., NW
Washington, DC 20506

Dear Woods:

The other day I was in a taxi from La Guardia and the cabby asked me what I did and I said architecture. We were then driving down Park Avenue, and he looked around at the steel and glass buildings and said, "I don't know anything about architecture, but there certainly seems to be more and more of

less and less." And in just this way we arrive at a mute and barren world when a new utopia attempts to avoid the past.

But then what are we to do about your little problem with history? I myself am more disposed toward something like Oliver Goldsmith's saying, "History owes its excellency more to the writer's manner than to the material of which it is composed." Or perhaps I am closer still to a throw-away by I guess it was Voltaire, "Histories are but fables that have been agreed upon."

My cabby then said, "In buildings, I'm for brick. Brick, tried and true for 3,000 years." For brick, as well as for the building blocks of thought. Which is how it is, really, really, really. I'm completing a text about the nineteenth century, in which I oppose France and the plan with England and the elevation. Among other things. You will presumably be quarrelsome about it.

But then your persistence on getting it right about how it was in the past is dear but too obsessive. Do read a few of the better detective stories, where you will find that collecting facts never solves the mystery. Instead, it is the detective who reflects on the matter who arrives at a solution. The detective is able to connect to the real solution an apparent set of relationships conceived early on as an elegant formula in the mind, well before all the facts are in.

Veritably (and wearily),
Colin Rowe

22 August 1986

Colin Rowe
Architecture/Sibley
Cornell University
Ithaca, NY 14853

Dear Colin Rowe:

I, too, have felt that good historians would be attracted to detective novels, since detective and historian operate in similar ways – up to a point at least. In fact, I was addicted to mysteries long before my interest in architectural history developed. But one fundamental difference does exist between detective and historian, which is wonderfully apparent in *The Name of the Rose*.[27] Even though Umberto Eco permits his sleuth, William of Baskerville, to arrive at a correct solution on the basis of William's faulty hypothesis, William nevertheless has been led to the perpetrator of the crimes, wily, blind Jorge, and it is Jorge's admission of what he's done that enables William to adjust and correct his analysis.

William as an historian, however, never has a Jorge to clarify and confirm the interconnections of past events. Consequently, control of an historical analysis can only be achieved by understanding the motivations that are revealed through examining the more inclusive setting.

Juxtaposing situations derived from the past with what appear to be similar ones in the present abuses this setting, and the architect who then uses this information fabricates myths divorced from reality. When that separation is extreme, society tends to refer to it as insanity. The next query in this line of thought is, I suppose, what is reality? You take my meaning, however, and I leave this question be, which in any event is too far from the point at which I began.

Sleuthfully,
Hyrcanian

Picture postcard from Colin Rowe to Hyrcanian Woods of an airview of Hadrian's villa at Tivoli: "Wasn't Hadrian brilliant! An enormous villa complex – a small city really – constructed from bits and pieces of reconstructed historical buildings that he had seen during his travels."

26 September 1986

Colin Rowe
Architecture/Sibley
Cornell University
Ithaca, NY 14853

Dear Colin Rowe:

Your postcard reminds me that my concern about reading sense into statements by locating them within their context suggests two corollaries, or more specifically, two liabilities in establishing a rationale for the making of design today on the basis of forms extracted from the past. The first is that any specific situation from the past is not easily understood, for it is inevitably dense with conflicts and unclarities. When considering an architecture from the past, the specific hierarchy of values of that time needs to be established and the particular meanings ascertained with which those forms were imbued.[28] To establish a context, and to explore intention on the basis of that context, requires perseverance in equal measure to insight. This plodding labor is necessary, a practical reason for the professional historian. It tells us why buildings turned out as they did.

Nor is this observation limited to matters of historical discourse. That segment of architectural practice today that uses a formal element from a past setting as appliqué in a contemporary design collapses as a legitimate enterprise in the very act. At first glance it appears an easy way of providing a design with meaning, a message, significance. But the meaning of an architectural element in one context can never be automatically transferred into a different one. To do this, you would have to transport the entire social and cultural paraphernalia from one place and time to another, an absurd proposition since you would then be in that past rather than your own present. Meaning is not available by snipping a quotation from one text and gluing it onto a different sheet of paper. When a building is a pastiche, it is lost to sense. Though Louis Kahn was impressed by the greatness of the Roman vault, the vaults of the Kimbell Museum are not vaults taken from ancient Rome.[29]

A second liability comes into play when the work of establishing a context is not undertaken. A design rationale extracted from the past without this necessary control is actually a polemic given the semblance of legitimacy by historical trappings. Here the past is manipulated to bear false witness. Without acknowledging its true nature, the polemic banks on the authority of history to justify what it asserts. This device can be potent and persuasive. A polemic achieves clarity through its singleness of purpose, whereas a particular historical setting is complex and elusive. If a polemic is masked as history, the past seemingly provides an obvious message, whereas in reality it is not the historical circumstance but the polemic that is clear and certain. Parallels between past and present become dramatic when isolated assertions are separated from their setting and juxtaposed to other assertions similarly isolated. As Mussolini put it, describing antique monuments transformed by *svrentramenti,* or the stripping away of all surrounding construction, they "loom gigantic in their necessary solitude."[30] In this exaggeration the buildings have been lost to their meanings.

Both historians and architects, it seems to me, have suffered the consequences of these liabilities. Historians have contemplated several decades of buildings put up in America since World War II, duly noting the preponderance of the tall, steel-framed building sheathed in a skin of glass sheets and thin metal frames. They have then cast back to Mies's multi-storied buildings of the twenties and thirties, observed his American work of the forties, and with these images in mind, characterized the American skyscraper as Miesian – in this suggesting that Mies single-handedly shaped the direction of American architecture.[31]

Some effort has been made to reassess this conclusion by showing that architectural attitudes similar to Mies's were evolving in America during the 1930s and 1940s.[32] When the authority of Mies's architecture was joined with this indigenous tradition, a powerful and persuasive position was established. But the question of why so many dubious performances were produced in this mode continues to nag. Here again, Professor Rowe, I believe that context comes into play, though from a different vantage point.

In his embracing analysis of architecture, Quatremère de Quincy distinguished between type and model, the first being an attitude or set of principles, the other an imitated object.[33] "The word 'type' presents less the image of a thing to copy or imitate completely than the idea of an element which ought itself to serve as a rule for the model. . . . The model . . . is an object that should be repeated as it is; the type, on the contrary, is an object after which each [artist] can conceive works of art that may have no resemblance."

I suspect that much of the skyscraper problem can be understood, at least at one level, from this vantage point. Many makers of the postwar American highrise observed certain existing buildings, as Mies's perfected 860-880 Lake Shore Drive Apartments, accepted them as models, and designed variations on this theme. They did not examine the process that led to the making of these buildings, as I outlined it in my earlier letter. They designed from the model rather than the rule.

Yours,
Hyrcanian

Notes

1. William J. R. Curtis, *Modern Architecture Since 1900* (Englewood Cliffs, N.J., 1982), p. 266.

2. Peter Ackroyd, *New York Times Book Review,* January 19, 1986, p. 3.

3. Colin Rowe, *The Mathematics of the Ideal Villa* (Cambridge, Mass., 1976), specifically the essays, "Mannerism and Modern Architecture" of 1950; "Character and Composition; or Some Vicissitudes of Architectural Vocabulary in the Nineteenth Century" of 1953-54; "Chicago Frame" of 1956; and "Neo-'Classicism' and Modern Architecture I" of 1956-57.

4. Rowe, "Chicago Frame" (note 3), pp. 99-101.

5. Ibid., p. 106.

6. As the new architecture was labeled in Germany; see Norbert Huse, *"Neues Bauen" 1918 bis 1933. Moderne Architektur in der Weimarer Republik* (Munich, 1975).

7. Ludwig Mies van der Rohe, "Hochhausprojekt für Bahnhof Friedrichstrasse in Berlin," *Frühlicht* 1 (1922), pp. 122-124.

8. Ludwig Mies van der Rohe, "Bürohaus," *G. Zeitschrift für Gestaltung* (Berlin) 3 (June 1923). Mart Stam, *ABC Beiträge zum Bauen* (Zurich) 3/4 (1925), pp. 4-5, recognized this disjuncture between structure and form, and proposed a possible though still not very precisely detailed construction that resulted in a redesigning of Mies's tower.

9. Steven K. Peterson, "Idealized Space: Mies-conception or Realized Truth?" *Inland Architect* 21, 5 (May 1977), pp. 4-11.

10. Mies's pronouncements about the project in: Mies, "Bürohaus" (note 8). F. von Emperger, *Handbuch für Eisenbetonbau*, 4 vols. (Berlin, 1907-09), provides a thorough overview of reinforced concrete technology as it had developed by the first decade of the twentieth century. The engineering of Mies's office building, to the extent that it is revealed in surviving documents, was also discussed with David P. Billington and Robert Mark in June 1984.

11. The Concrete Country House of 1922-23 reveals a similar form/structure disjuncture. This single-family house, the point of closest association with an individual's private life, was not presented primarily as reinforced concrete construction, but in a way that challenged the traditions of the house, certainly for Weimar Germany of that time. A flat roof, expansive horizontal windows, and unimpeded spaces flowing openly into one another resulted in a design that was so unlike the traditional house that even Gropius, on first seeing the model of it in 1923, did not recognize it as a house: Gropius letter to Mies, June 7, 1923, Library of Congress.

12. The frame consisted of columns, beams, and joists. Details of the structure are listed in the official catalogue for the Weissenhof exhibition, for which the building was put up, *Werkbund Ausstellung die Wohnung* (Stuttgart, 1927), p. 25.

13. Ludwig Mies van der Rohe, "Zu meinem Block," *Bau und Wohnung* (Stuttgart, 1927), p. 77: "Der Skelettbau ist hierzu das geeignetste Konstruktionssystem. Er ermöglicht eine rationale Herstellung und lässt der inneren Raumaufteilung jede Freiheit."

14. This type of layout – i.e., stairs serving apartments to right and left at each landing, and the service core, kitchen, and bath clustered along the stair wall – can already be found in a Berlin housing project of 1849-50; see D. Rentschler and W. Schirmer, *Berlin und seine Bauten*, IV B (Berlin, 1974), p. 8. Mark Stankard, a graduate student in the history of architecture program at Cornell University, pointed to these and other examples in a seminar paper that he prepared in the fall of 1984. Mies's moveable partitions within each apartment, however, meant that the internal arrangements of rooms could be different for each unit, a situation that clearly distinguished his plan from standard bearing-wall housing.

15. See drawings 469 and 474 in the Mies van der Rohe Archive, Museum of Modern Art, New York, for a full presentation of the façades. A few poorly reproduced photographs of the building under construction in *Bau und Wohnung* show the three-dimensional configuration of the frame in relation to the windows and wall infill. Construction drawings in the Mies Archive further explicate the frame and its joining with other components of the building.

16. Franz Schulze, *Mies van der Rohe: A Critical Biography* (Chicago, 1985), pp. 146-151. Additional visual materials in the "Mies van der Rohe Centennial Exhibition," Museum of Modern Art, February 10-April 15, 1986.

17. This statement should be slightly modified and augmented. At the far edge of the Adam Store, a floor slab is just visible behind the sheathing. Because it is so thin, Arthur Drexler has suggested that Mies may have intended the slabs to be steel: "Mies Centennial Exhibition," Museum of Modern Art, label caption. The glass sheathing is drawn down as a narrow strip at the top of the ground story, creating a delicate shadow joint and suggesting an abstract entablature above the abstract columns of the structure – should one be inclined to read the building as a kind of classicism. A low wall along the sidewalk obscures where the columns stand on the ground, lending the building an ephemeral quality, or perhaps a certain lack of specificity, which is inherent as well in the treatment of the sheathing and floor slabs.
In the presentation drawings of the Stuttgart Bank, some of the vertical supports are visible behind the glass, suggesting, though barely, an architectural interaction between sheathing and structure. The buildings in the Alexanderplatz competition are depicted more schematically than the store and bank, but the structure/sheathing argument appears to be the same.
At this point, it can be noted that in Mies's projects for Friedrichstrasse of 1929 and the Reichsbank of 1933, the structure/sheathing dialectic is not engaged. Mies investigates only the character of the flat curtain wall in these undertakings.

18. The factory is discussed in Wolf Tegethoff, "Industriearchitektur und Neues Bauen, Mies van der Rohes Verseidag-Fabrik in Krefeld," *Archithese* 13 (May/June 1983), pp. 33-38. Philip C. Johnson, *Mies van der Rohe*, 3rd rev. ed. (New York, 1983), illustrates the Administration Building project on pp. 128-130. Also see "Mies Centennial Exhibition," Museum of Modern Art.

19. Mies's office assistant Eric Holthoff prepared line drawings of the 1937 project and Mies then applied shading to them. As depicted on these renderings, a point especially emphasized by the shading, the sheathing is continuous and flat, an exaggerated version of Weissenhof, since the window glass is placed on the same plane as the stucco rather than being slightly recessed.

20. Dates of the IIT plans and buildings still await clarification. Kevin Harrington, who has studied the IIT undertaking and is the editor of a forthcoming book on the campus design, has kindly shared his knowledge and insights about the IIT building history with me. Johnson (note 18), pp. 131-153, offers the most complete published documentation of the projects and buildings to 1947. Schulze (note 16), pp. 218-230, is briefer about specific proposals, as was the "Mies Centennial Exhibition."

21. Schulze (note 16), p. 226, although focusing his attention on the corner detail of the building, elegantly summarizes this design strategy: " . . . the real structure of Alumni Memorial Hall, though suppressed, is expressed: what one knows is there is not what one sees, but is made evident by what one sees. Mies's reasoning is . . . to demonstrate that the supporting steel frame is the basis, or essence, of the building, it is indicated, rather than shown, externally; to acknowledge that what shows, moreover, is not fact but symbol of fact, the columnar covering plate and the skin I-beam stop short of the earth."

22. Ibid., pp. 241-243, for specific information about the project.

23. Marvin Trachtenberg, "Modern Architecture," in Marvin Trachtenberg and Isabelle Hyman, *Architecture From Prehistory to Post-Modernism/The Western Tradition* (New York and Englewood Cliffs, N.J., 1986), p. 538, emphasizes this point in his discussion of the Seagram Building: "Just as the column had been used from antiquity to the

nineteenth century to express gravitational forces within structure, the structural I-beam would be visually omnipresent in small scale as a truth symbol of the new structural reality."

24. Colin Rowe, "The Present Urban Predicament," *The Cornell Journal of Architecture* 1 (Fall 1981), pp. 16-33, discusses the polarity of "physics envy" and "Zeitgeist worship" in the making of modern architecture.

25. See Rowe (note 3), p. 122, for the citations in this paragraph.

26. Paul Goldberger, "His Buildings Have the Simplicity of Poetry," *New York Times,* February 16, 1986. Another more sophisticated attempt to associate Mies's architecture with ornament is: Thomas Hall Beeby, "Vitruvius Americanus. Mies' Ornament," *Inland Architect* 21, 5 (May 1977), pp. 12-15. Beeby argues that Mies, in his "search for a valid modern architecture," sought a "unity of common [architectural] convention," which he found by applying "the abstract methodology of ornament" to his buildings. Beeby finds this methodology in the "grid-derived ornament" illustrated in Franz Sales Meyer, *Handbook of Ornament, A Grammar of Art, Industrial and Architectural Designing in all its Branches, for Practical as well as Theoretical Use,* translation of *Handbuch der Ornamentik,* 8th ed. (Leipzig, 1890), which he associates with Mies's "grid-derived architecture," as seen in the Barcelona Pavilion and his IIT buildings. The discipline of ornament is analogous to Mies's design approach, resulting in a "complete" and "convincing" style of powerful "authenticity." Beeby concludes that, "The architecture of Mies van der Rohe was consciously conceived in this light to become *ARCHITECTURE,* and to a great degree succeeded." Beeby's argument is elaborated with references to neoclassicism, constructivism, and "rational construction," but its thrust concerns Mies's relation to ornament. Although ingenious, this consideration imposes a position on Mies and his work that is alien to both. Gridding and structure are related to Mies's pursuit of architecture in a technological age, as he perceived it, not to any discourse with which he was involved about an ornamental system.

27. Umberto Eco, *The Name of the Rose,* translated from the Italian by William Weaver (New York, 1984). Originally published as *Il Nome della Rosa* (Milan, 1980).

28. This observation is indebted to the analysis in an exceptional Cornell dissertation by Mark R. Ashton, "Purpose and Purposes in the Study of Art," 1981.

29. "My mind is full of Roman greatness and the vault so etched itself in my mind that, though I cannot employ it, it's there always ready." *Light is the Theme: Louis I. Kahn and the Kimbell Art Museum. Comments on Architecture by Louis Kahn,* compiled by Nell E. Johnson (Fort Worth, Tex., 1975), p. 33. The Kimbell and its cycloid vaults can be studied in this publication, as well as in *Louis I. Kahn, Sketches for the Kimbell Art Museum,* organized by David M. Robb, Jr., essay by Marshall D. Meyers (Fort Worth, Tex., 1978).

30. Spiro Kostof, *Third Rome: 1870-1950, Traffic and Glory* (Berkeley, 1973).

31. See, for example, William H. Jordy, *American Buildings and Their Architects: The Impact of European Modernism in the Mid-Twentieth Century* (New York, 1976), especially chapter 4, in which Jordy discusses Mies. Or Schulze (note 16), p. 220: "Mies's sway over post-World War II architecture can be measured on the one hand by the rectilinearization of the skylines of all major international cities and on the other by the force of the rebellion against his principles which rose up after his death in 1969."

32. Christian F. Otto, "American Skyscrapers and Weimar Modern: Transactions between Fact and Idea," *The Muses Flee Hitler* (Washington, D.C., 1983), pp. 151-165.

33. See Quatremère de Quincy, "Architecture," in *Encyclopédie Méthodique,* vol. 3, pt. II (Paris, 1825). This quotation is from the translation in "Quatremère de Quincy, Type," Introduction by Anthony Vidler, in *Oppositions* 8 (Spring 1977), pp. 147-150. More recently, Françoise Choay has developed these ideas philosophically and historically in relation to the built domain, distinguishing between Alberti's use of the rule, which possesses generative power, and the model proposed by Moore, which is copied: Françoise Choay, *La règle et le modèle* (Paris, 1980).

Excellence: The Culture of Mies as Seen in his Notes and Books

by Francesco Dal Co

Areté: it comes to mind that the work of Mies van der Rohe can be summarized with this singularly beautiful word. Or at least, it was a word to which he always returned; he would dwell on it attentively, reading Plato's *Republic* with a stoic's eyes. *Areté* does not mean "conquest" or "aim"; in relating its meaning to Mies's oeuvre it is especially important to avoid assigning this Greek word the meaning of "goal" or "target." *Areté* is the essence of *operari,* even in the Schopenhauerian sense: a form of experience motivated by contraction of the will into a specific historic time, such as the modern age, which makes it necessary to "sacrifice God for nothingness," as Nietzsche maintains in *Beyond Good and Evil,* concluding that "this paradoxical mystery of the final cruelty was reserved for the generation that is now coming up: all of us already know something of this."[1]

Mies is one of the foremost exponents of this generation. That, no doubt, was one of the reasons he studied the above-mentioned work of Nietzsche with such voracity that one is led to conjecture whether those very pages might not constitute the premise for the unfolding of the parable that is his original, peaceful approach to his work.

If one considers the characteristics of Mies's work from the perspective outlined in *Beyond Good and Evil,* one begins to grasp the conflict that arises between the *areté* of *operari* and its historical definition. This is borne out by an examination of the distinction, so often made by Mies (and not only in reference to his own work), between *Architecture* and *Baukunst* [literally, the "building art"]. By noting, in this connection, how the English language has no expression equivalent to the German word – so wonderfully succinct and packed with meanings – Mies seems to allude precisely to the difference which *areté* embodies, making *Baukunst* a spiritual expression, a practice liberated from need and from the slavery of necessity.

"Architecture," on the other hand, interprets the prevalence of function, the mechanical conjoining of forms and needs *through* the project, the limiting of experience inside the horizons imposed by necessity. "Architecture" is mere "naturalism," a manifestation of the Nietzschean *laisser aller. Baukunst,* by contrast, is spiritual art, a virtuous exercise of invention through the observance of solid laws and customs, and at the same time it is intellectual defiance, dangerous transgression. *Baukunst* shuns the *new* and favors the *good,* to use words that Mies seems to have taken from a beautiful passage in Nietzsche that he dwelt on at considerable length, a complex passage that merits being quoted here in full, as it clearly contains numerous suggestions that ought to be taken into consideration in any interpretation of the German architect's work.

> Every artist knows how far from any feeling of letting himself go his "most natural" state is – the free ordering, placing, disposing, giving form in the moment of "inspiration" – and how strictly and subtly he obeys thousandfold laws precisely then, laws that precisely on account of their hardness and determination defy all formulation through concepts. . . . What is essential "in heaven and on earth" seems to be, to say it once more, that there should be *obedience* over a long period of time and in a *single* direction.[2]

It might be interesting to try to think what Mies's reasons were for dwelling on this passage, but in any case they were clearly important. Here Nietzsche is overturning the "romantic" notion, so to speak, of freedom of inspiration as the origin of the work of art. Inspiration is not so much tension given to the production of meaning as, rather, the event of an encounter between signification and the work. Inspiration thus is not in this sense the fulfillment of the human productive faculties, nor the "naturalistic prison" of the intellect, but the conclusive act of the mind's laborious preparation for a decisive encounter. Taking off from this overturning, it is probably safe to add, extending the distinction made by Mies, that if "architecture" is the expression of a naturalistic dimension of the project, *Baukunst* is instead a manifestation of the pertinacity of the

1. Museum for a Small City project, 1942, collage

spirit, and the freedom it exercises within the law. This freedom has nothing to do with the will; it implies persistence, adherence to rules, clear and well-aimed choices. If one considers the radical antinaturalism of Mies's projects, the perseverance with which he insists on his own linguistic constructions, the slowness of his method with its wealth of innovations, what emerges are so many aspects of a practice that has many points of tangency with the wonderful synthesis presented in the passage from Nietzsche cited above. There is no lack, moreover, of confirmation of these connections in the various, well-informed studies that have been recently devoted to the master from Aachen.

But we can hardly claim to have exhausted the subject we have just introduced here, given the limitations of this essay. Mies's persistent dwelling on the unequivalence of *Baukunst* and architecture provides further useful means for interpreting both the mastery of construction and the axiology toward which his work tends. But in order to proceed in this direction, we must turn our attention to one dimension of Mies's case that merits further investigation and, in any event, cannot be ignored. As Wolf Tegethoff and Franz Schulze have pointedly illustrated, recounting in full detail numerous episodes of Mies's life, Mies's *operari* is dominated by the dimension of waiting, like a musical score dominated by suspensions.[3] Not unlike Nietzsche, Mies believes "that a thought comes when 'it' wishes, and not when 'I' wish."[4] The wait for this sort of event, for inspiration's self-assertion, creates the need for freedom which guides the existential choices made by the German architect. These choices, moreover,

seem themselves determined by a kind of predisposition to "idleness" – here intended, once again, in a strictly Nietzschean sense. Also connected to this predisposition is another choice that marked the architect's life, as numerous scholars have pointed out: the choice of solitude. A solitude that seems lived and conceived in accordance with Nietzsche's exhortation: "Choose the *good* solitude, the free, playful, light solitude that gives you, too, the right to remain good in some sense."[5]

Solitude and waiting. It would be reductive if, in covering these two complementary aspects of Mies's vision, we were to favor considerations of personality and psychology. From up close, isolation and pause are attributes of an existential condition that confirms and broadens the meaning now ascribed to the notion of "inspiration." Inspiration is not the fruit of a choice made with production in mind, nor does it represent the full attainment of perfect naturalness by the planning intellect. Rather it is the occurrence of an unknown, unexpected encounter; it is, paradoxically, the moment of inspiration's appearance within inspiration itself.

As a not inconsiderable reader of Konrad Fiedler and Alois Riegl, Mies realizes that the origin of the work lies in the work's own self-revelation to the "mind." The origin is, therefore, always a showing, the thought's arising into presence. The recognition and acceptance of the necessity of a patient wait are indispensable conditions for this manifestation, as are also "idleness" and that virtue which predisposes the mind to receiving the "thought" at the instant at which "it" decides to unveil itself. The decisions involved in this system of relationships are not, however, ordered according to a scale of values: indeed, the determination to wait is as essential as the resolution effected by that which is waited for when it reveals itself, fulfilling the wait itself.

Far from partaking in the modern celebration of the primacy and rootless freedom of invention, Mies prefers to linger and listen. It is no accident that suspension is the salient feature of his design, or that chance predominates in his collages (fig. 1).

Solitude feeds on extended pauses. It scorns the *prestissimo* rhythm of the constant search for novelty propelling the experiments of modernism. It is perfectly understandable, therefore, that Mies should have been particularly struck by yet another axiom from *Beyond Good and Evil:* "A German is almost incapable of *presto* in his language."[6] Slowness feeds on drawn-out pauses, and it is the "form" of the tempo required by the event and by the architecture which, according to Mies, is granted a privileged glimpse of the essential image of an epoch. In executing his own architecture, the master from Aachen indeed works like a "real German," without haste, allowing himself long periods of time, as Franz Schulze repeatedly points out in his biography.

These "waits" make way for the concentrated tension of the listening, which is destined to be fulfilled, according to Max Scheler (another of Mies's favorite authors), with the appearance of the "truth in the fact." Truth, however, can be observed and heard only after one has taken the necessary distance from those appearances that mask "the true" from its own time. This detachment reinforces the need for solitude in which the "listening creator" must learn to live. Mies's isolation finds full expression in the austerity of the languages he uses (fig. 2).

It would, of course, be meaningless to put the systems of communication used by the German architect all on the same level. As an interpreter of the radical choices facing the "vigilant spirits" of "his generation," he expresses himself perfectly in a single language, that of his great architecture, whose shadows can only filter through the lines of this study, which is devoted instead to examining a number of hypotheses concerning the nature of what could be called Mies's "second language." And yet the inventive brilliance, precision, and power of Mies's architectural "scores" are also reflected in the aphoristic verve of his rare theoretical statements. This is because in these instances as well, the language is shaped according to the idea, shared by Scheler, that only the instantaneousness of the event offers one a chance to encounter the "truth of the fact."

Listening and waiting thus come together in the "slow German language" spoken by Mies. But listening requires silence, and the greater the will to hear, the more *quiet* there must be. Mies's work does in fact create silent spaces and volumes, the sheltering purpose of which is not aimed at satisfying the *natural* inclinations of the inhabitants, as Mrs. Tugendhat perceived, but at attending to the spirit and to the potential for thought. The quest for silence is the guiding thread of Mies's constructions, whether they take the form of the highest tectonic perfection or express themselves in the extreme concision of a theoretical observation. And whether he is working on the articulation of his ascetic spaces or constructing his spare aphorisms, what prevail are procedures, attitudes, and thoughts aimed toward negation, as Mies himself acknowledged when explaining their incommunicability to Frank Lloyd Wright.[7]

This tendency is confirmed in the fact that Mies, whenever possible, is more inclined to subtract than to add. It would be useful here to recall the famous assertion by Mies that, given the analogy between architecture and language, it is possible to think of the architect as refining a tectonic language which, depending on its consistency, can attain the purest form of prose and thus the heights of poetry as well.[8] But the analogy of which Mies speaks is without question determined by negativity and by essentially "antinaturalistic" practices. The proof of this lies in the reference to poetry. In fact, poetry for Mies does not represent the culmination of a productive activity, the harmonious conjunction of a polyphony of sounds in meaning. Meaning and – after further mediation – symbol are not "producible": they arise from the attainment of fullness in the word, and this fullness is represented by essentiality. Only a purely essential word is suitable for the poet's language. Just as the "truth of the event" is represented by the "fact," so the meaning of every expression lies in its greatest simplification. For this reason, tectonic perfection and poetry share the value of essentiality. Language, in all its manifestations, is a continuous and inexhaustible tending toward a perfect substantiality, or, in other words, toward a state of quiet represented by the "moment" at which nothing can be added to or subtracted from every construction (fig. 3).

Projected toward this condition, the work substantiates the product of the careful listening in wait for possible events, and it justifies the "idleness." Tension, which the work halts but does not resolve, thus motivates Mies's choice to accept the *beautiful* only as an implication of the *good* – this being the ultimate meaning of the sentence in Mies's famous letter to Walter Riezler: *"Alles Wie wird getragen von einem Was"* (All "how" is supported by a "what").

This "acceptance" is for Mies a synonym for *projecting*, although the project, as we shall see, is not taken up purely in accepting/listening. However, while for modern architectural culture and artistic practices the project is realized in the new and constructed as a program of dominion over the future and of form imposed on time, for Mies, formal research is the extreme tension created within a spiritual exercise, the main

2. Bismarck Memorial monument project, Bingerbrück-Bingen, 1910

3. Barcelona Pavilion, 1929

task of which is to think itself. This exercise may lead to the occurrence of the beautiful, though Mies understands the "beautiful" in Saint Thomas Aquinas's terms, emphasizing its differences from and proximity to the "good." This conception seems also to show the influence of Jacques Maritain, whose work was apparently of interest to Mies. *Art and Scholasticism,* in particular, which the German architect read in an English translation around the mid-1940s, presents a confirmation of the conception of the *beautiful* as an expression, in the work of art, of the fusion of *wholeness* and *clarity* in accordance with the rules of *proportion* and *order.*

The concept of order is essential to an understanding of Mies's work and thought. If there is a salient value in his axiology, it is represented in this concept. We shall see further on how, in as much as the question is by now apparent, a rather strict relationship is established between *order* and *quiet* in the architect's work, a connection that determines the combination of theory and practice in Mies's experience. In this regard, Mies's mind show a close connection to the thought of Romano Guardini, one of the authors most quoted in the records and notebooks that Mies left behind. The understanding that underlies Mies's opinions on such important issues as the nature of the work of art and the characteristics of the modern age is strikingly consistent with the opinions of Guardini, a theologian born in Italy who wrote in German. Like Guardini, Mies believes the industrially and socially advanced modern age to have a profound need for *order.* This need springs from the mechanisms governing the world's pulse – the "second world" (to use Guardini's terminology), which is dominated by technology [*tecnica*] and the processes of standardization. According to the common understanding of our two protagonists, this need can only be fulfilled by *organization.*

Mies dwells insistently on this conviction, while at the same time imputing to technique [*tecnica*], as the generative phenomenon of those mechanisms, a significance that can be easily illustrated with the words of Guardini. What are, then, the characteristic features of this "second world" that aspires to order through organization and to form through technique? In order to find a satisfactory answer, even if it be partial, it is necessary to understand that Mies and Guardini begin from the same premises, though by different routes. We can get a good sense of these premises in a brilliant observation made by Hans Urs von Balthasar, to whom we owe many pointed interpretations of Guardini's thought: the world that the generation announced by Nietzsche, of which Guardini and Mies are part, must live in is "an artificial world that has lost its coordination and has splintered into many parts which, because of their lack of interconnection, lacerate man and create extreme anarchy."[9]

It is not unusual to find, among Mies's notes, the word "chaos" underscored or with various notations, but always intended as in radical opposition to the notion of "cosmos," which is instead an expression of order and, more importantly, of organic harmony between the whole and its parts. In his use of this expression, Mies summarizes Guardini's analysis in the most concise manner possible. Mies counters Guardini's "world without center" with rigid demands for order, as though interpreting Guardini's thought, designing his own rigorous, Schinkelesque volumetric compositions to encompass ascetically shaped spaces.

The formal characteristics of Mies's demands for order are, however, difficult to decipher and thus open to misinterpretation. If we consider the great care with which the architect read Guardini's 1926 *Briefe vom Comer See* (and from which he took more than a few quotations), we may find some useful clues to this problem. In using the adjective "rigid" to describe Mies's approach, I intend it not only on the formal level, but as a quality emphasizing the *rigorous compulsion* that we are ascribing to Mies's program. And I should add that such demands are never expressed – even on a strictly architectural level – through abstract languages, contrary to what is usually believed. Even Mies's most concise, limpid, and penetrating representations shun abstraction. And even on a strictly formal level of analysis, no confusion between the concepts of "abstraction" and "spirituality" is admissible. The need for order embodied by Mies's constructions and projects – from the most profound of his poetic compositions to the most radical of his typological experiments, from the Pavilion of Barcelona to the square blocks of the Afrikanischestrasse in Berlin (fig. 4) – always expresses a programmatic rejection of abstraction. From this perspective, any ambiguity that might be encountered on a formal level is resolved on the theoretical level. The rejection of abstraction is, in fact, perfectly consistent with Mies's reasons for favoring order as a typically modern value. Abstraction, on the other hand, is the most obvious and deeply rooted characteristic of the "second world"; it lies at the origin of the "chaos" which Mies, like Guardini, would counter with faith in organization.

All this might be better explained by the final words of the "Third Letter" of Guardini's *Briefe vom Comer See,* a statement with which Mies most certainly would have agreed:

> All civilisation has from the beginning possessed this abstract quality. But once modern thought, conceptual and mathematical thought, began to spread, and once modern technology became part of the work world, this abstract quality became decisively predominant. It determined, in a definitive manner, our relation to the universe, our direction, and consequently, our existence.[10]

Mies's available declarations and notes show him to be closer to this vision of the nature of the modern world than to Oswald Spengler's ideas, to which they have not infrequently been compared. But Mies's readings and sources cannot be

4. Municipal Housing Development on the Afrikanischestrasse, Berlin, 1926-27

traced according to any orthodox criteria, and often seem to be the result of intermingling and unexpected overlappings. This is why the influence of Spengler's *Decline of the West* (though we should not forget *Preussentum und Sozialismus*, the 1929 Munich edition of which was in Mies's library) can indeed be found in Mies's continual arguments appealing to the dichotomy between *Kultur* and *Zivilisation* as an essential given of the abstraction shaping the modern world; but this typically Spenglerian theme is also much in evidence in Guardini, who on this matter assumes theoretical and analytical positions that are not incompatible with those taken, but with a different slant, by both Ernst Troeltsch and Georg Simmel, both of whose works were familiar to Mies.

From *The Decline of the West* and from the author of *Die Grossstädte und das Geistesleben*, Mies derives the idea of the metropolis as an epiphenomenon of the Guardinian "second world," through a synthesis that is not orthodox but certainly neither very unusual. In the metropolis, the progressive *Vergeistigung* [the "process of spiritualization and abstraction"] (to use a term dear to another author read by Mies, Werner Sombart) creates the process of the general uprooting of the modes of life, while transforming things into abstract fetishes. If in the *Grossstädt* ["large city"] studied and described by the architect's loyal friend Ludwig Karl Hilberseimer, man becomes the mere subject of "a system of spiritual edifices which form without our personal collaboration,"[11] as Sombart maintains, an analogous process takes place involving the forms, relations and things that make up the urban environment.

Guardini's analysis of the nature of modern processes of alienation has numerous points of tangency with the philosophical tradition here invoked. Since they share the premises of this web of problems, Mies's positions regarding the relations between "beautiful" and "good," between form and function, between abstraction and essentiality, between usefulness and the project in the area of research, would bear fruitful examination in the light of a significant passage from the Berlin philosopher Georg Simmel's *Philosophie des Geldes*, the relevance of which to the various matters thus far discussed should be clear:

Now this whole development from value in terms of usefulness to value in terms of beauty is a process of objectification. When we say something is beautiful, its qualities and meaning are independent of the disposition and need of the subject in a manner entirely dif-

5. Aerial view of the campus at IIT, looking north, 1986

ferent from when we say that something is merely useful. When things are only useful, they are fungible, one is replaceable by another, each has the same effect as the other.[12]

The "facts" that Mies strips from the masks of the new are the products of this process of objectification. And within this process, the architect intends to create order.

In the "'hominized' (*hominisierte*) world . . . , power (*Macht*), man's instrument for dominating the world, overcomes man's subjugating force and makes him a slave: formerly a person, he becomes a thing."[13] Thus, von Balthasar on Guardini. The process of general *Vergeistigung* can neither be stopped nor reversed; if anything, it can be "shaped," that is, "organized." In a world inhabited by "things" possessed of the nature attributed them by Guardini and Simmel, Mies's architecture speaks the dry language of the ordering mind, promising nothing, fully aware that "life" may find refuge only in solitude (figs. 5, 6). Indeed, as Guardini maintains, "Man now lives in the abstract. And of course the abstract, the conceptual, is not 'spirit'! Spirit is life."[14] The task of ordering, organizing, and showing this world forces Mies to opt for extreme concreteness in his own practices, which concede nothing to abstraction.

For Mies, too, the values of *Kultur* founder in *Zivilisation*'s processes of objectification. Mies absorbed the dichotomy thus designated through the filter of his "German readings" and continually called it to the attention of his interlocutors. The implications stemming from this *Entfremdung* ["alienation"] can once again be summed up with the words of Guardini: "To me it is as though our heritage has ended up among the gears of some monstrous machine that makes a hash of everything. We are becoming poor, utterly poor."[15]

This last statement, though not surprising, is of considerable importance. Mies's poetry, in its essentiality, reaches conclusions similar to Guardini's. Defining the architectural form of modern *Vergeistigung* means showing the progressive impoverishment of life, the rapid decay of the spirit, the madness of things overwhelmed by their own usefulness. *Giving form* is nothing other than giving order to the chaotic foundering of all residual experience in an irreversible *Armut* ["poverty"]. Faced with "chaos," Mies does not, however, accept the role of detached observer. When noting that the shadows of the sunset are beginning to extend over the entire world, no longer covering just the "West," he does not cast the complacent gaze of someone witnessing a distant shipwreck.

6. Opposite page: Crown Hall, IIT, Chicago, 1950-56

His detachment from things and, therefore, from the "new" is instead a conscious choice aimed at determining the exact distance at which the eyes might bring the "truth," the "essentiality of facts," into focus. Mies's thought, like Guardini's, is not nostalgic but lucidly disillusioned: "Whatever is not totally authentic, in itself and in our souls, will fail. This is how it must be. Perhaps we are on the verge of nothing but a more real essentiality."[16] But while in Guardini there is a shadow of doubt surrounding this end, the same is not true for Mies, since his architecture unveils this essentiality for "a 'second world' [where] the gods are no longer possible and [where] at best technology produces 'a confused numinosity.'"[17]

In one series of notes Mies lucidly encapsulates his aversion to the *new* without showing any nostalgia for the old, though he expresses his *Sehnsucht* ["longing"] for the seduction of the traditional *Baukunst*. This aversion is articulated in an original manner in the idea that it is necessary for architecture to side with the *super-rational* against the *rational,* and with the *invisible* against the *visible.* In such assertions one notices not only a logical articulation of the analysis of the modern mechanisms of the objectification of life as formulated in Simmel's terms; one also hears an echo of the very particular relations Mies had with the avant-garde movements of his time. We need not go into detail to point out, for example, how the above assertions call to mind the architect's long association with Theo van Doesburg, which began in the early 1920s. And on the other hand, if we were to examine Mies's positions in the light of Piet Mondrian's meditations and experiences, it would take us too far away from our central concerns. What is important to underscore here is that in Mies's appeals to the need to regard the "new" with circumspection at the very least, looking past the appearances in which modernity wraps itself, one perceives, aside from a reflection of the architect's experiences during that period of the 1920s in which he collaborated on the magazine *G,* the results of a long meditation on the notion of *appearance,* seen as a determinant component of modern *Zivilisation.* Thus, as though by contrast, the meaning that the architect attributes to *Kultur* becomes clearer, with *Kultur* appearing more and more as a synonym for the "tendency toward the truth" in Scheler's sense, and as an opening of the spirit toward the spheres of "super-rationality" and the "invisible."

These considerations also make it possible to understand the reasons why Mies so energetically insisted that his work was not in the field of "architecture" but in that of "architecture-as-language." The search for truth in fact applies first and foremost to language, when culture is identified with the will to give back to words – reduced to empty reverberations in modern compositional practices – their real significance. In attempting to determine the meaning of things, Mies constructs, in his most successful moments, poetic texts that

avail themselves of technology in order to remove both the "numinosity" and "confusion" from it. The formal clarity that results is in some cases astonishing, and it is untouched by doubt when, by virtue of its radicality, it is forced to confront the problem of repetition. In this respect as well, there is a great distance separating Mies's work from modern architectural stylistics caught in the coils of this particular aspect of the "objectification" of the time. One cannot speak of "reproducibility," in the sense intended by the most well-known artistic expressions of the modern avant-garde, when referring to the details or the compositional "scores" of the German master's work. Mies counters reproducibility with *repetition.* Repetition is choice – radical, solitary decision. Reproducibility is an expression of "naturalistic mechanism"; it is the assumption of a state of necessity; and it is motivated by the prevalence of the useful. It is, in a word, "architecture." Repetition, on the other hand, is a dissolution of the appearances that veil the misery which reproducibility mystifies. The repetitive aspects exhibited with desperate courage in Mies's last works require appropriate means, refined techniques (fig. 7). There is no room in them for any nostalgia, though it is very clear that for Mies no innovation can be made when the ties to tradition have been severed.

At this point we can hardly ignore the relations that Mies entertained with tradition. The question has, on the other hand, been the subject of more than a few misunderstandings. This has been due, by and large, to the usually prevalent tendency to consider the question of tradition, and its relation to Mies's work, in light of the connections between the developments of Mies's research and the experiments of such important figures in modern architecture as Karl Friedrich Schinkel, Bruno Paul, Peter Behrens, and H.P. Berlage. However useful it might be in a general sense, any attempt to trace a sort of evolutionary genealogy for Mies's work will be of little use in an historical investigation. Indeed, in taking such an approach one risks confirming the idea that identifies tradition with the renewed persistence of compositional practices and attitudes. In order to avoid this sort of banalization, it is useful to reverse our analytical presupposition and to try to think of Mies's relation to tradition in the negative terms to which his thought should by now have accustomed us. The respect that the architect showed for the work of Schinkel tends to confirm this hypothesis.

Schinkel is a giant of his century. As Arthur Moeller van den Bruck states in some exceptional pages, Schinkel is an architect who made a "heroic attempt" to give a style to his age, his nation, his city, and to "his" prince. The *Neue Wache* bears the stamp of *Preussentum,* which it celebrates with the spirit of a nation that has emerged victorious from a final test. In the simplicity and power of the large masses skillfully composed by Schinkel, the spirit of the *Tekton* – literally, the

7. Aerial view of 860-880 and 900-910 Lake Shore Drive Apartments, Chicago, 1986

"builder of the prince's house," as Karl Boetticher explains in his *Die Tektonik der Hellen,* a volume of which Mies possessed a rare edition after having probably become acquainted with it at Behrens's studio – is momentarily revived. Schinkel, as Moeller states, finished Gilly's work, striking the final chisel-blow to the "classical Prussian style."

With Mies the word takes root, rigorously and through a language of luminous clarity – the word as the last real *inhabitant* of the "second world" described by Guardini. Exposed to the *Nervenleben* ["nervous life"] analyzed by Simmel and transferred onto film by the collaborators of *G,* this world is an immobile spectator of the modern *Vergeistigung* and the Spenglerian "decline." It is not the *style* of this world which finds expression in Mies; this world, as Adolf Loos well knew, already had its own style, and one had no need of architects' mediation in order to appreciate it. Mies lays bare the nature of this style, the form of all-inclusive objectification, and grasps and represents its essence.

While Schinkel celebrates the destiny of a nation preparing to shape the destinies of the world, Mies analyzes, with the precision of an anatomist, what the world has become. He recognizes its rootless, extraordinary power, which is no longer ordered by a "prince," no longer guided by benevolent "gods."

In the modern, turbulent, noisy void, the architect's responsibilities become all the greater, despite all appearances; so much so that the planner must take upon himself the dangerous task of committing, as Mies says, "mortal sins." This is why Mies constantly comes back to confront the same question raised in the pages of *G,* each time rethinking the meaning of so important a word as *Bauen,* which he reconsidered in the famous letter to Walter Riezler and in the 1938 speech to IIT. By thus positing the problem of finding a *tertium quid* between "non-form" and "excess of form," between "what does not exist" and "what is pure appearance," Mies shows how the aspiration to the truth of essential form cannot result in a style, but is instead grounded in a sense of tradition, and thus in the firm resolve of repetition. But "tradition," in this instance, has nothing in common with the notion of "process"; tradition is not a becoming, nor an organic transformation. Tradition is, then, the work of Schinkel, immobile in its distance and diversity, unsettling in its power to illuminate the

8. Seagram Building, New York, 1954-58

present without pity. Tradition is not the amicable side of the past, but the troubling closeness of what stands in the distance.

Mies has no debts to settle with Schinkel's *style.* Yet he does share with Schinkel the conviction that tradition is *at once* presence and distance, the source of an irresolvable *Sehnsucht.* Tradition, thus, is also the irremediable separateness of *Kultur,* which is nevertheless present at the spectacle offered by the contortions of *Zivilisation,* as Guardini also clearly perceived.

Tradition as paradox, then – but this paradox is what guides Mies's hand in his search for the *tertium quid* between nothingness and excess. The path to follow must be sought – once again in keeping with Mies's laconic suggestions – in "ancient and medieval philosophy," to which the architect owes the configuration of his own thought, and from which springs the secret of his architecture and the wisdom of his *ornaments.*

Ornament for Mies, however, is quite different from the "superfluous" that insistently survives on the surfaces of modern architecture. Ornament finds its proper significance in the traditional medieval conception, whereby what incurs condemnation is not "decoration" but excess of ornament. In this

sense it is clear that if we are to formulate a judgment of his work, our attention should focus not on the presence of decoration but on the possible excess of same. Mies operates at the borderline separating excess from ornament, the line protecting form from the prevalence of use. This choice implies a privileged relationship with technique and materials, the very "facts" laid bare by Mies's language.

In the resistence that the German architect puts up against the objectifications caused by the prevalence of "use" and "function" – against the progressive conformity of all things to the physical traits of "washability," to use Ernst Bloch's distinctive expression – in this firm resolve, we can also hear the echo of one of the "ancient medieval philosophers" whom Mies loves so much to cite. The words of Meister Eckhart come to mind, from the sermon *Iustus in perpetuum vivet et apud dominum est merces eius:* "Your works are all dead, until some motive should impel you to act; and even should God impel you to act from without, these works are truly all dead. If instead your works should live, God must move you from within, from the depths of your soul, where they must live: that is where your life is, and only there do you live."[18]

Medieval scholastic thought does not call into question the necessity of ornament, but judges its appropriateness. Mies's architectural solutions subscribe to the same principle. Just as ornament constitutes the very root of the definition of *architectural order* (as Ananda Coomaraswamy demonstrated and René Guénon argued in his discussion of the idea of "measure"), in the same way, in Mies's case, form is essentially *order*. By *demonstrating* this discipline, the project manifests its own tendency toward *truth*.

Ornament, measure, order: these are the essential characteristics of the Miesian *operari* (fig. 8). Ornament means the knowledge and appropriate use of materials, the only decorations admitted into the spaces designed by Mies; measure is the occasion provided for the *beautiful*, Thomistically represented by proportion; order is the rejection of the masks of modern objectification; and organization, finally, is the clarity of the decisions made in the face of the poverty of "facts."

Ornament is the secret that *Baukunst* keeps to allow the *Tekton* to display the values of which he is guardian. And to conclude this point, it may be useful to remember one of Mies's more felicitous aphorisms. When the architect states that architecture begins where two bricks are carefully joined together, our attention should not fall on the curious, reductive image of the "two bricks," but on what is required for their joining to create something architecturally significant – "carefully" is the key word here. Planning, building, and *Baukunst* imply continual *care*. And such attention demands dedication, "idleness" and time – irrevocable decisions, as Nietzsche instructs. To build is thus to provide protection for the possibility of the event – it is a rejection of the "new" and a love of tradition. *Baukunst*, finally, is the *art of time*.

In a 1939 letter to Mies, Lilly Reich suggests that he read Ernst Junger's *Blatter und Steine* (which she calls *"Steine u. Blatter"*). The zeal of her praise for Junger's book was probably shared by Mies, who already possessed the 1934 first edition. Moreover, he also became familiar with the great writer's thought through the volume *An der Zeitmauer* (1959), which contains entire pages that could provide valid information toward locating the *place* where Mies decided to live, and from which he observed man inexorably approaching the "wall of time" where "the world's disillusionment ends in the void." Courageous in their capacity for repetition and so perfect as to elicit a comment such as that made by Aby Warburg concerning the special preference that the gods give to detail – here a synonym for measure/order – Mies's works possess qualities similar to those which make Junger's best pages so riveting in their ability to capture, with the "slightest stroke," details that require the attention of an entomologist.

There cannot, however, be any will in details – how else could God's dwelling-place be an expression of arbitrary free-

9. New National Gallery, Berlin, 1962-67, detail of the model of the column exhibited at The Art Institute of Chicago, 1968

dom? But details are points at which ornament exhibits its full potential for display (fig. 9). Moreover, *through* detail the good Lord exerts his ordering power over the whole construction, as many pages of Mies will attest.

Enemies of excess and heralds of order, details prolong, through their very constitution, the search for *quiet* underlying Mies's praise of order and organization. *Quiet* is the key to Mies's architecture and thought. It is an incontestable value, the significance of which lies rooted, once again, in medieval tradition, which we find wonderfully exemplified in the following sermon of Meister Eckhart, *In omnibus requiem quaesivi:*

> If I was to state briefly what the creator's intention was when he created all the creatures, I would say: quiet. If I was then asked what the Holy Trinity always seeks in its every action, I would answer: quiet. If, then, I was asked what the soul seeks in all its movements, I would answer: quiet. And if I was asked what all creatures sought in all their natural inclinations, I would answer: quiet. . . . No creature resembles God as much as quiet does.[19]

Such resemblance is the goal of Mies's work, which, in its care for things, is nevertheless well aware that this quiet is unattainable for the "facts" of the world. The "German slowness" of the language spoken by Mies takes the form of a never-ending wait, an "idleness" that is, nevertheless, but a delay at quiet's doorstep. Quiet shines in the distance, and is thus a torment for the project. Mies would not have understood Guardini so well had he not read the above-cited Eckhart sermon with earthly hope; it, in itself, probably clarifies better than anything just what Mies believes the essence of architecture to be.

If we accept the definition of architecture as "the expression of the inner structure of our epoch and the slow unfolding of its soul," we must, however, admit that this definition is neither original nor particularly significant. Such elegant phrasing might satisfy a distracted public, but it does not sufficiently answer the more radical questions formulated by Mies over the course of his life's work. How can the slow flowering of time's soul appear as truth? What form contains this truth? From Ben Solomon, through Saint Thomas, Mies gets his final response, though in fact it answers only some of his questions: truth is *adequatio rei et intellectus.* But beyond the architect's responsibility toward the truth of fact," a more radical question arises regarding exclusively the planner. As Mies said to a London audience in 1959, "'Where we go from here' does not make sense." What does make sense, and constitutes architecture, lies in the necessary repetition of another question: "What architecture is?" [*sic*]

The paradox is unavoidable: the *truth* lies in this question for which there is only one answer: the endless repetition of the question itself. It is a question that accepts only itself as answer.

For these reasons, I shall conclude this brief commentary by stealing the words of Elias Canetti, who says that "in everything [he] said, there reigned an order which enchanted." The enchanter here described was, however, Robert Musil. But this distortion of the text is perhaps not inappropriate, for like the author of *The Man Without Qualities,* Mies van der Rohe "traced boundaries around all things, as well as himself. He was wary of mixtures and brotherhoods, effusions and exaggerations. He was a man in the solid state and kept his distance from liquids and gases."[20]

Translated from the Italian by Stephen Sartarelli.

Notes

This essay analyzes a particular side of Mies van der Rohe's cultural background, the one that we encounter upon examination of his writings, the handwritten material located in various archives, and the books he read and kept in his library.

All quotations presented here have been taken from volumes in Mies's library or else were quoted in his notes. Since this study intends simply to provide a hypothetical reading and basis for further interpretative discussion, it is not furnished with reference notes of its own, which, given the specific nature of the research behind this study, would have to be so extensive that they would further weigh down its contents. A thoroughly systematic treatment of the subjects here touched upon would, moreover, require a great deal more space. For these reasons I have decided to condense the text as much as possible, relying on a strictly essayistic approach and on the reader's understanding of the nature of the material presented.

I should also mention that most of the research I conducted for this essay was done in the United States beginning in 1980. I should like to express my gratitude for the generous support given to my research by the Dipartimento di Storia dell' Architettura of the Istituto Universitario di Architettura di Venezia and by the Graham Foundation for Advanced Studies in the Fine Arts, Chicago. I also owe particular thanks to the Center for Advanced Studies of the National Gallery of Art, Washington, D.C.

1. Friedrich Nietzsche, *Beyond Good and Evil,* trans. Walter Kaufmann (New York, 1966), p. 67.

2. Ibid., pp. 100-101.

3. Wolf Tegethoff, *Die Villen und Landhausprojekte von Mies van der Rohe* (Essen, 1981), trans. as *Mies van der Rohe: The Villas and Country Houses* (Cambridge, Mass., 1985), and Franz Schulze, *Mies van der Rohe: A Critical Biography* (Chicago, 1985).

4. Nietzsche (note 1), p. 24.

5. Ibid., p. 36.

6. Ibid., p. 40.

7. See Schulze (note 3), pp. 237-238.

8. Quoted by Kenneth Frampton earlier in this volume; see p. 41.

9. Hans Urs von Balthasar, *Romano Guardini. Reform aus dem Ursprung* (Munich, 1970), Italian trans. *Romano Guardini. Riforma dalle origini* (Milan, 1970), especially chap. 1.

10. Romano Guardini, *Briefe vom Comer See* (Mainz: M. Grunewald Verlag, n.d.).

11. Werner Sombart, *Deutscher Sozialismus* (Berlin, 1934), chap. 2, sec. 2.

12. Georg Simmel, *Philosophie des Geldes* (Leipzig, 1900); 7th ed. (Berlin, 1977), chap. 1, sec. 1.

13. Von Balthasar (note 9), chap. 1.

14. Guardini (note 10), third letter.

15. Quoted by von Balthasar (note 9), chap. 1.

16. Ibid.

17. Ibid.

18. Meister Eckhart, *Sermoni tedeschi* (Milan, 1985); for the original German texts, see J. Quint, *Meister Eckhart,* 4th ed. (Munich, 1977).

19. Ibid.

20. Elias Canetti, *Das Augenspiel, Lebensgeschichte 1931-1937* (Munich and Vienna, 1985). The two quotations are from part 3, the chapter entitled "Musil."

[This essay was in production when Fritz Neumeyer's *Mies van der Rohe, Das kunstlose Wort, Gedanken zur Baukunst* (Berlin, 1986) appeared. The reader is urged to compare Professor Dal Co's thoughts with Neumeyer's treatment of some common issues, namely, Mies van der Rohe's notebooks and philosophical readings, and the influence of Romano Guardini on Mies. See also Neumeyer's "Mies as Self-Educator" in the IIT exhibition catalogue, *Mies van der Rohe: Architect as Educator* (Chicago, 1986), which appeared when this volume was at press. – Ed.]

miMISes READING: does not mean A THING

by Peter Eisenman

Architecture has traditionally been thought of as producing an object with meaning. Recently this meaning has been confused with a different idea, that of an architectural text. The presumption is that simply because something has meaning, the now fashionable term "text" can be applied to it. A text, however, may be distinguished from an object. While an object (whether concrete or written) may also be a text, a text differs from an object in that it is a reading or an analysis of another object. Hence, while all texts can be objects, not all objects are necessarily texts. Texts always contain something else. That something else is the approximation or simulation of another object. A text does not represent or symbolize this other object, it attempts to reveal or simulate its structure.

An aspect of this confusion of text and meaning has been the assumption that either a formal analysis or a symbolic analysis of any architecture would reveal its textual structure. Such is not the case. A formal analysis can only investigate the object as object; a symbolic analysis can only investigate the traditional meaning of the object; it cannot reveal its textual structure. Meaning, form, and text are different objects. Since a text is a structural simulation of its object, it is necessary to undertake a textual analysis to reveal the operations of its simulation.

Textual analysis differs from both formal analysis and symbolic analysis in the following respect. Formal analysis looks for formal order, such as sequences, closures, or proportions: the interval between columns, the relationship of wall lengths, the ratios of solids to voids or parts to the whole. While formal analysis is concerned with the aesthetic aspect of architectural metaphysics, symbolic analysis is concerned

1. Concrete Country House project, 1923, model

with its traditional meaning. This meaning unfolds in the analysis of metaphor, of something which is described in terms of something else: the facade as a face, the chimney as a backbone, etc. The "meaning" revealed by a textual analysis is, however, a structural meaning, not a metaphoric one. A structural meaning is one in which there is a differentiation and not a representation. Symbols are metaphoric; they are objects that represent other objects. Signs, however, are textual in that they differentiate one element from another in a set of structural, rather than formal or metaphoric, relationships. Signs are notational devices that will not yield to formal and symbolic analysis and, therefore, are self-referential: that is, they do not participate in a formal or symbolic whole. For example, the slot in the facade of Mies van der Rohe's Concrete Country House (fig. 1) is a sign (not a symbol) of the absence of the floor plane. The slot signals the difference between presence and absence, and it is, therefore, neither a formal nor a symbolic element, but a textual one. A sign of difference and a trace of presence are textual notations. It is the operation of these kinds of notations which is usually ignored by the traditional analysis of meaning; the textual level is left unconsidered, because of a fixation on symbol-as-metaphor that suppresses sign-as-difference. Thus, the idea of text must be "teased out" from the systems of conflicting notation – formal, symbolic, and textual – that may be present in any object.[1]

Traditionally in literature – in which the simulating or analytic text is always outside of or parallel to the object – it is thought that object and text are different. This notion has been challenged by the deconstructionist critique, which suggests that there is no difference between an analytic text and an object, that they are mutually imbedded.[2] Similarly, while architecture has always enjoyed a tradition of the external text in the form of architectural criticism, there has always been another text imbedded within its object. As opposed to language, where signs represent "absent" objects, in architecture the sign and the object are both present. Thus, the problem for a textual analysis of architecture is different from that of language. It suggests that while in language there is a need for a congruence between sign and object, in architecture the reverse may be true. Since the sign and the object in architecture exist in reality together, there may be a need to uncouple them if a sign is to be disengaged from a symbol. This textuality is found in architecture when symbol and form can be extracted from the object. This extraction discovers two things: one, the object stripped of its former symbolic content; two, a structure that simulates (since it cannot be the object without its former context) this condition. This structure can be considered a text.

The work of Mies van der Rohe has never been examined in the light of this possible textuality. Even Manfredo Tafuri and Francesco Dal Co, who in their provocative writings propose a non-traditional interpretation of Mies, do not view the work as text.[3] Nonetheless, it is possible to see in Mies's work a strong textuality, especially in his preoccupation with precise dissonances that cannot be ignored. Although these may seem to have no symbolic or formal significance, it is precisely because of this lack, it will be argued, that they are the essence of what is textual.

Text emerges in Mies's architecture when the symbolic connection between man and the object (and hence symbol and object) loses its relevance and thus can be taken apart. Instead of simulating the vertebrate structure of man, Mies's architecture simulates a textual structure. The separation of an architecture from the mimesis of man is the production of a simulation; this is the nature of a text. The "text" in this context can be seen in the attempt to break away from the symbolism, hierarchy, and mimesis that linked the symmetrical axis of objects to the vertebrate axis of the human body. When this break occurred, Mies's objects became unstable, non-hierarchical. Their asymmetry signalled that the elements had broken apart from their vertebrate or organic structure. With Mies's break from mimesis there was also a break from traditional representation. This break for Mies is manifested in an unusual juxtaposition, the contamination of the modern by the classical.[4]

The key here is the reintroduction of classical elements (axiality, symmetry, etc.) in a non-classical manner. This contamination is not so much a dialectical insertion of the classical into the modern (the object into the text) as it is a damming up or a transgression of the classical. It is presented in the context of a rupture with traditional representation. Consequently, Mies's work should be read as an argument that proposes something apart, a suspension as the unresolved condition of being. It is important to see the work in this non-synthetic light.

Mies van der Rohe's projects from 1923 to 1935 fall into three phases that form an internal, almost self-referential narrative: the early work (namely, the Brick and Concrete Country Houses); the middle work (the Barcelona Pavilion and the Tugendhat House); and the late work of this period (summarized in the Hubbe House and, to a lesser extent, in the Ulrich Lange House). The narrative has two aspects. First, one detects a movement from a formalist (classical aesthetic concern) through a modernist (break up of the subject and object) to a textual architecture, where imbedded in the formal (useful, meaningful, and sheltering) object is a parallel discourse – a text (or a series of textual notations). Second, this narrative is not a sequence of signs that refer to other objects, but a narrative that indicates the differences between objects – presence, absence, process, etc. – which can be considered textual. It is important to understand that text does not deny

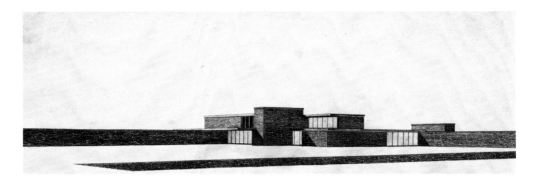

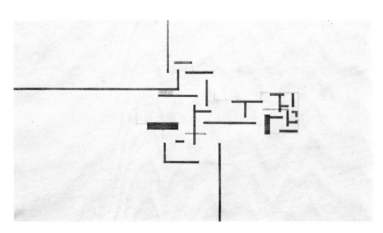

2. Brick Country House project, 1923-24, perspective and plan

the presence of a meaningful, aesthetic, useful shelter. It suggests rather that the representation or symbolization of these issues is no longer its primary concern. Mies van der Rohe was not conscious of this idea of text; he did not intend "textuality" in his work. Yet the evidence of a growing and evolving "textuality" is powerful; it is only necessary to find the way to it. In order to do this, Mies must be misread, that is, read from inside, as if from his own unconscious.

The first indication in Mies's work of textual notation is found in the Brick Country House (fig. 2).[5] This project begins to explore the limits of the independence of the object from the subject and how these limits can be articulated. It is concerned with a first order of textuality, the reduction of symbolic objects to mere objects, i.e., objects without the traditional narrative of man. With the Brick Country House, Mies begins to deploy the elements of architecture as textual counters. The first of these is the wall. Here the walls speak to the fact that there is no space in the house. The walls do not define space; rather, they define their own condition of being – that is, their capacity to support and their capacity to divide.

Traditionally, walls are read as the perimeter of space: they either contain, enclose, or exclude space. But the walls in

the Brick Country House are merely object presences, divisions where there is no space to divide or where the space has been removed and only surfaces exist. Van Doesburg's 1918 painting *Rhythm of a Russian Dance* (fig. 3), which is often cited as the original model for the Brick Country House, in fact does not reflect such an attitude toward space. It utilizes no such absence of space; in it space is active as a ground. For Mies, the absence of space eliminates a major classical element – the ground – leaving the walls as suspended figures. It is merely a case of Mies recognizing in van Doesburg a vehicle from which to elaborate these ideas.

Likewise, the glass planes in the Brick Country House do not contain; again, they are merely a void presence. It, too, signals a breakdown of the idea of the house as a metaphysical enclosure and abandons the traditional distinction between inside and out. The house encloses and shelters, but it does not represent or symbolize shelter and enclosure. Above all, the house remains an object in the metaphysical sense, although there is a displacement from classical mimesis.

This displacement of mimesis is only a part of the entire thesis of the Concrete Country House (fig. 4), for here there is a second development. Whereas in the Brick Country House

3. Theo van Doesburg, *Rhythm of a Russian Dance*, 1918, oil on canvas, 135.9 x 61.6 cm

there is the absence of space, here that absence is marked by a sign. This is the first indication of a text. It is neither a representational nor an aesthetic gesture. It is now the object-as-sign, a sign of the object's own condition. This marks the pivotal shift from the object as a representation of the condition of man to the idea of a text within the object.

Mies begins this shift with a negation of man's plane. Even though there is a classical podium, it is used to signal that the symbolic plane of man, the ground plane, is stripped as such from the object. In the elevation drawing, the plane of the floor is read as a slot. There is an actual floor plane inside, but it is not marked on the façade. This cut in the vertical surface also denies an expected relationship to the windows above. While there are many different window solutions that would have related to the rest of the fenestration, Mies chose, instead, to mark the floor plane with a cut that both marks the absence of man's plane and suggests that the metaphor of support in the concrete wall is being eroded. It is as if Mies purposely undercut the wall's "meaning" as clear and logical support.

The Brick and Concrete Country House projects were followed by the Barcelona Pavilion and Tugendhat House, which exemplify the next period of Mies's work. In the Barcelona Pavilion (fig. 5), particularly, one can discern an important stage in Mies's ongoing confrontation with the classical notion of enclosure and the enclosing wall. Here Mies converts two additional architectural elements into textual counters: the column and the roof. Though the theme is the court house type, Mies, instead of enclosing a court, breaks it open to reveal the column and the roof. The two elements previously employed textually, the wall and the podium, operate in the same way. Again, the wall is not the wall of finitude – the wall that makes space and symbolizes the classical relationship between man and object. These walls cleave space; they begin and end in response to no greater order; rather, they obey only their own mute existence.[6]

The podium in the Barcelona Pavilion, as in both of the earlier houses, is not entered axially. (As will be seen, axial entry will become a textual counter when classical elements become imbedded in Mies's work.) In fact, the early schemes in many of Mies's projects have a formalist bias. These are then worked through until they ultimately become textual. In the early studies of the Barcelona Pavilion there are further tentative gestures toward what might be termed a "latent classicality," for example, the alignment of the pool with the main podium (see figs. 6, 7). This alignment would have caused the direction of the main entry to be reinforced by the line of the podium and the pool, thus erecting a virtual barrier between the outside and the inside. In the realized project, the pool is pushed out into the landscape, up against the corner of the wall. It is no longer framed by a terrace (fig. 8), but now pene-

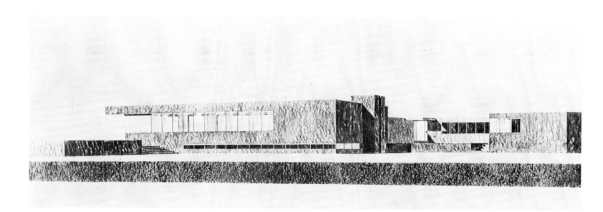

4. Concrete Country House project, 1923, perspective

5. Barcelona Pavilion, 1929

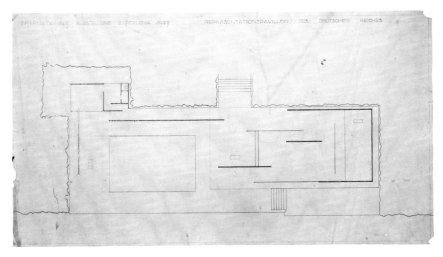

6. Barcelona Pavilion, Plan I, 1928, pencil on transparent paper, 48.4, x 91.4 cm

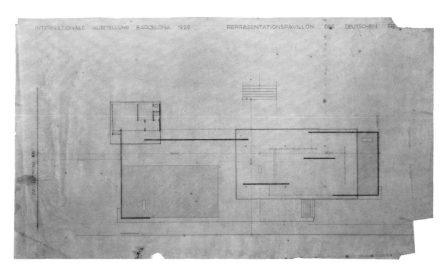

7. Barcelona Pavilion, Plan II, 1928, pencil and colored pencil on transparent paper, 47.7 x 87.3 cm

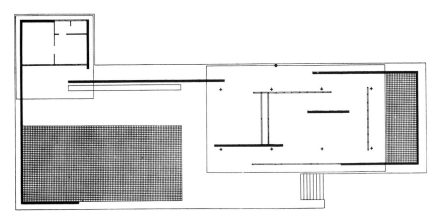

8. Barcelona Pavilion, final plan

trates the wall, seeming to intrude from the outside. In the early schemes the entire podium except for the small utility pavilion was enclosed by an uninterrupted perimeter rectangle. In the realized scheme, this perimeter is fractured at every corner, almost imperceptibly but enough to engender instability. The principal motive for the fracturing is to disengage the roof plane formally from the floor plane, and then to engage it as a signifier, i.e., as another textual counter. The condition of the roof plane in the Barcelona Pavilion is in opposition to Le Corbusier's Maison Domino (fig. 9), where the stature and status of man is symbolized by the roof plane/ podium as coupled horizontal datums. With the Barcelona Pavilion, the hovering roof, formerly a symbol of shelter and enclosure, is stripped of this meaning. It hovers, but symbolically shelters and encloses nothing – it is extracted from its former symbolic presence and recast as a sign. Indeed, there is no interior space in the pavilion; its symbolic presence is one of spatial continuity and the denial of usable interior space.

The Barcelona Pavilion is the first use of the column in Mies's work; it, too, becomes a notational device. For Le Corbusier the column was the quintessential symbol of the new architecture. His columns were typically round and set back from the façade, creating the canonical "free plan" and "free façade" that were to become trademarks of modernist archi-

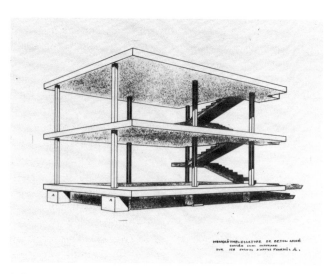

9. Le Corbusier, Maison Domino, 1914

10. Barcelona Pavilion

11. Tugendhat House, Brno, 1928-30, entrance

12. Tugendhat House, dining room

tecture. For Mies, the column is employed as a sign, not a symbol. In the Barcelona Pavilion, the columns, though detached from the walls, are set forward rather than back; because of their cruciform shape they seem intended to define the corners of an en suite sequence of square bays (fig. 10). But, in fact, they signify the absence of corners. This is emphasized by Mies's use of reflective stainless steel, which causes the columns to mirror and double their own infinitude – their absent presences.[7] When the corners disappear, the negative space is read as presence (even though void). The glass planes further mirror and enforce these voids as presences (echoing the roof's function – to shelter nothing), thus becoming the signs of absent enclosure. (In fact, the glass doors were intended to be taken down every day and only put up for security at night.) The stainless steel mullions that divide and frame the glass also provide yet another level of optical self-reference and the signification of absence – they seem as absences in a present glass screen.

In the Tugendhat House, Mies introduces another aspect of text: the reduction of shape and texture to a system of signs (see Frampton, figs. 11, 12). In it are found two curved forms: one is the entry staircase (fig. 11) and the other separates the main living area from the dining area (fig. 12). The curve of the staircase is in opaque glass, that of the living room is in wood. Typically, a curve-ended staircase is used somewhat arbitrarily to create a formal tension and interest in an otherwise uninflected orthogonal scheme, or to accentuate function. In the Tugendhat House, Mies inflates this form into a larger text. It is no accident that Mies intersects the wooden curve with the opaque glass plane. If any of the white walls is taken as a neutral datum, it is seen as solid in contrast to the opaque, glazed curve of the entry staircase. Yet, remarkably, when the same opaque glazing – now as a "flat plane" – is seen against the wooden curve of the living room, the opacity dematerializes by the force of the abrupt contrast. The two similar curves articulated in dissimilar materials textually engage the physicality of the opaque, planar walls in a dialogue of difference. The same "opaque glass" material becomes, in each case, a different sign – in both cases negative: in the former case it is a positive shape; in the latter, a "negative" or neutral shape.

In the Tugendhat House there is also a use of furniture as text. In most of Mies's projects there are two Barcelona chairs side by side and another placed away from the pair. Landscape architects group trees this way to create the appearance of a natural ensemble and to allow a flowing continuity through space. In the Tugendhat House there is an even number of chairs (three Barcelona, three Tugendhat), which are grouped such that a symmetry is established and then abruptly denied by a destabilizing third (fig. 13). Significantly, this strategy contravenes normal function (disrupting

13. Tugendhat House, living room

the groups of two or three), thereby suggesting that there is another intention to the grouping.

The final period of concern here, the years 1933-35, is distinguished by the return of openly classical elements imbedded in a modernist setting, as exemplified by two houses with similar plans: the Ulrich Lange House (fig. 14) and the Hubbe House (fig. 15).[8] This imbedding raises an interesting problem. On the one hand, classical elements are being imbedded in a modernist setting, while on the other hand, this strategy is being used to separate the traditional symbolism of man from architecture. The Hubbe House is a modernist house which contains its opposite – a classical insertion. But this imbedding of the classical is not a "negative object" (since architecture is always a constructive project).[9] Nor is it a void, the traditional idea of the negative in architecture.[10] Instead, it is absence as a constructive presence. It is a modernist object hosting an alien simulation; the text of a classical object imbedded within it. It is an object of superposition. Superposition differs from super*im*position of figure on ground: the courtyard house as modernist ground and the row of columns as classical ordination superimposed on it. This kind of layering and transparency can be found in Cubist collage and in Le Corbusier's plans: the overlay of two systems that resolve themselves as figure and ground. But the Hubbe House is not the same. It becomes a textual object in which a simulation of a classical object is superposed with a modernist object. There is no ground but, instead, a relationship of figure to figure.

Figure to figure suggests a possible condition of textuality; an architecture without origin in shelter use, form, or symbol; rather, a free-floating set of interchangeable integers. The erosion of the traditional iconic structure of architecture is achieved by this superposition, the simultaneous presence of two systems (classical/modern, symmetry/asymmetry, absence/presence).

The textual mark or trace as the presence of absence is further signalled in the Hubbe House by the unresolved nature of the figures. Like the Barcelona Pavilion and the Ulrich Lange House, the Hubbe House is a courtyard house that has been broken apart, irreparably split into two figures. The first fracturing is generated by a double row of symmetrically placed cruciform columns which split the house in two. Unlike the columns of the Barcelona Pavilion which run with the grain, these run counter to it. At Barcelona they signal a modernist ground; at Hubbe, a classical intrusion. They signify both the introduction and denial of a classical ordination. It is this state of being and non-being, of imbedding and contamination, which becomes the textuality of the house. These columns first introduce and define an axis of symmetry that becomes an eroding device. This is then itself systematically eroded. The columns are asymmetrically placed within both the long (front to back) side of the house, and the short, closed sides of the house, initiating a textual reading. The first pair of columns is symmetrical within the terrace that is pushed forward of the house, but asymmetrical in terms of the exterior

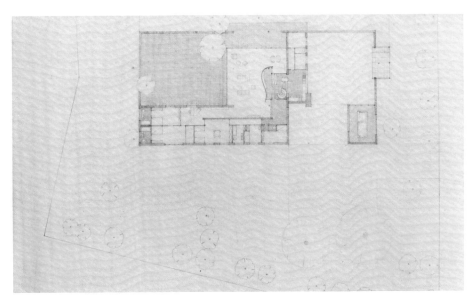

14. Ulrich Lange House project, Krefeld, 1935, final plan, pencil on tracing paper, 55.2 x 95.9 cm

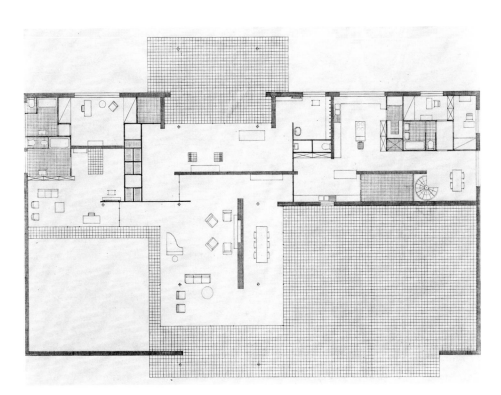

15. Hubbe House project, Magdeburg, 1935, plan

wall. The second pair of columns is symmetrical in terms of their flanking walls, but the furniture in the entrance bay is arranged asymmetrically to them. In fact, each bay contains a sequence of quite precise and detailed countermanding symmetries and asymmetries. In the second bay, for example, the wall, which seems to have broken off from the exterior closure, is both too long to fit into its "former" position and is shifted away from it. In the third bay, the fireplace wall is asymmetrical about the vertical axis of the bay but symmetrical about the horizontal axis. The fireplace wall becomes a conceptual screen, a cleavage for two symmetries on either side, neither of which, however, operates symmetrically with the other. Within the wall, the fireplace itself is placed symmetrically with its edge aligned with the absent axis of the table on the other side. The seating, placed symmetrically about the fireplace opening, further accentuates the shift. On the other side of the wall the dining room table is symmetrically placed with respect to the wall. Hence, the wall becomes a textual fulcrum for the countermanding symmetries with their opposite asymmetries indicated as absences by edges rather than centers. These always occur about a wall-as-fulcrum, i.e., as text. The sequence of free-floating wall elements, seemingly fragments of a former symbolic cruciform, is the final stage of Mies's reconsideration of the wall from structure to text, from symbol to sign.[11]

A focal point of this notation of absence, the transition from symbol to sign, can be located in the single odd column that can be found in the Hubbe House (see fig. 15). How is it to be explained? Possibly as a sign that there are other missing columns, which would be present either as a spine along the length of the middle of the building or as an entire field of columns. In any case, the isolated presence of this single column can only imply absences, including its own. This column is textual, a sign, because it is neither supporting, aesthetic, nor indicative of the history of the column. It is detached from the history of the symbolism of "the column."

Furthermore, in the architecture of Mies, there is a level of detailing as an indication of significant gesture that has resisted interpretation. It is necessary to penetrate this resistance – the inclination to ignore what are significant details – in order to effect a textual analysis. For example, if the notations of the relationship of tile gridding to monolithic floor material are taken as significant, then a series of fractured cruciforms for which there is no resolution can be seen. The first of the cruciforms has three whole arms and one fractured. The horizontal arms are formed by the living quarters, the lower vertical arm is the living/dining area, and the upper vertical arm is erased by the superposition of the tile pattern of the forecourt (fig. 16). Not only is this cruciform fractured, but its arms are also in a state of imbalance: the left arm is widened and the right arm is elongated. Two smaller cruciforms to the right and left of the larger one are similarly fractured

and imbalanced, echoing the larger cruciform. Together these fractured cruciforms are signs of the destabilization of the whole.

Finally, the Hubbe House raises another textual issue of the court house. The court house as a type is an attempt to enclose space; yet it also encloses nature. In the Hubbe House, Mies explores textually the inversion of man and nature. Tafuri and Dal Co in their view of Mies van der Rohe propose the idea that the courts of Mies's court house were not so much contained within the walls looking out on nature, but in fact were the framing of nature behind glass; i.e., nature was reduced to an unnatural object, a sign of nature.[12] There is thus another absence, real nature, made present as absence by the use of unnatural, man-made nature as a sign.

Mies's court house simulates nature by a virtual enclosure of it. With the rupture of the type in the Hubbe House, unnatural nature is ironically contaminated by exposing it to real nature. The glass that separated man from nature is now a glass that separates man from the simulation of nature; unnatural nature becomes framed behind glass (fig. 17). Glass, rather than being seen as the outside of the inside, is now the inner-outside of the outside. This glass frames neither man nor space, but frames nature in an unresolved duality.[13] The type is now not merely a simulation of nature, but rather becomes nature as text. In the Hubbe House, Mies objectifies the denial of nature into a sign, with all its meaning and symbolism.

The design of negatives, that is, both presence and absence, and the reversal of symmetries and asymmetries are Mies's signature. The absence of space becomes the sign of a sign, the sign of a text and the denial of symbolized, functional, aesthetic, meaningful shelter. The sign of a sign is a redundancy produced by opposites. Mies's signification is achieved through the very fact of the opposition, through the seeming irresolution of the system. The expectancy of the system as a whole is betrayed by an order which itself is broken apart, and neither of which is dominant. These signs or texts do not symbolize nor represent. They function but do not make function their theme. Rather, they split symbolic and objective reality, which have become, since the Renaissance, powerfully unified in the linking of man's vertebrate axis with the pitched roof, symmetrical hearth – symbolic of the axis of the world.

Texts that split symbol from object in order to form signs dislocate architecture. But architecture is sustained by this dislocating energy, which is creative and critical rather than stabilizing and institutionalizing. Mies's separation of symbol and reality creates the dislocation of the metaphysic of architecture necessary for its maintenance. The history of architecture is a constant struggle enacted between the limits of maintenance and dislocation.[14] Mies van der Rohe's texts probe those limits.

16. Hubbe House, model

17. Hubbe House, interior perspective drawing, pencil on illustration board, 48 x 67.3 cm

Notes

1. See Barbara Johnson, "The Critical Difference," *Diacritics* 8, 2 (1978), p. 3.

2. See J. Hillis Miller, "The Critic as Host," in *Deconstruction and Criticism* (New York, 1979), pp. 217-253.

3. See Manfredo Tafuri and Francesco Dal Co, *Modern Architecture* (New York, 1982), pp. 153-157.

4. This idea has been suggested by Tafuri and Dal Co (note 3), but not for the reasons of text.

5. Although the Concrete Country House is chronologically prior to the Brick Country House, it is not the first in the textual sequence. The ideas in the Concrete Country House can only be understood after the statement of the Brick Country House.

6. This is as opposed to the organization of walls in any of Le Corbusier's projects which obey a proportional order that is ultimately linked to his modular proportional system. While based on the Fibonacci series, the dimensions of the modular are linked to an ultimate anthropomorphism in the figure of modular man.

7. Colin Rowe has, from a different point of view, maintained that an analysis of the changing column section in Mies van der Rohe would make a useful thesis, as well as a way to understand the formal development of Mies's work.

8. Although the Ulrich Lange House was done after the Hubbe House, it is in some ways its precursor. Compared to the Hubbe House, however, it is unresolved and lacks the separation of sign and symbol. The Ulrich Lange House is neither a criticism, an elaboration, nor a transformation of the Hubbe House. It "sounds" and looks like the Hubbe House, but it does not have quite the same meaning.

9. See Jacques Derrida, "The Maintenance of Architecture" (Trento, Italy, 1986), for a discussion of the idea of architecture as a constructive project.

10. See Tafuri and Dal Co (note 3), p. 157.

11. This is different from the Tafuri and Dal Co proposition of the impossibility of significances in the work of Mies. For them, the signs in Mies are "no longer organic components of a language. Where the avant-garde was projecting continuity, Mies designed separations. His architecture isolates itself: meditation on the impossibility of dialogue, it reduces itself to a montage of signs that have mislaid, with never a trace of nostalgic regret, the universe of significance." Tafuri and Dal Co (note 3), p. 153.

12. Ibid., p. 155: "Nature was made part of the furnishings, a spectacle to be enjoyed only on condition that it be kept impalpably remote."

13. Ibid., p. 157: "The natural relationship with the surroundings is a mystification to be replaced by an artificial construction." It is my contention that this artificial construction is a text.

14. See Derrida (note 9) for a more complete discussion of this idea.

Mies van der Rohe and his Disciples
or
The American Architectural Text and its Reading

by Stanley Tigerman

If one assumes that architecture is essentially textual in nature, then it is both reasonable and profitable to engage in a discussion of the nature of reading, decoding, or interpreting that text in a way that is analogous to that in which literature is conventionally examined. By so doing, it is possible to discover certain features about architectural textuality. Alternatively, because it is also equally possible to infer that architecture has traditionally been perceived of in terms of the "faith" one might place in it, over and against its interpretation, a re-examination of the constituent features of that faith might reveal new territory in the architectural landscape. In either of the above scenarios, the establishment of a religious connection to architectural textuality is intrinsic to the theories presented, since both "interpretation" and "faith" are representative of equal, but uniquely different relationships between God and man. It is in the context of religion in its relationship to architecture that the following arguments are couched.

Because the twentieth-century architectural giant Mies van der Rohe was elevated to a God-like position by his disciples (a status not specifically related to the ways in which Mies perceived himself), it is possible to assert that his architecture, textually speaking, was positioned either to effect an interpretive response or simply to elicit faith in its being. If, on the one hand, Mies's architecture was clearly understood in all of its manifestations, then the conventional ways in which it has been perceived (read) and measured retain their authority. Yet, if that same architecture was intrinsically "mute" – i.e., bereft of those conventions normally associated with cultural traditions (insofar as architecture is typically measured in terms of its deference to such standards as an "original" or "cultural referentiality," or just plain "usefulness") – then one could claim that Mies's text may well deserve another reading.

The methods by which Mies van der Rohe's architectural production has been analyzed thus far are conventional in nature. Either by locating his oeuvre well within the realm of the modern movement (but significantly after Le Corbusier and Gropius engaged in the original skirmishes that led to the apparent defeat of the classical language of architecture); or, referentially, by placing his text in juxtaposition to certain convenient historical movements (specifically, the Gothic, because that tradition has been interpreted as falling conveniently within the structurally rational element of architectural history), attempts have been made to verify Mies and his text from an historical point of view. Therefore, if one were to suggest either that Mies van der Rohe's architectural production induced faith, or by contrast, that his architecture required an intrinsically interpretive response, knowledge about the architecture, or indeed how it was perceived (or used) might well result from such an analytic comparison.

Mies's work falls neatly into two chronological as well as geographical sections: the initial part relates to the first half-century of his oeuvre executed in his native Germany, and the second, the three-decade portion spent largely in the United States. Given that Mies van der Rohe was exiled from the Germany that was the site of his own early, optimistic explorations and that he arrived at a time when modernism was deriving its strength from post-Wrightian deformations of the historically conventional Cartesian approach common to the classical language of architecture, it is not unreasonable to suggest that Mies's American architectural production was essentially culturally displaced. The possibility of his cultural displacement is supported by a recent suggestion that Mies, near the end of his tenure as director of the Bauhaus in Berlin, despaired of the future of modernism, a mood brought on in part by his reading of Oswald Spengler's *Decline of the West*.[1] Certainly, it is clear that his twenty-five-year absence from the land of his birth (most particularly, the wartime years) significantly diminished his influence on the post-World War II generation of German architects. In Berlin today, for example, Mies's awesome twentieth-century museum, the New National Gallery, raises precious little polemical debate among

1. Perls House, Berlin-Zehlendorf, 1910-11

the architectural avant-garde. On the other hand, the more significant way in which his reputation in Germany has been formed relates to his early, historically pre-modernist productions (the first Perls House [fig. 1], the unbuilt Kröller-Müller project, etc.), though these are more of an expression of Karl Friedrich Schinkel's influence on Mies than anything else.

These early examples of Mies's work exercise little influence on an architectural intelligentsia that is more particularly interested in "neorational," postfunctionalist architecture, than it is in furthering the cause of "neoclassicism." Examples of the twentieth-century neoclassical architecture by Paul Schultze-Naumburg, Albert Speer (fig. 2), Heinrich Tessenow, and Paul Ludwig Troost (fig. 3), relating as they do to the official architecture of the Third Reich, have created such repugnance on the part of most post-World War II German architects that any architectural image connected with the classical language of architecture elicits a mildly hysterical response (one can almost hear the cry "Fascismus"). Since the perception of Mies van der Rohe, in large measure, is generated by his early classical work, it is little wonder that his reputation is less influential in Germany today than one might imagine.

On the other hand, Mies's influence on post-World War II American architects, as well as on the culture they infected, has been and remains immense, if for no other reason than because of the plethora of architectural productions he engaged in for the last thirty-one years of his professional life.

Being more solidly rooted in the conventions of the day than Mies himself (who was, after all, a stranger in an alien land, disconnected by the lack of a common language) and, by extension, being less morally driven by the larger, epochal transformations that Mies saw himself engaged in as a primary force in the modern movement, Mies's American disciples felt the need to interpret or to make practical the meaning of his work so as to affirm its "usefulness." It is equally reasonable to assert, however, that the meaning of the Miesian text had little to do with the cultural and practical extensions to which his disciples subjected that text. If it is true that the Miesian text was intrinsically mute and inaccessible, since it implied so little about culture, history, and metaphor (that is, any of the conventions normally associated with architecture), then its "practical" interpretation by his disciples was basically extrinsic to its deeper meaning. All of which leaves one with the overwhelming urge to suggest that faith, not interpretation, was the central feature of Mies van der Rohe's architecture as perceived by his disciples, and that feeling of faith overwhelmed all others to such a degree that whatever resulted from that posture established the true, and only, meaning of the Miesian text.

The question of reading, therefore, is essential to any understanding of the truth of a given text, and while it is tempting to suggest that Mies van der Rohe's American disciples were trained to "have faith" in the master's philosophy and, by extension, in his architectural production, I would

2. Albert Speer, Zeppelinfeld, Nürnberg, 1935

3. Paul Ludwig Troost, House of German Art, Munich, 1933

submit that the truth of the matter is more closely associated with the interpretation of, rather than the belief or faith in, that philosophy. Certainly, if it is true that Mies van der Rohe's architectural text was beyond conventional "reading," then there can be little doubt that interpretation – not faith – was required to make the text accessible. The question of textual understandability, or by contrast textual opacity, is centered on discerning whether literalism or abstraction was the driving force underlying the intentions of that text, since those characteristics establish whether a particular text is accessible or not.

If, on the one hand, literalism drives a particular text, then its cultural references must be apparent so that its meaning is successfully conveyed. On the other hand, if abstraction is the constituent feature of a particular text, then that text must be decoded in order to attain cultural comprehensibility, or it remains mute, and by definition inaccessible. In Mies van der Rohe's case, there can be little doubt that cultural sensibility was not the driving force behind the crafting of this American architecture. If that had been the case, the appearance of culturally derived forms (tripartition, anthropomorphic referentiality, symmetry, and the like) would be intrinsic to his work. It is at once fascinating and mysterious that much of his work – certainly the body of it that brought him American disciples – was essentially hermetic, encoded within the seeming transparency of "structure." That hermeticism, however, was not the basic reason for the formation of a constituency, as I will attempt to explain.

One may assume that abstraction, not literalism, informed the Miesian text, and that it was essential, for good cause, that his disciples decode that abstraction to verify their claims about the validity of modernism itself. One may also assume that by making Mies's philosophies accessible to an audience larger than the one composed of his acolytes and sycophants, his disciples might generally verify their own interpretations of his text. With that verification, they might well go on to establish legitimacy for their own architectural productions, just as religious denominations, after attaching themselves to a divine being, lay claim to an equally sacred position by virtue of their proximity to the original. The problem inevitably faced by the Miesian descendancy is the very same problem faced by any individual or group that lays claim to legitimacy or attempts to verify its existence through acts of mimesis: they necessarily commit themselves to a state of imperfection, since mimesis is, by definition, incapable of perfection.

Interpretation is, clearly, in and of itself an immensely dangerous game, since the motives underlying the interpretation, more often than not, establish the value of the exegetic operation itself. If, in the most noble of cases, the interpreter selflessly engages in an exegesis wishing nothing more than

to decode, or to make clear that which is otherwise silent, one set of values can be assigned to such an operation. But if, on the other hand, the reasons for engaging in interpretation are based on verifying a set of acts by the interpreter that resulted specifically from his personal understanding of that text, then another, quite different set of values may be assigned to that operation.

In the case of Mies van der Rohe and his American disciples, before judgment can be assessed or values ascribed to the exegesis relating to the master's text, the nature of the text itself must be defined. The central constituent of Mies van der Rohe's abstract architectural text – i.e., measurement – is the very same one employed throughout the Bible, as its editors went about the business of describing visual phenomena and things generally existential primarily through measurement alone, often detached from other descriptive methods. (The cubit, for example, is the only element consistently employed in describing the temple of Solomon [I Kings 5-9], as well as Ezekiel's vision of a temple in anticipation of a Messianic age [Ezekiel 40-43].) Thus, it is not unreasonable to assert that the meaning underlying Mies van der Rohe's architecture may conceivably relate to his use of measurement as a means of speculation, which in turn defers to the sacred way in which measurement confirms "being" as described in the Bible. Certainly, his fascination with philosophy, and by extension theology, has been well documented.[2] For example, Mies's interest in the writings of both St. Augustine and St. Thomas Aquinas has been interpreted by historians as helping him to establish a philosophic attitude; but, in addition, it may well be that those same readings helped him to position himself theologically as well, reinforcing a relationship between his architectural text and the Bible.

Indeed, by suggesting that Mies van der Rohe was effecting a theological posture, it is possible to contend that his insistence on informing his work by significantly marking his production by means of measurement and proportion, i.e., mathematics, is at the core of understanding the abstract characteristics of his work, and that the source of his mathematical fascinations was centered on the sacred biblical text. Certainly, Mies's apparent repugnance with utilizing anthropomorphically acceptable, historically conventional architectural forms was not necessarily informed only by his being located in the midst of the major twentieth-century architectural revolution. Yet, more than with Le Corbusier and Gropius, Mies's architectural text can be construed to have been driven by the well-known stricture of the Second Commandment that forbade iconography not only from worship but from "being" as well, since Mies's architecture is significantly more opaquely mathematical (and thus, abstract) than is the work of either of these two contemporaries. By citing these particular examples of Miesian abstraction (one might submit that there are many more), it is possible to assert that the absence of conventionality – within the realm of what Mies chose to make present by virtue of that which he chose to make absent (namely, literalism displaced by abstraction) – is at the core of the as yet mute portion of Miesian textuality.

But are these issues of philosophy and theology, literalism and abstraction, really central to those committed to the interpretation of the Miesian text? I would submit that they have had no influence at all on the ways in which that text has been interpreted. Indeed, I would dare say that the true reasons for the interpretations entertained by Mies van der Rohe's American disciples have no such noble implications, but that they are in fact only an extension of his disciples' desires to verify the ways in which that original text could be manipulated in capitalistically informed, practical possibilities intended for their own personal verification. If Mies's interpreters had been interested in the abstract way in which his architectural production could be expanded upon, the results of such fascination would have helped to make clear, for example, the very nature of his utilization of measurement as a means of speculation. By now, for instance, the literature on Mies might well have included diagrammatic information about: 1) the underlying characteristics of his systems of proportions; 2) the methods underlying his use of modulation; 3) the mythical numerical ratios as they relate to his work; and many other features elaborating upon the abstract nature of his production. Such an approach would not at all have divested him of his mythological position in twentieth-century architectural lore, but simply better "informed" the body of knowledge of his oeuvre already in place in the public realm.

Such is not the case however, and as time continues to pass and as one continues to speculate about the insistent obsessions connected with neo-Miesian interpretation, one cannot help but believe that the reasons for this continuous, mindless stream of interpretively mimetic architectural production are rooted in capitalist production more than in pure architectural scholarship. The dozen or so books on Mies van der Rohe's work, his life, and his students' projects purport to flush out the myth of Mies, but merely add to it by not examining substantively the intrinsic characteristics underlying the Miesian text. But the innumerable examples of built work by acolytes and sycophants most tellingly reveal just how intellectually and morally corrupt his disciples are with respect to believable textual interpretation.

If Mies van der Rohe's text was encoded to conceal an intrinsically architectural hidden agenda, one could not possibly know it from the built work of his American disciples. Their architectural production is overwhelmingly mimetic, with any sense of interpretation limited only so as to justify whatever modifications are necessary to make the production "useful" primarily in its physical presence. Mies's text is never

deconstructed to examine its intrinsic nature, since such an approach would belie the reasons for its interpretation by his disciples in the first place. In other words, Mies van der Rohe's text seems to have been seen by his disciples as source material to be drawn upon only to make its usefulness the central constituent of that production. In so doing, they removed any trace of morality, ethics, and sacred presence lest such factors embarrassingly reveal a side to that architectural production not considered useful in the most practical sense of the word, to say nothing of the potential embarrassment created for the disciples by the absence of any moral, ethical, or sacred presence in their own work as well.

Now, it is true that innocent acts of interpretation by those who are distanced from the source of their fascination and are engaged in exegetic acts so that they may comprehend the nature of things, may sometimes inadvertently result in perceptions not intended by the original author. By extension, it is also possible that consensus may be reached by large numbers of people whose perceptions about a text may be infected by cultural and other extrinsic conditions removed from any or all of the intentions implied by original authorship. When, however, the distance of such casual observation is removed (and with it, the innocence of the interpreter), and in turn is replaced by a conscious effort to locate the interpreter in proximity to the original author to verify the resulting mimetically driven work, then not only may the motives for that interpretation be dissonant with the author's original intentions – the mime may find a use for his work entirely different from the central reasons underlying the work of the original author – but usefulness as verified by proximity to an authentic original itself may be the driving reason behind the interpretation in the first place.

But authenticity is not the condition that contaminates a mimetically driven American architectural Miesian descendancy, even though it is unquestionable that the condition of the particular author informing the work of that descendancy – Mies, himself – was an authentic original. America is a practical place after all, populated by pragmatists who are not always affected by questions of morality. The moral, ethical, or even sacred elements of the architecture of Mies van der Rohe have essentially nothing to do with the ways in which that work was seen by self-anointed disciples as potentially paradigmatic.

One is somehow always able to ascertain what is the work of Mies van der Rohe and what is the work of his disciples. Not requiring verification in and of itself, the original is always studied assiduously in terms of its proportion, its modulation, its precision of detailing – in a word, its consistency and, thus, its correctness. Never a quick study, Mies labored intensively to convey an authentic way in which the technology of American production could be translated through the

4. David Haid and Associates, Abraham Lincoln Oasis, Tri-State Tollway, South Holland, Illinois, 1965-67

artful vehicle of his architectural text. Only residually affecting his earlier, European interpretations of post-Wrightian, neo-de Stijlian planar juxtapositions, his American architectural production was predominantly informed by a return to the principles of language – architectural language to be sure, but language all the same. The popularizers of that language, his disciples, in making Mies's work accessible, did so quite casually, at the expense of sacrificing the essentials of the language with which Mies himself was clearly so concerned. One might go so far as to suggest that, whereas in Mies's work language was present, in his disciples' work, language was absent. By literalizing the Miesian abstract text, his disciples removed the original, and perhaps only meaning of that text, subverting it to popular conveyance for their own convenience, not the least intention of which was their desire to verify, indeed to rationalize their own architectural production.

A few examples may be helpful here. First, David Haid's Tri-State Tollway Oasis (1965-67; fig. 4) does not conform to Mies's use of the "golden section" in establishing the system of proportion apparent in his American architecture (note the gusset plates that subdivide the spandrel below the mullioned glass without a recognizable proportional system consistent with the window subdivision). Furthermore, the number of modules bisected by the columns (five, fifteen, five) more clearly conforms to the commonly understood structural ra-

tionale establishing an appropriate double cantilever (i.e., one, three, one) than to anything within Mies's personal aesthetic tradition of precise visual adjudication.

Second, Joseph Fujikawa's Illinois Center (fig. 5), by dividing the short ends of the towers into an even number of bays (four), dispensed with the Hellenic tradition of an odd number of bays (which placed man, rather than a column, at the center), a tradition Mies observed in his American architectural production. It is well known, of course, that four structural bays of approximately thirty feet in dimension (or 120 feet overall) represents the ultimately rational width for a commercially derived, speculative office tower. It is this obsession with practicality that drives the Mies acolytes, rather than any extension of Mies's concerns with the development of an architectural language.

Third, Peter Carter in the Hambro Life Centre (fig. 6) not only removes any perceivable proportional system that might have been identified with Mies, he also deletes the vital surface modulating element of the applied H-section mullion so crucial to an understanding of the value of repetition in measurement. And yet, curiously, the measurement Carter did establish in organizing the window mullions is centered on the column, creating a different sized window pane adjacent to that column. Where Mies's modulation speaks of an understanding of dimensionality and physicality (e.g., thickness of elements), Carter's repetitiousness is simply mute.

5. The Office of Mies van der Rohe, Architect, Joseph Fujikawa, Project Architect, Illinois Center, Chicago, 1967-70

6. Peter Carter, Architect, and YRM Architects, Hambro Life Centre (now Allied Dunbar Centre), Swindon, England, 1977-80

7. Nuns' Island Apartment Buildings, Montreal, 1966-69

Finally, Dirk Lohan's Proposed Convention Center for New York (see cat. no. 123) implies that a Miesian concept is mimetically self-referential. By doggedly repeating the brilliant Chicago exposition hall proposal in another location because he was requested to do so, Lohan makes a joke of the earlier proposal by implying that one concept destined for the Chicago lakefront is equally useful on New York's West Side. Ironically, by such an action, Lohan confirms the long-held popular suspicion that Mies's "glass boxes" are, after all, repeatable.

But is it not the American way to make ideological signification useful in practical terms so as to make it accessible for public consumption? Mies van der Rohe's disciples were not any more or less amoral than any descendancy committed to conveying original concepts by the removal of the myth and the replacement of it with usefulness. One might even take the position that the American architectural production of Mies van der Rohe implicitly suggested its own popularization by concerning itself with American technology. The tragedy lies neither in making accessible selected portions of the unique conditions of the language of a master, nor even the usury implicit in the obsessive behavior of a descendancy determined to verify its own existence through proximity, but rather in what has been consciously overlooked in the Miesian text in the drive to popularize certain aspects of it. That which is still inexplicable in the text may not have been particularly important in the context of American pragmatism, but its suppression in favor of a less savory, albeit culturally recognizable interpretation suggests a lack of morality in a discipline

desperately in need of every ounce of moral certitude available.

But it was not only the disciples whose practical interpretations of the Miesian text trivialized any deeper meaning intrinsically buried in that text, it was equally his American clientele whose concerns were also invariably centered on "usefulness." It is common knowledge, for example, within the architectural discipline that Mies desired a free-plan organization for the internal apartment organization for his glass towers (860-880 Lake Shore Drive Apartments, 1948-51), only to be thwarted in his efforts by his developer-client, Herbert S. Greenwald, who subverted those intentions in order to make the project "useful" (conventional rooms, with conventional doors, etc.). It might not be as commonly known, however, that Greenwald's descendant organization, Metropolitan Structures, headed by Bernard Weissbourd, also subverted the readability of the Miesian frame enclosed by its superstructure girded with slender, superimposed mullions, by adding balconies on a Mies highrise – once again in favor of usefulness – on Nuns' Island, Montreal (1966-69; fig. 7).

And yet, was not the suggestion of all of this usefulness implicit in Mies's American architectural production? Examples of both client and disciple perceiving practical extensions of Mies's work are neither coincidental nor particulary innocent; they suggest that Mies's silence on the deeper meaning of his work, in combination with an intelligentsia limited in its interest in hidden meaning, can only be conceived of as the way in which Mies continuously concealed the true meaning of his architectural text. Unlike a European architectural cognoscenti trained in dialectical operations, and thereby eminently equipped to receive textuality that it dissects to establish meaning, Mies's American disciples suffered from no such cultural qualifications. Their perceptions of him and his text were clearly vocational both in their training (one could not consciously accuse Mies's regime at IIT of ever being particularly Socratic in its architectural posturing) and in their professional subservience to their clientele. (American capitalistically driven clients have a persuasive way of dispensing with architectural ideas, as they displace them with useful – i.e., functional – features.)

There is no doubt that Mies van der Rohe's paradigmatic position as the most influential architect of the twentieth century is directly related to the ability of his disciples, as well as his clients, to popularize his architectural philosophies. If they had not, the more hermetic side of his architecture would not have been made intelligible. Notwithstanding this fact, it is crucial that the whole of the Miesian text be made clear, since its intrinsically architectural nature is the grist by which epochal movement is made possible, and since the popular side of language is not the stuff of speculation but rather of verification. Without the potentiality connected with the future, there is only the memory of the past upon which to draw. A dependence upon hindsight alone only leads to despair and the loss of innocence, for it is innocence that is the constituent feature of the optimism native to architecture and it is innocence that is essential to the hope manifest in any examination of the future. After all, Mies van der Rohe not only described his own epoch through the vehicle of his work, he also used that same work simultaneously to speculate about the future, suggesting that his American architectural production was intrinsically optimistic, even as he employed that work in order to extend the language of architecture.

Notes

1. This influence was the subject of two separate 1983 lectures in Chicago given independently by Arthur Drexler and Peter Eisenman.

2. See Fritz Neumeyer's recent publication *Mies van der Rohe, Das kunstlose Wort, Gedanken zur Baukunst* (Berlin, 1986).

A Note on the Exhibition

The exhibition "The Unknown Mies van der Rohe and His Disciples of Modernism," for which this volume serves as catalogue, was designed to examine some aspects of Ludwig Mies van der Rohe's career in relation to those of his contemporaries, colleagues, and disciples by exhibiting less well known drawings and models selected from a variety of private, institutional, and corporate collections. The core of the exhibition, however, comes from the permanent collection of The Art Institute of Chicago, principally through the generosity of the students of both Mies van der Rohe and Ludwig Karl Hilberseimer, in particular A. James Speyer and George Danforth. Many of the objects included in the exhibition have never been shown before; a selection of these objects is reproduced in this section.

Following a brief section of personal memorabilia, the second of the five sections of the exhibition places Mies van der Rohe's European projects from the late 1920s through the 1930s in context with the work of other German architects and planners, particularly his friend and colleague Ludwig Hilberseimer. The items on display show us that although Mies and Hilberseimer often drew and published large-scale projects, the harsh economic realities of the depression of the early 1930s and the subsequent rise of National Socialism, with its antagonism toward much of the alleged Communist orientation of the Bauhaus, prevented them from realizing many of their dreams, even the small-scale ones such as Mies's Hubbe House of 1935 and his own mountain retreat of 1934. Also of special importance in this section are the competition drawings for an office building and bank in Stuttgart from 1928. These items were rediscovered and saved some twenty-five years ago by Martin Werwigk, the architect of the Württembergische Landesbank, and they are being shown for the first time in this country in this exhibition. (See Appendix II for excerpts from the official record of the competition.)

In the late 1930s many architects, like Mies and Hilberseimer, fled Nazi Germany to start their careers anew in the United States. The third section of the exhibition is especially devoted to the work that Mies and Hilberseimer did at the Illinois Institute of Technology. This section also displays houses and other small-scale, low-rise buildings and interior spaces by Mies, Hilberseimer and their followers, namely, Daniel Brenner, Peter Carter, George Danforth, Edward Duckett, Joseph Fujikawa, Myron Goldsmith, David Haid, Dirk Lohan, Reginald Malcolmson, A. James Speyer, and Gene Summers. One can see from the works presented here that Mies and his young colleagues continued to receive the kind of commissions for low-rise structures that he had executed in Germany, though these American projects began to be built, especially after World War II, with increasing frequency.

The fourth section of the exhibition is given over to Mies's participation in the post-World War II reconstruction of West Germany. Although his New National Gallery (1962-67) in Berlin is the only executed German work from this period, he had plans for other sites, including a National Theatre (1952-53) in Mannheim, and an Administration Building (1961-63) for the Krupp Corporation in Essen. Items chosen for this exhibition from collections in Mannheim and Essen bring Mies home, figuratively, to German soil and, in the latter project, document the contribution of disciple Gene Summers.

Although Mies designed skyscrapers in the twenties and thirties, it was not until his move to America in 1938 that he was able to design and construct large steel and glass buildings. More specifically, it was the building boom following the war that enabled Mies and his disciples to change the face of the American cityscape, and, in particular, the skyline of Chicago, Mies's base for thirty years. The fifth and final portion of the exhibition focuses on drawings for some of the early apartment buildings of the late 1940s that were financed by Herbert

Greenwald, the farsighted developer who catapulted Mies toward his dream of building skyscrapers for work and habitation. In addition, related works by Hilberseimer, Brenner, Carter, Fujikawa, Goldsmith, Jacques Brownson, and Charles Genther of Pace Associates are displayed. These include a special featuring of models and documents for Mansion House Square in London, one of Mies van der Rohe's last major projects, the design of which was continued by Peter Carter until the project was finally stopped, after much public discussion, in 1985. Finally, we have also included a number of professional renderings for commercial buildings in Chicago and elsewhere to give the viewer the feeling of this active building boom.

This exhibition, then, explores Mies van der Rohe in his professional and aesthetic kinships with his disciples through less well known objects – principally drawings and models – that come from collections outside the massive archive of Mies's work in the Museum of Modern Art. We hope that this exhibition and catalogue, along with the other events that are part of the international celebration of Mies's centenary, will bring forth other unknown artifacts and reveal more of the interrelationships between Mies and his followers.

John Zukowsky, *Curator of Architecture*
The Art Institute of Chicago

Catalogue

N.B. The dimensions given in the following checklist are in centimeters, with height preceding width. Lenders to the exhibition are indicated as such, and all donations to The Art Institute of Chicago are credited as gifts of their respective donors.

Part I. Ludwig Mies van der Rohe (1886-1969)

1. Robert Damora. Autographed portrait photograph of Ludwig Mies van der Rohe, c. 1947. Published in *House and Garden,* November 1947. Photoprint, mounted on board, 24 x 18.8. Lent by Mrs. Herbert S. Greenwald. (See cover illustration.)

2. John Cromelin. Profile Caricature of Ludwig Mies van der Rohe, c. 1949. Published in the *Bulletin of the Chicago Chapter, American Institute of Architects*, September 1949, p. 10. Charcoal and prismacolor on tracing paper, 42.5 x 39.6. Gift of L. Morgan Yost.

3. Ludwig Karl Hilberseimer. Library display cases containing manuscript material, photographs, memorabilia, and sketches of buildings by Mies van der Rohe, Peter Behrens, Le Corbusier, Louis Sullivan, and Frank Lloyd Wright that Hilberseimer used in writing his books. The Hilberseimer Collection, Gift of George Danforth. (On display in Chicago only.)

Part II. Ludwig Mies van der Rohe and the European Context

A. Housing and City Planning

4. Ludwig Karl Hilberseimer. Pitched roof houses, perspective, c. 1920. Ink on heavy paper, signed on verso, 33.2 x 46.4. The Hilberseimer Collection, Gift of George Danforth.

4.

5. Ludwig Karl Hilberseimer. Housing project, Berlin; two perspective studies, c. 1925-29. Pencil on tracing paper, 30.6 x 23.5. The Hilberseimer Collection, Gift of George Danforth.

6. Ludwig Karl Hilberseimer. "Hochhausstadt" (highrise city), north-south street, 1924. Published in *Die Form*, 1926, p. 174, and *Groszstadtarchitektur*, p. 18, ill. 23. Ink and watercolor on paper, 97 x 140. The Hilberseimer Collection, Gift of George Danforth.

7. Ludwig Karl Hilberseimer. "Hochhausstadt" (highrise city), east-west street, 1924. Published in *Groszstadt-architektur*, p. 19, ill. 24, and *G*, March 1926. Ink and watercolor on paper, 96.5 x 148. The Hilberseimer Collection, Gift of George Danforth.

8. Ludwig Karl Hilberseimer. "Anwendung des Prinzips auf Berlin" (application of the principle on Berlin), c. 1929-30. Published in *Die Form*, 1930, p. 608, and *Entfaltung einer Planungsidee*, p. 23, ill. 8. Collage, photograph with ink on paper, 17.2 x 25.2. The Hilberseimer Collection, Gift of George Danforth.

6.

7.

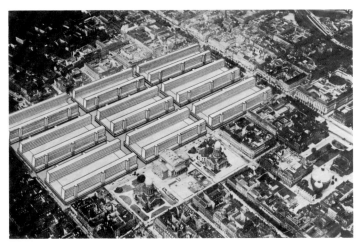

8.

111

9. Ludwig Karl Hilberseimer. "Blick vom Balkon" (perspective view from balcony); mixed housing development, c. 1929-30. Published in *Entfaltung einer Planungsidee,* p. 37, ill. 25. Ink on heavy paper, 36.9 x 50.6. The Hilberseimer Collection, Gift of George Danforth.

10. Ludwig Karl Hilberseimer. "Mischbebauung. Mietshäuser. . ." (mixed type settlement: apartments . . .), c. 1929-30. Published in *Entfaltung einer Planungsidee,* p. 37, ill. 26; *Contemporary Architecture,* p. 151, ill. 126; and *Berliner Architektur,* p. 67. Ink on heavy paper, 20.1 x 26.6. The Hilberseimer Collection, Gift of George Danforth.

9.

10.

11. Ludwig Mies van der Rohe, Architectural Coordinator. The Weissenhofsiedlung, Stuttgart, 1927. Model from 1982 by Fa. Enz in cooperation with the Staatliche Hochbauamt III, Stuttgart. Wood, 120 x 280 x 200. Lent by Staatliche Hochbauverwaltung Bundesrepublik Deutschland.

12. Ludwig Mies van der Rohe. Apartment building in the Weissenhofsiedlung, 1927. Photograph by Hermann Nägele, 1985, with restoration in progress. Colored photoprint, 40.4 x 60.5.

13. Weissenhofsiedlung, Stuttgart. Aerial photograph dated September 21, 1927, by Strähle Luftbild. 1986 photoprint on paper, approximately 101 x 152.

14. Ludwig Karl Hilberseimer. "Mietshausprojekt" (apartment house project), Kanstrasse, Berlin, c. 1930. Published in *Entfaltung einer Planungsidee*, p. 124, ill. 103. Pencil on heavy paper, 72.9 x 10 x 101.8. The Hilberseimer Collection, Gift of George Danforth.

15. Ludwig Karl Hilberseimer. "Kleinstwohnung im Treppenlosen Haus" (small flat in the house without a staircase), Berlin, 1930. Plates 6 and 7: plan; section and elevation. Ink on heavy paper, each 83.5 x 59.5. The Hilberseimer Collection, Gift of George Danforth.

11.

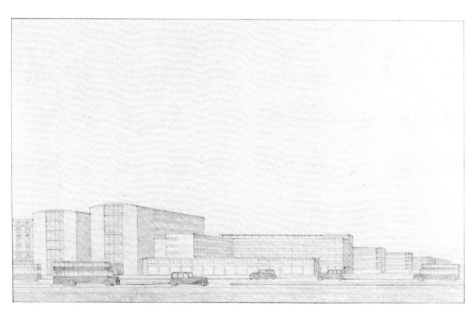

14.

B. Commercial, Public, and Multi-Use Buildings in Relation to City Planning

1928 Competition for a Bank and Office Building, Stuttgart

The following twenty-five items represent part of nine competition entries for a bank and office building at Hindenburgplatz and Lautenschlagerstrasse in Stuttgart, also called the Württembergischen Sparkassen und Giroverband (now the Württembergische Landesbank). The competition was held from August 21, 1928, to December 1, 1928. All items lent by Martin Werwigk, Architect of the Landesbank, Stuttgart.

16. Adolf Abel. Photomontage, matted. Photo: 15.6 x 27.1. Perspective rendering. Pencil on tracing paper, mounted on board, 49.3 x 64.7.

17. Paul Bonatz and F.E. Scholer. Photomontage, mounted on board. Photo: 15.8 x 22.1; board: 32 x 41.9. N.B. This entry was actually constructed, although it did not receive first prize.

18. Richard Döcker. Elevation Lautenschlagerstrasse, elevation Hindenburgplatz. Blueline print on paper, 58.6 x 82.3.

19. Alfred Fischer. Two photomontages; small photo: 12.1 x 23.1; large photo: 35.2 x 49.1; mounted on board, 49.9 x 65. "Zeichnung für die Lichtreklame" (drawing showing neon signs), elevation Lautenschlagerstrasse, at night. Pencil, pastel, white ink, yellow watercolor on paper, mounted on black board, 28 x 49.

20. Carl Krayl. Photomontage, isometric drawing, elevation Hindenburgplatz, elevation Lautenschlagerstrasse, detail of the facade. Various techniques on board, 72.6 x 101.6.

17.

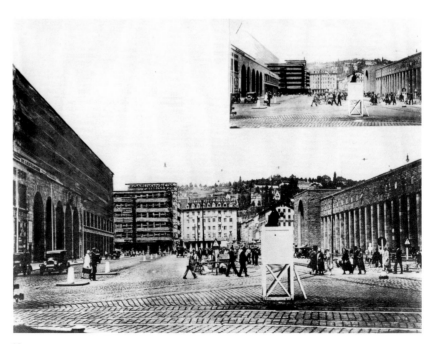

19.

114

21. G. Schleicher and K. Gutschow. a) Photo-montage, mounted on paper; photo: 12.2 x 20.8; paper: 20.9 x 33.9. b) Photo of the model, mounted on board; photo: 47.3 x 59.5; board: 65.5 x 75.2. c) Four perspective renderings at night. Washed ink on paper, mounted on board; each drawing: 10.4 x 21.7; board 65.7 x 75.8. N.B. The Schleicher and Gutschow entry was premiated.

21. a

21. b

22. Adolf G. Schneck. a) "Vorschlag für Lichtreklame" (proposals for neon signs), perspective renderings. Watercolor on paper, 7.1 x 15. b) Photomontage, mounted on board; photo: 12.7 x 22.8; board: 24.8 x 32.3.

23. Ernst Stahl. Detail of the facade. Blueline print on paper, 58.5 x 109.2.

24. Heinz Wetzel und A. Schuhmacher. Photomontage and site plan, mounted on board; photo: 15.2 x 20.8; plan: 50.6 x 53; board: 95.8 x 63.8. Elevations Lautenschlagerstrasse, Hindenburgplatz, Alleenstrasse, detail of the facade. Blueline print on paper, 95.5 x 63.2.

25. Ludwig Mies van der Rohe. a) Photomontage, mounted on wood, 95 x 150.
b) Nine drawings, pencil on tracing paper mounted on board, each 44 x 90.5: 1) elevation Lautenschlagerstrasse and elevation Hindenburgplatz; 2) section and elevation of the court; 3) eighth-floor plan; 4) floor plan of a regular story, pencil; 5) second-floor plan, pencil and colored pencil; 6) first-floor plan, pencil and colored pencil; 7) basement plan, pencil and colored pencil; 8) floor plan of safe basement; 9) site plan, colored pencil on blackline print mounted on board.

26. Ludwig Karl Hilberseimer. Perspective view, Stadthalle (state theatre), Nürnberg, 1929. Ink on heavy paper, 43.1 x 60.2. The Hilberseimer Collection, Gift of George Danforth.

27. Ludwig Karl Hilberseimer. Two aerial perspectives, mixed living planning concept, c. 1934. Similar in concept to drawing published in *The New City*, p. 97, ill. 70. Ink on paper, approximately 28.65 x 85.3 and 29.1 x 85.3. The Hilberseimer Collection, Gift of George Danforth.

28. Ludwig Karl Hilberseimer. Lake Front Development, Zurich, 1935. Published in *Entfaltung einer Planungsidee*, p. 125, ill. 105. Pencil on heavy paper, 60 x 90. The Hilberseimer Collection, Gift of George Danforth.

22. b

25. a

116

29. Ludwig Karl Hilberseimer. Perspective view of proposed hotel, c. 1933-35. Pencil on heavy paper, 72.7 x 100. The Hilberseimer Collection, Gift of George Danforth.

30. Ludwig Karl Hilberseimer. A View of the Business and Administration Zone – The Decentralized City, c. 1933-35. Published in *Entfaltung einer Planungsidee,* p. 52, ill. 41. Ink on heavy paper with pencil notes, 36.2 x 50.8. The Hilberseimer Collection, Gift of George Danforth.

31. Ludwig Karl Hilberseimer. Isometric plan of University of Berlin, 1937. Published in *Entfaltung einer Planungsidee,* p. 126, ill. 107, and *Berliner Architektur,* p. 78. Ink on heavy paper, 38.1 x 51.8. The Hilberseimer Collection, Gift of George Danforth.

32. Ludwig Karl Hilberseimer. "Gartenstadt Eichhorst Berlin – Waidmanns Lust." Signed and dated, Berlin, June 8, 1938. Pencil on tracing paper, 36.8 x 38. The Hilberseimer Collection, Gift of George Danforth.

C. Private Residences and Related Low-Rise Buildings

33. Ludwig Mies van der Rohe. Model of proposed Krefeld Golf Club, 1930, made by Raimund Schröder, Krefeld, 1981. Plywood, 9 x 130 x 145. Lent by Krefelder Kunstmuseen – Kaiser Wilhelm Museum, Museum Haus Lange, Museum Haus Esters. (On display in Chicago only.)

34. Ludwig Mies van der Rohe. Two sheets: perspective study of an interior with a wall mural; and perspective sketches, plan, and elevations of a house with a projecting canopy, c. 1934. Ink on paper, each 31 x 21. Gift of A. James Speyer.

35. Ludwig Mies van der Rohe. Elevation studies for the proposed Mountain House for the Architect, near Meran, South Tyrol, 1934. Ink on paper, 15.7 x 21.4. Gift of A. James Speyer.

36. Ludwig Mies van der Rohe. Two sheets: perspective sketches for the proposed Mountain House for the Architect, near Meran, South Tyrol, 1934. Pencil on paper, each 15.3 x 21.5. Gift of A. James Speyer.

29.

37. Ludwig Mies van der Rohe. Two sheets: bird's-eye view and perspective sketches of the proposed Mountain House for the Architect, near Meran, South Tyrol, 1934. Pencil on paper, each 21.6 x 26.4. Gift of A. James Speyer.

38. Ludwig Mies van der Rohe. Two sheets: a) perspective study of proposed Hubbe House, Magdeburg, 1935; and b) elevation study of the proposed Mountain House for the Architect, near Meran, South Tyrol, 1934. Pencil on paper, each 21.6 x 27.6. Gift of A. James Speyer.

39. Ludwig Mies van der Rohe. Two sheets: a) plan and perspective study for a house with two courts; and b) plan detail sketch, c. 1934. Pencil on paper, each 21.4 x 29.9. Gift of A. James Speyer.

40. Ludwig Mies van der Rohe. Two sheets: plan sketches for a house with two courts and skylight, c. 1934. Pencil on paper, each 21.6 x 29.8. Gift of A. James Speyer.

38. a

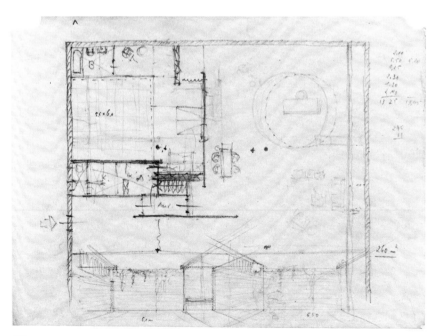

39. a

118

41. Ludwig Mies van der Rohe. Two sheets:
a) perspective and b) plan and perspective
studies for a court house or, possibly, the
proposed Hubbe House, Magdeburg,
c. 1934-35. Ink on paper, each 21.6 x 30. Gift
of A. James Speyer.

42. Ludwig Mies van der Rohe. Two sheets:
plan details; and site plan of property for
proposed Hubbe House, Magdeburg, 1935.
Pencil on paper, each 21.4 x 24.9. Gift of A.
James Speyer.

43. Ludwig Mies van der Rohe. Two sheets:
plan studies and sketch elevation of the proposed Hubbe House, Magdeburg, 1935.
Pencil on paper, each 21.5 x 29.9. Gift of A.
James Speyer.

44. Ludwig Mies van der Rohe. Two sheets:
a, b) perspective studies for the proposed
Hubbe House, Magdeburg, 1935, with a perspective doodle, lower right (b), of an
unidentified house. Ink on paper, each 21.6 x
30. Gift of A. James Speyer.

45. Ludwig Mies van der Rohe. Two sheets:
plan, elevation, and perspective exterior and
interior sketches for the Hubbe House, Magdeburg, 1935. Pencil on paper, each 21.5 x
29.5. Gift of A. James Speyer.

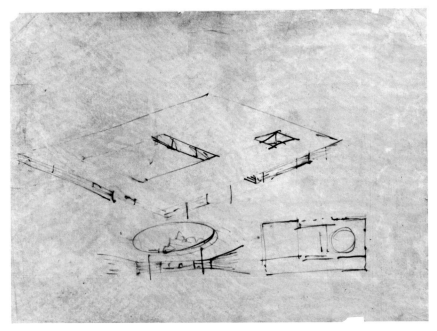

41. b

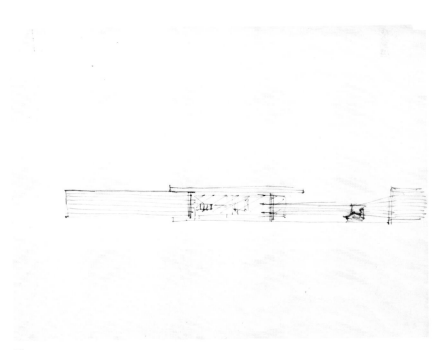

44. a

46. Ludwig Mies van der Rohe. Two sheets:
a) plan and elevation, and b) two plans of the
proposed Hubbe House, Magdeburg, 1935.
Pencil on paper, each 21.4 x 29.9. Gift of A.
James Speyer.

47. Ludwig Mies van der Rohe. Two sheets:
a) perspective study of house interior, possibly for the Hubbe House; and b) a mural
study, c. 1935. Ink on paper, and pencil and
colored pencil on paper, each 21.4 x 29.9.
Gift of A. James Speyer.

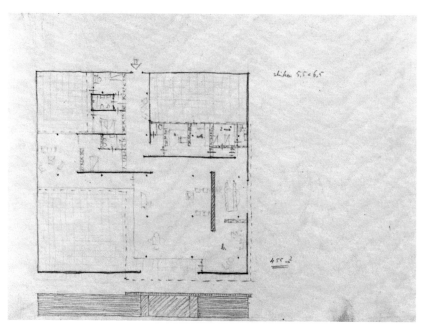

46. a

47. b

48. Ludwig Mies van der Rohe. Two sheets:
a, b) court house sketches (possibly Hubbe
House), showing slab roofs, c. 1935. Ink on
paper, each 21.4 x 29.9. Gift of A. James
Speyer.

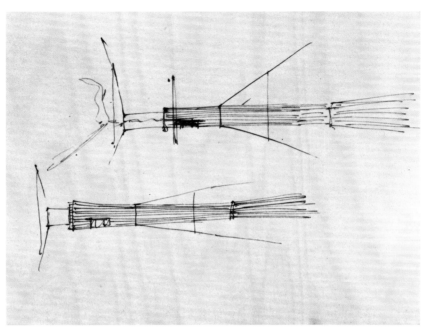

48. a

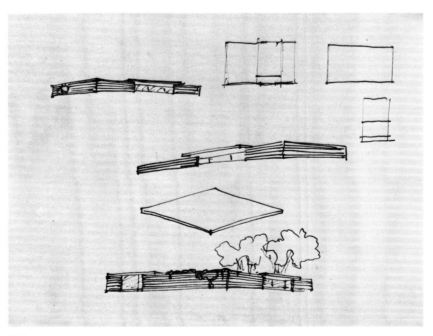

48. b

D. Furniture and Furnishings

49. Ludwig Mies van der Rohe. MR Chair, 1927. Chrome steel tubing and green leather, 80 x 53.3 x 35.6. Restricted gift of the Graham Foundation for Advanced Studies in the Fine Arts (1970.403). (On display in Chicago only.)

50. Ludwig Mies van der Rohe. MR Side Chair, 1927. Chrome steel tubing and tan leather. Private Collection, Chicago. (On display in Chicago only.)

51. Ludwig Mies van der Rohe. Two sheets: drawings for bent tubular steel chairs, showing numerous designs in profile and perspective, with German annotations, probably regarding the exhibition halls at the Gewerbehalleplatz, Stuttgart, 1927. Pencil on cream paper, 21.7 x 29.9 and 21.7 x 30.4. Gift of A. James Speyer.

52. Ludwig Mies van der Rohe. Chair Studies, c. 1927-30. Green pencil on paper, 20 x 58 (image). Lent by A. James Speyer.

53. Ludwig Mies van der Rohe. Chair Sketches, c. 1927-30. Green pencil and pencil on paper, 43.5 x 52 (image). Lent by A. James Speyer.

54. Ludwig Mies van der Rohe. Lamp fixture, Lange House, Krefeld, c. 1928-29. Glass and metal, 17 x 55. Lent by Krefelder Kunstmuseen-Kaiser Wilhelm Museum, Museum Haus Lange, Museum Haus Esters. (On display in Chicago only.)

49.

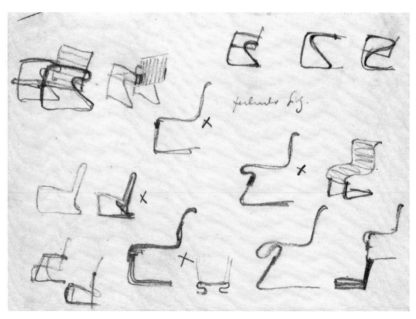

51. (detail)

55. Ludwig Mies van der Rohe. Two sheets: a) drawings for lounge chairs, with German annotations, such as "eventuell auch in der lage verstellbar" (possibly also adjustable position), "montiert, auf den Boden auf Fahrzeugen" (mounted, on the floor on vessels), "aber als mobile" (but mobile), and "leicht metall gepresst, metall überzogen" (pressed light metal, chromeplated); and b) lounge chairs and side chair details, c. 1930-35. Pencil on cream paper, each 15 x 21. Gift of A. James Speyer.

56. Ludwig Mies van der Rohe. One sheet of furniture studies, with German annotations, "Stapel" (stacked), "Verstärkungsprofil" (reinforcing rod), and "Liegestuhl" (chaise lounge), along with a newspaper clipping of an aerial observation spotter in a chaise lounge entitled "Der Liegestuhl wird Kriegsgerät" (the chaise lounge becomes war material), c. 1935. Pencil on paper, 21.5 x 30, and printed newspaper, approximately 20 x 28. Lent by A. James Speyer.

57. Ludwig Mies van der Rohe. Two sheets: nine elevations of chairs, and four sketches of a conchoidal-tractor seat chair, with German annotations, c. 1930-35. Ink on paper, 21 x 30.4, and pencil on paper, 21 x 29.9. Gift of A. James Speyer.

58. Ludwig Mies van der Rohe. Three drawings of furniture studies on note paper and a piece of newspaper dated September 25, 1936, with German annotations, "Sitz und Liege möbel" (chair and chaise lounge) and "aus federndem Werkstoff lackiert" (with lacquered spring-frame). Pencil on paper, 29 x 6.7, 5 x 31, and 5 x 32. Lent by A. James Speyer.

59. Ludwig Mies van der Rohe. Chair and tractor stool, c. 1930-35. Ink on paper, 19 x 28.6. Gift of A. James Speyer.

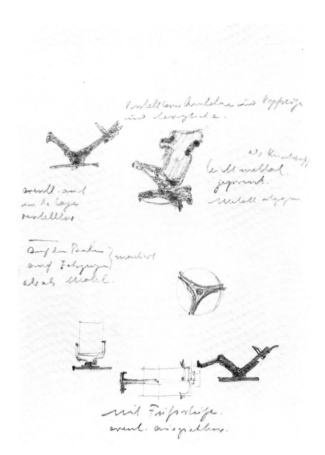

55. a

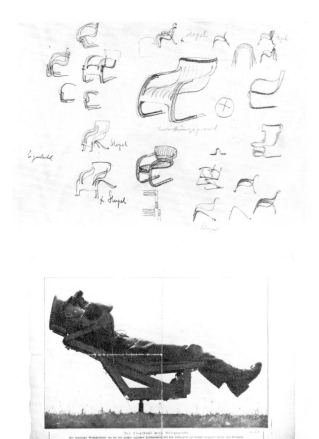

56.

60. Ludwig Mies van der Rohe. Two sheets: a) chair arm studies, c. 1935-37; and b) chair studies and lamination sketches, with numerous German annotations, c. 1936-37. Pencil on paper, each 21.7 x 30.1. Gift of A. James Speyer.

61. Ludwig Mies van der Rohe. Two sheets: studies for conchoidal chairs, one with German annotation "Doppelfahne" (double curved slat), c. 1935-37. Pencil on cream paper, 21 x 29.6. and 21.2 x 30. Gift of A. James Speyer.

62. Ludwig Mies van der Rohe. Two sheets: a,b) studies for conchoidal or pleated chairs, c. 1937. Pencil on paper, each 21.5 x 32. Gift of A. James Speyer.

63. Ludwig Mies van der Rohe. Two sheets: a,b) chair sketches, with German annotations, on Lilly Reich's stationery, c. 1937. Pencil on paper, 29.8 x 21.2 and 27 x 22. Gift of A. James Speyer.

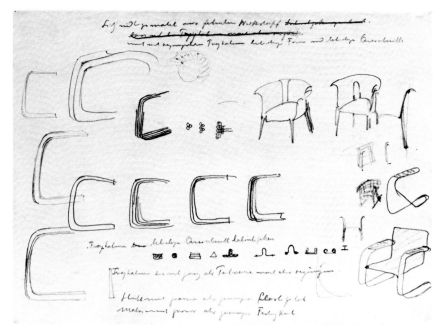

60. b

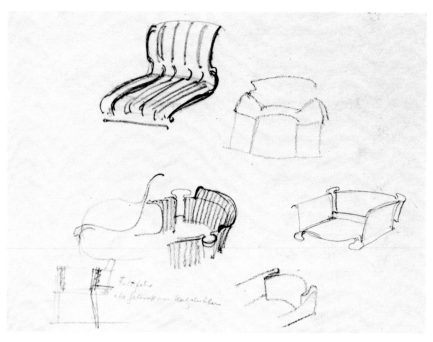

62. b

III. Ludwig Mies van der Rohe Moves to America

A. Houses and Housing

64. Ludwig Mies van der Rohe. Perspective sketch of a court house with garden sculpture, c. 1931-38. Ink on paper, signed, 21 x 30. Lent by A. James Speyer. (See frontispiece.)

65. Ludwig Mies van der Rohe. Perspective sketch of a court house with mural, c. 1931-38. Ink on paper, signed, 30 x 21. Lent by A. James Speyer.

66. Ludwig Mies van der Rohe. Two sheets: perspective studies for the interior of a court house, c. 1931-38. Ink on paper, each 21 x 30.1. Gift of A. James Speyer.

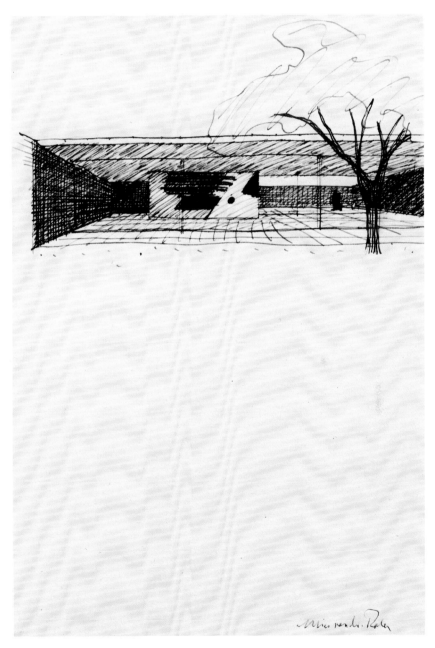

65.

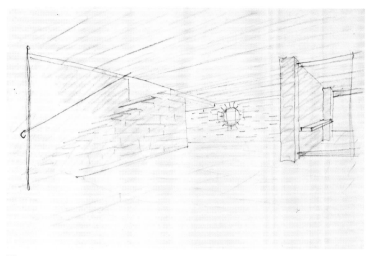

67. a

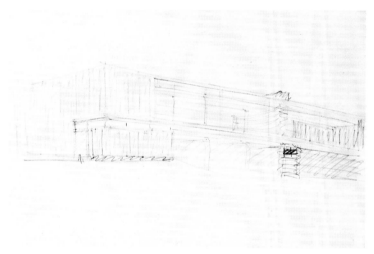

67. b

68. a

67. Ludwig Mies van der Rohe. Two sheets:
a) perspective study of the entrance foyer,
and b) exterior of the proposed Resor House,
Jackson Hole, Wyoming, c. 1937-38. Pencil
and yellow pencil on paper, 21.9 x 33. Gift of
A. James Speyer.

68. Ludwig Mies van der Rohe. Two sheets:
a, b) perspective sketches of a house in a
mountainous terrain (either the proposed
Mountain House for the Architect, 1934, or
proposed Resor House, 1937-38) on Stevens
Hotel stationery, Chicago, probably drawn
c. August-September 1938. Ink on paper,
each 22 x 28. Gift of A. James Speyer.

69. Ludwig Mies van der Rohe. Two sheets:
a) perspective study of living room, probably
for proposed Resor House, Jackson Hole,
Wyoming, c. 1937-38; and b) perspective
study of living room and mantel, probably
for the proposed Hubbe House, Magdeburg,
1935. Pencil on paper, 21.7 x 28.2 and 22.4 x
28.4. Gift of A. James Speyer.

70. George Danforth. Two student sketches
for a court house, 1940. Pencil and colored
pencil on tracing paper, each 30.5 x 53 cm.
Gift of George Danforth.

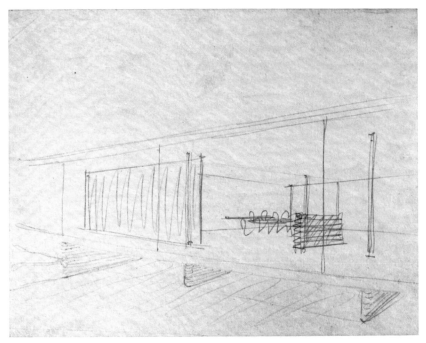

69. a

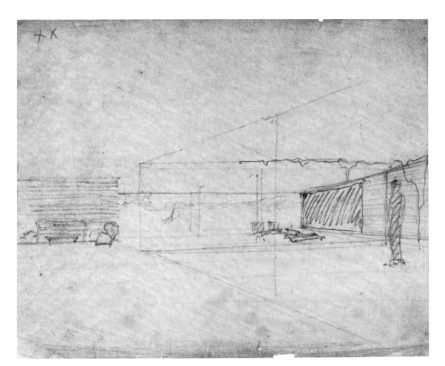

69. b

71. Ludwig Karl Hilberseimer, possibly with Alfred Caldwell. Bird's-eye view of L-shaped houses for 80 people per acre, c. 1943. Published in *The New City,* p. 95, ill. 69, and *Entfaltung einer Planungsidee,* p. 36, ill. 22. Ink on buff paper, 39.5 x 50. The Hilberseimer Collection, Gift of George Danforth.

72. David Haid and Associates. Factory fabricated housing, 1968. Published as "Städtebauliches Sanierungsschema" in *100 Jahre Chicago Architektur.* Model. Mixed media, 90.5 x 90.5. Lent by David Haid.

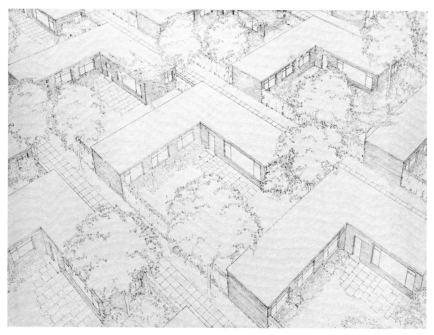

71.

72.

73. Myron Goldsmith with Earl Bluestein,
Associate Architect. Two sheets: a) plan, and
b) sections and elevations of proposed house
for Stuart A. Borovay, Glencoe, Illinois,
March 12, 1948. Pencil on tracing paper;
plan, 65 x 92; elevations: 64 x 92. Gift of
Myron Goldsmith.

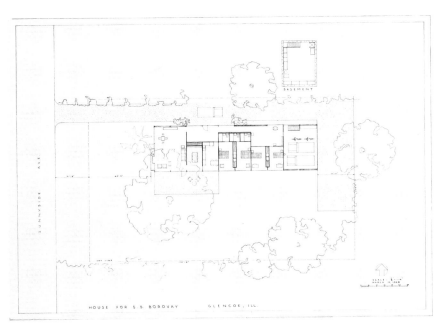

73. a

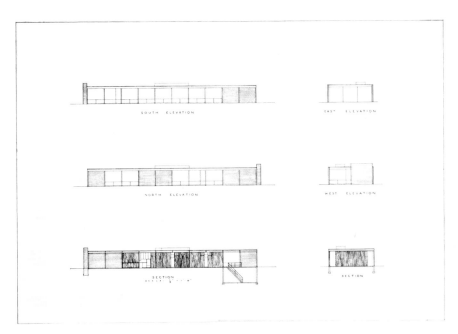

73. b

74. Ludwig Mies van der Rohe. Two sheets:
a) bird's-eye view, and b) elevation of a variation on the 50 by 50 House, c. 1950-51.
Pencil on note paper, each 15.5 x 21.7. Lent
by A. James Speyer.

75. Ludwig Mies van der Rohe. The
Farnsworth House, Plano, Illinois, 1951.
Photopanel, 72.2 x 101.7. Lent by Hedrich-
Blessing, Photographers.

76. A. James Speyer. Preliminary plan for
the Rose Residence, Highland Park, Illinois,
1952. Pencil on tracing paper, 50.7 x 82.7.
Gift of A. James Speyer.

77. A. James Speyer. Four preliminary elevations for the Rose Residence, Highland Park,
Illinois, 1952. Pencil on tracing paper, 49 x
87. Gift of A. James Speyer.

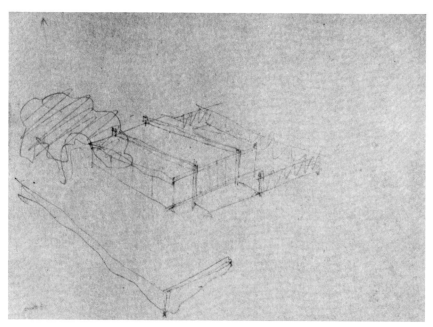

74. a

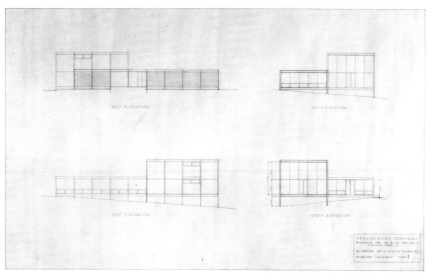

77.

78. David Haid and Associates. Pavilion on the site of the Rose Residence, Highland Park, Illinois, 1974. Autographed photopanel. Lent by Hedrich-Blessing, Photographers.

79. David Haid and Associates. Plan of pavilion on the site of the Rose Residence, Highland Park, Illinois, 1974. Pencil on tracing paper, 76.2 x 90.5. Lent by David Haid.

80. David Haid and Associates. Pavilion on the site of the Rose Residence, Highland Park, Illinois, 1974. View of shop-fabricated steel building components (17). Pencil on tracing paper, 76.2 x 90.5. Lent by David Haid.

81. Daniel Brenner. Six drawings for a guest house on the Brenner property, Ellison Bay, Wisconsin, c. 1974. Pencil on gridded paper, 28 x 43. Gift of Rachael, Jon, and Ariel Brenner.

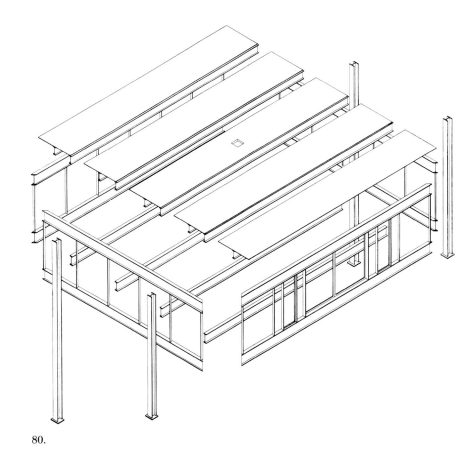

80.

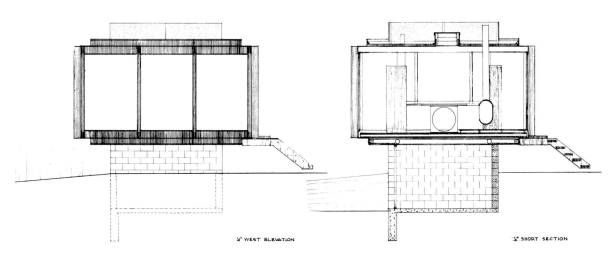

81.

B. Illinois Institute of Technology and Related Work

82. Ludwig Mies van der Rohe. Two sheets: sketch plans for the campus of IIT, c. 1939-40. Pencil on paper, each 15.2 x 17.9. Gift of A. James Speyer.

83. Ludwig Mies van der Rohe. Perspective sketches of a typical building, IIT, c. 1940-41. Pencil on note paper, each 15.3 x 21.5. Gift of A. James Speyer.

84. Ludwig Mies van der Rohe. Presentation study of typical classroom, laboratory, or faculty office building prototype for IIT, c. 1940-41, partly delineated by George Danforth. Crayon and pencil on illustration board, 50.8 x 76.2. Gift of A. James Speyer.

85. Ludwig Mies van der Rohe. Two sheets: a) corner detail sketch, and b) perspective sketch, probably for the proposed Administration Building, IIT, c. 1944. Pencil and ink on paper, each 15.1 x 21. Gift of A. James Speyer.

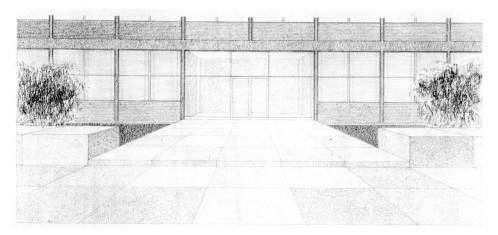

84.

85. a

86. Ludwig Mies van der Rohe. Two sheets:
a, b) perspective sketches for buildings at
IIT (Engineering Building?), c. 1944. Pencil
on note paper, each 15.3 x 21.5. Lent by A.
James Speyer.

87. Ludwig Mies van der Rohe. Rendered
study of proposed Administration Building,
IIT, c. 1941-44, partly delineated by George
Danforth. Pencil and charcoal on illustration
board, 76.4 x 101.8. Gift of A. James Speyer.

86. b

87.

88. Ludwig Mies van der Rohe. Perspective rendering of proposed Chemistry or Metallurgy Building, IIT, c. 1944. Pencil and charcoal on illustration board, 76.9 x 101.8. Gift of A. James Speyer.

89. Ludwig Mies van der Rohe, Architect, with Friedman, Alschuler and Sincere, Associate Architects. Elevations of the Chemistry Building, IIT, March 1, 1946. Pencil on tracing paper, approximately 66 x 101. Gift of Friedman, Alschuler and Sincere.

90. Ludwig Mies van der Rohe, Architect, with Friedman, Alschuler and Sincere, Associate Architects. First-floor plan of the Chemistry Building, IIT, March 1, 1946. Pencil on tracing paper, approximately 66 x 101. Gift of Friedman, Alschuler and Sincere.

91. Ludwig Mies van der Rohe, Architect, with Friedman, Alschuler and Sincere, Associate Architects. Window details for the Chemistry Building, IIT, March 1, 1946. Pencil on tracing paper, approximately 66 x 101. Gift of Friedman, Alschuler and Sincere.

92. Ludwig Mies van der Rohe. Two sheets: a,b) elevation studies for a proposed theatre, IIT, c. 1947. Pencil on paper, each 15.3 x 21.5. Gift of A. James Speyer.

93. Ludwig Mies van der Rohe. Two sheets: elevation and perspective studies of a proposed theatre, IIT, c. 1947. Pencil on paper, each 12.8 x 20.5. Gift of A. James Speyer.

94. Ludwig Karl Hilberseimer. Plan variation, sketch with notes, possibly IIT, c. 1947-50. Pencil on tablet paper, 21.5 x 5.2. The Hilberseimer Collection, Gift of George Danforth.

95. Ludwig Karl Hilberseimer. Study sketch, aerial view, IIT campus, c. 1947-50. Ink on insert paper, 21.5 x 28. The Hilberseimer Collection, Gift of George Danforth.

88.

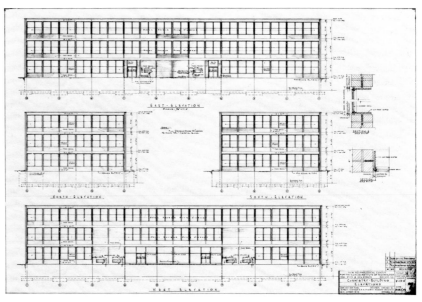

89.

96. Ludwig Karl Hilberseimer. Plan variation, possibly IIT, c. 1947-50. Pencil on
reverse of ad for *Airports Magazine*, 28 x
21.6. The Hilberseimer Collection, Gift of
George Danforth.

97. Ludwig Karl Hilberseimer. Study sketch,
plan, IIT campus, c. 1947-50. Ink on tracing
paper, 38.5 x 26.5. The Hilberseimer Collection, Gift of George Danforth.

98. Ludwig Mies van der Rohe. First scheme
perspective sketches of the chapel, IIT,
c. 1949-52. Red pencil on paper, 15.3 x 21.5.
Gift of A. James Speyer.

99. Ludwig Mies van der Rohe. Exterior per-
spective studies of the chapel, IIT, c. 1949-52.
Red pencil on note paper, 15.3 x 21.5. Gift of
A. James Speyer.

100. Ludwig Mies van der Rohe. Two sheets:
perspective sketches of the chapel, IIT,
c. 1949-52. Red pencil on paper, each 15.3 x
21.5. Gift of A. James Speyer.

101. Ludwig Mies van der Rohe. Two sheets:
a) plan and interior perspective view toward
altar; and b) interior perspective sketch toward rear of the chapel, IIT, c. 1949-52. Red
pencil on note paper, each 15.3 x 21.5. Gift of
A. James Speyer.

102. Ludwig Mies van der Rohe. Two sheets:
preliminary perspective studies of the steel-
framed interior of the chapel, IIT, c. 1949-52.
Pencil on paper, each 15.2 x 20.2. Gift of A.
James Speyer.

103. Ludwig Mies van der Rohe. Two sheets:
drawings of the interior and exterior, and
structural studies of the chapel, IIT,
c. 1949-52. Red pencil on note paper, each
15.3 x 21.5. Gift of A. James Speyer.

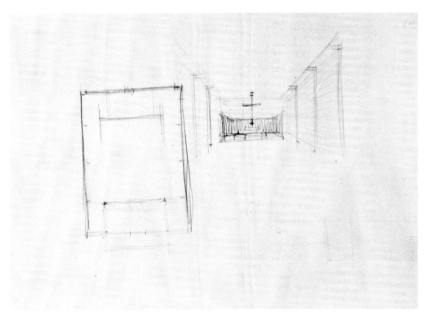

101. a

101. b

104. Ludwig Mies van der Rohe. Perspective rendering of the chapel, IIT, c. 1949-52. Pencil and charcoal on illustration board, 75.7 x 100.2. Gift of A. James Speyer.

105. Ludwig Mies van der Rohe, Architect, with Pace Associates, Associate Architects. Crown Hall, IIT, 1955. Autographed photo-panel, 89 x 117. Lent by Hedrich-Blessing, Photographers.

106. Ludwig Mies van der Rohe. Presentation plan of the School of Social Service Administration Building, the University of Chicago, c. 1964. Ink on illustration board, signed by Mies van der Rohe to Dean A. Linford, 76 x 101.5. Lent by the School of Social Service Administration of the University of Chicago.

104.

Mies van der Rohe with Dean Linford at the groundbreaking ceremony for the School of Social Service Administration Building, University of Chicago, October 17, 1963

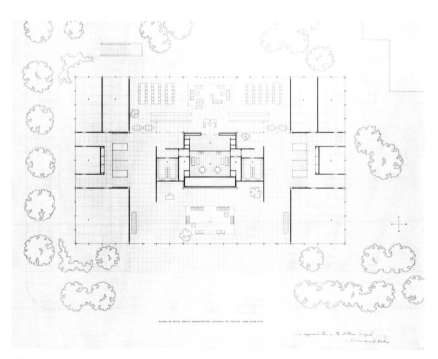

106.

C. Disciples of Modernism

107. Reginald Malcolmson. Perspective study of "An Airport," 1937. Ink and wash on paper, 66 x 49. Lent by Reginald Malcolmson.

108. George Danforth. Collage for small art museum, 1942. Photograph, halftone reproduction, ink, and paper on board, 76.7 x 101.5. Gift of George Danforth.

109. Daniel Brenner. Student collage for a concert hall, 1946, after a collage by Mies van der Rohe, 1942. Paper, oil, and wood veneer on photo enlargement, 36 x 74.2. Gift of Rachael, Jon and Ariel Brenner.

110. Ludwig Karl Hilberseimer. Chicago area; diagram for its proposed replanning; preliminary sketch. Initialed and dated November 3, 1940. For final design, see *The New Regional Pattern*, p. 158, ill. 104. Ink on tracing paper, 62 x 50.5. The Hilberseimer Collection, Gift of George Danforth.

111. Ludwig Karl Hilberseimer. Manhattan; a diagrammatic sketch of its replanning, 1944. Published in *The New City*, p. 159, ill. 109. Blue ink on tracing paper, pencil borders, 29.2 x 22.8. The Hilberseimer Collection, Gift of George Danforth.

107.

108.

112. Ludwig Karl Hilberseimer. Detroit area; diagram for its proposed replanning; preliminary sketch. Initialed and dated March 1945. Published in *The New Regional Pattern,* p. 173, ill. 114. Ink on tracing paper, 47.2 x 38.2. The Hilberseimer Collection, Gift of George Danforth.

113. Ludwig Karl Hilberseimer. Part of Eastern Europe; arterial settlement belts; preliminary sketch. Initialed and dated April 1946. Published in *The New Regional Pattern,* p. 177, ill. 115. The Hilberseimer Collection, Gift of George Danforth.

114. Reginald Malcolmson. Interior view of a theater, 1948-49, after a collage by Mies van der Rohe, 1947. Colored paper, aluminum foil collage, and India ink on illustration board, 76 x 101.5. Gift of Reginald Malcolmson.

115. Reginald Malcolmson. Perspective of the structure of a proposed Museum of Natural Sciences, 1957. Ink on paper mounted on board, 76 x 101.5. Gift of Reginald Malcolmson.

116. Reginald Malcolmson. Perspective of the interior of a proposed Museum of Natural Sciences, 1958. Photomontage and India ink on illustration board, 76 x 101.5. Gift of Reginald Malcolmson.

117. Ludwig Mies van der Rohe, Architect, David Haid, Project Architect. Proposed sculpture garden and site plan, Museum of Fine Arts, Houston, 1958. Pencil on illustration board, 76.2 x 101.6. Lent by David Haid.

118. Ludwig Mies van der Rohe, Architect, David Haid, Project Architect. Proposed sculpture garden, Museum of Fine Arts, Houston, 1958. Collage on illustration board, 76.2 x 101.6. Lent by David Haid.

109.

118.

119. David Haid and Associates. Elevation study, Abraham Lincoln Oasis, Tri-State Tollway, South Holland, Illinois, 1965. Pencil, conté, and charcoal on paper, 91 x 217.5. Gift of David Haid.

120. Gene Summers assisted by Tom Burke, both of C. F. Murphy Associates. McCormick Place, Chicago, c. 1969-70. Published in *Architectural Record,* May 1971, p. 103. Photocollage on board, 91.5 x 91.5. Anonymous gift.

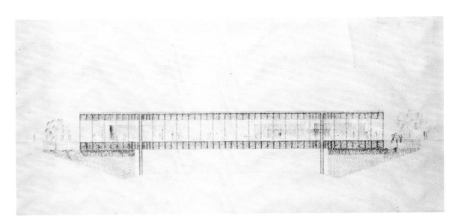

119.

120.

139

121. Gene Summers of C. F. Murphy Associates. McCormick Place, Chicago, 1970. Autographed photopanel, 61 x 101.5. Lent by Hedrich-Blessing, Photographers.

122. Reginald Malcolmson. Collage of an interior view of proposed Hall of Sport and Culture, 1971-73. Photographs, colored paper, and India ink on illustration board, 76 x 101.5. Gift of Reginald Malcolmson.

123. Dirk Lohan of Fujikawa, Conterato, Lohan and Associates, with joint venture architects Emery Roth and Sons and Tuckett and Thompson. Bird's-eye view of proposed Convention Center for New York, rendered by Dick Howard Associates, 1977-78, an adaptation of Mies van der Rohe's Convention Hall project for Chicago, 1953, applied to a New York site on the Hudson River. Ink on paper, 70.5 x 91.3. Gift of FCL and Associates.

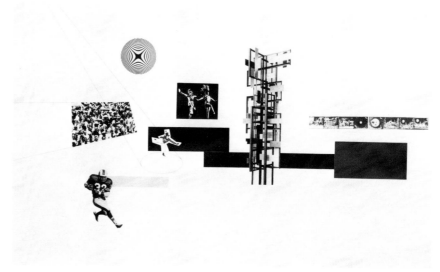

122.

123.

140

124. Peter Carter, Architect, and YRM Architects. Elevation study of the Hambro Life Centre (now Allied Dunbar Centre), Swindon, England, 1977. Photomontage, colored papers, clear acetate, and sliced foam filter, 53.3 x 76.2. Lent by Peter Carter.

124.

D. Interiors and Furniture

125. Ludwig Mies van der Rohe. Barcelona Chair, designed 1929, manufactured by Knoll Associates 1957. Tan leather, chrome steel frame, 74.9 x 74.6. Gift of Mr. and Mrs. George B. Young (1984.719). (On display in Chicago only.)

126. Ludwig Mies van der Rohe. Entrance staircase of The Arts Club, 109 East Ontario Street, Chicago, 1951. Photograph by Robert McCullough, approximately 42 x 34.5. Lent by The Arts Club of Chicago.

127. Ludwig Mies van der Rohe, assisted by Joseph Fujikawa. Model for The Arts Club, 109 East Ontario Street, Chicago, c. 1949. Masonite, cardboard, and wood, 30 x 75.5 x 144. Lent by The Arts Club of Chicago.

128. Ludwig Mies van der Rohe, Architect. Four working drawings for the Mies van der Rohe exhibition at the Fifth Biennial, Sao Paulo, Brazil, 1959, designed by Edward Austin Duckett and delineated by Philip Thrane. Ink, pencil, and pressure-sensitive colored film on mylar, each 94 x 117. Gift of Edward Austin Duckett.

129. Daniel Brenner. Details of the installation of the Louis Sullivan exhibition, The Art Institute of Chicago, 1957. Pencil on tracing paper, 63 x 94. Gift of Rachael, Jon, and Ariel Brenner.

PART IV. Ludwig Mies van der Rohe and the Reconstruction of Postwar Germany

130. Ludwig Mies van der Rohe, with Myron Goldsmith and David Haid, Project Assistants. Model of proposed National Theatre, Mannheim, c. 1952-53. Model made under the supervision of Edward Austin Duckett, Mixed media, approximately 40 x 20 x 100. Lent by Dr. Manfred Fath, Director, Städtische Kunsthalle, Mannheim.

127.

130.

131-138. Ludwig Mies van der Rohe, with Myron Goldsmith and David Haid, Project Assistants. Eight presentation drawings, by David Haid and Gene Summers, for the proposed National Theatre, Mannheim, c. 1952-53. Ink or ink and pencil on illustration board, each 76.5 x 101.5. Lent by Dr. Manfred Fath, Director, Städtische Kunsthalle, Mannheim.

131. Cross and longitudinal sections.

132. Two elevations.

133. Another set of two elevations.

134. Floor plan of the entire complex.

135. Site plan.

136. Floor plan and section of the smaller auditorium.

137. Floor plan and section of the larger auditorium.

138. Floor plan of the basement.

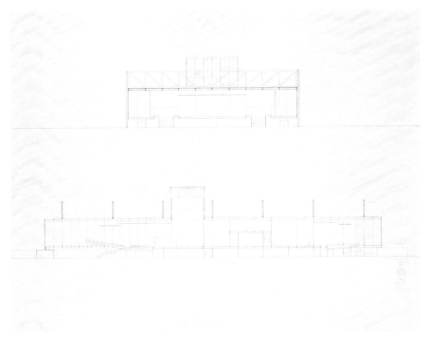

131.

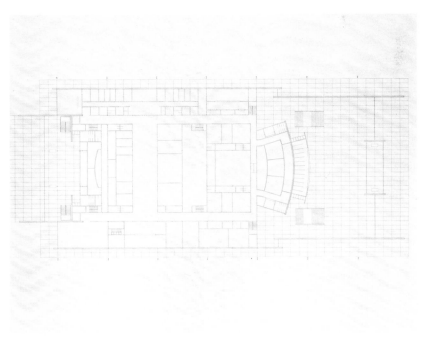

134.

139-144. Ludwig Mies van der Rohe. Six drawings, photographs, and prints for the proposed Friedrich Krupp Administration Building, Essen, 1961-63. All items lent by Dr. h. c. Berthold Beitz, President of the Alfred Krupp von Bohlen and Halbach Foundation.

139. Photograph of the model, view of the main entrance. Mounted on board, 49 x 104.5.

140. Elevation, north and west facades, dated July 31, 1961. Blackline print on mylar, 53.6 x 97.1.

141. Elevation and perspective rendering of the court yard, proposal 3, drawn by Albion. Ink and pencil on tracing paper, 35 x 68.

142. First-floor plan, signed by Mies van der Rohe. Blackline print on mylar, 73.6 x 96.8.

143. Proposals for the floor plan, shape, and distribution of offices on the third floor, scheme 2, drawn by Gene Summers. Pencil on tracing paper, 27.8 x 14.7.

144. Upper-floor plan, proposal 2, April 23, 1963, drawn by Gene Summers during a visit to Essen. Pencil on tracing paper, 41.9 x 75.6.

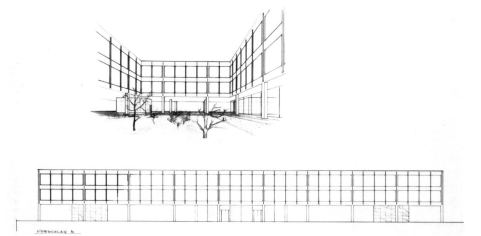

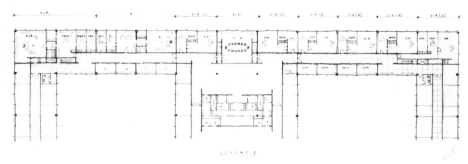

141.

143.

Left to right: Dr. Theodor Heuss, former president of the Federal Republic of Germany, Dr. h. c. Berthold Beitz, chairman of the board of directors of Friedrich Krupp GmbH., and Mies van der Rohe in the Villa Hugel in Essen, August 22, 1961

PART V. The Postwar Miesian Skyscraper

145. Ludwig Mies van der Rohe. Two sheets: highrise studies, one for a building termination, c. 1946-50. Pencil on paper, each 15.3 x 21.5. Lent by A. James Speyer.

146. Ludwig Mies van der Rohe. Two sheets: a, b) sketches for highrise towers, with curved tops, c. 1946-50. Pencil on paper, each 15.3 x 21.5. Lent by A. James Speyer.

147. Ludwig Mies van der Rohe. Two sheets: a, b) perspective sketches for a highrise building, possibly the Promontory Apartments, Chicago, c. 1946. Pencil on paper, each 15.3 x 21.5. Lent by A. James Speyer.

146. a

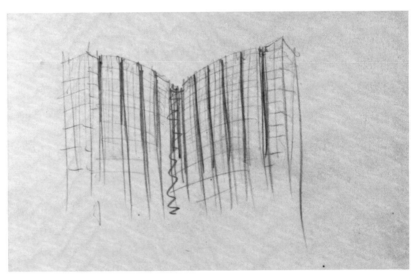

146. b

147. b

148. Ludwig Mies van der Rohe, with Pace Associates, Associate Architects. North and west elevations, the Promontory Apartments, Chicago, August 7, 1947. Pencil on linen, approximately 86.5 x 108. Lent by Charles B. Genther through the Chicago Historical Society.

149. Ludwig Mies van der Rohe, with Pace Associates, Associate Architects. Typical floor plan, Promontory Apartments, Chicago, 1947. Pencil on linen, approximately 86.5 x 108. Lent by Charles B. Genther through the Chicago Historical Society.

150. Ludwig Mies van der Rohe. Two sheets: perspective sketches, possibly for the Algonquin Apartments, c. 1948. Red pencil on paper, each 15.3 x 21.5. Lent by A. James Speyer.

151. Ludwig Mies van der Rohe. Two sheets: perspective sketches, possibly for the top of the Algonquin Apartments, c. 1948. Red pencil on paper, each 15.3 x 21.5. Lent by A. James Speyer.

152. Ludwig Mies van der Rohe, with Pace Associates, Associate Architects. South and east elevations for building no. 1 of the Algonquin Apartments, Chicago, November 19, 1948. Pencil on linen, 86.5 x 108. Lent by Charles B. Genther through the Chicago Historical Society.

153. Ludwig Mies van der Rohe, possibly with Ludwig Karl Hilberseimer. Sketch plan of a typical floor, Algonquin Apartments, Chicago, c. 1948. Pencil on tracing paper, 52 x 72. The Hilberseimer Collection, Gift of George Danforth.

154. Ludwig Mies van der Rohe. Two sheets: a, b) perspective sketches for highrise buildings, possibly the Promontory Apartments or 860-880 Lake Shore Drive, c. 1946-48. Pencil on paper, each 15.4 x 21.5. Lent by A. James Speyer.

155. Office of Ludwig Mies van der Rohe. Plot plan of 860-880 Lake Shore Drive, c. 1948. Blueprint, 61.7 x 92.5. Gift of D. Coder Taylor.

154. a

154. b

156. Ludwig Mies van der Rohe, Architect, with Pace Associates and Holsman, Holsman, Klekamp and Taylor, Associate Architects. Typical elevations of 860-880 Lake Shore Drive, Chicago, November 22, 1949. Pencil on linen, 116.4 x 91.5. Lent by Charles B. Genther through the Chicago Historical Society.

157. Ludwig Mies van der Rohe, Architect, with Pace Associates and Holsman, Holsman, Klekamp and Taylor, Associate Architects. Window details of 860-880 Lake Shore Drive, Chicago, November 22, 1949. Pencil on linen, 116.4 x 91.5. Lent by Charles B. Genther through the Chicago Historical Society.

158. Ludwig Mies van der Rohe, Architect, with Pace Associates and Holsman, Holsman, Klekamp and Taylor, Associate Architects. Photograph of 860-880 Lake Shore Drive by Hedrich-Blessing, Photographers, c. 1952. Photoprint, 32.3 x 25.1. The Burnham Library of Architecture, The Art Institute of Chicago.

159. Aerial photograph by Chicago Aerial Survey, 860-880 Lake Shore Drive, c. 1951-52. Photoprint, 28 x 35.5. Lent by Mrs. Herbert S. Greenwald.

160. Ludwig Mies van der Rohe. Barcelona Chair, designed 1929, manufactured by the Wells Furniture Makers and Jerry Griffith, Chicago, c. 1950. Leather, chrome steel frame, 76 x 75 x 75.3. Lent by George Danforth.

161. The Office of Mies van der Rohe. Anti-theft furniture anchors for the Barcelona Chairs in the lobbies of 860-880 and 900-910 Lake Shore Drive, c. 1950-55. Blackline print on paper, 21.5 x 28. Gift of Edward Austin Duckett, 1985.

162. Daniel Brenner. Two student drawings for an apartment building, c. 1949-1950. Pencil and colored pencil on yellow tracing paper, 34.5 x 71. Gift of Rachael, Jon and Ariel Brenner.

163. Daniel Brenner. Four drawings for a proposed apartment building, Chicago, 1956. Pencil on white paper, 49 x 67 and 37 x 53.5. Gift of Rachael, Jon and Ariel Brenner.

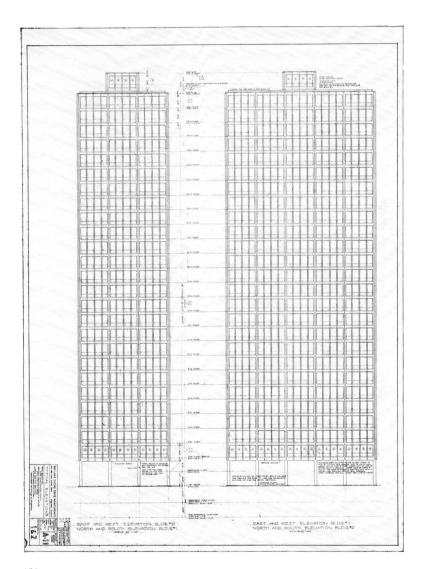

156.

164. Myron Goldsmith. Perspective rendering for "The Tall Building – Effects of Scale," a master's thesis at IIT, 1952. Ink on board, 76 x 102. Gift of Myron Goldsmith.

165. Ludwig Karl Hilberseimer, possibly with Alfred Caldwell. Studies of an apartment building, c. 1955. Blue ink on tablet paper, 20.9 x 29.6. The Hilberseimer Collection, Gift of George Danforth.

166. Ludwig Karl Hilberseimer with Ludwig Mies van der Rohe. Site plan study of Gratiot Project, Lafayette Park, Detroit, c. 1955. Ink with pencil additions on tracing paper, 53 x 41.2. The Hilberseimer Collection, Gift of George Danforth.

167. Reginald Malcolmson. Perspective view of "Metro-Linear: the Regional Metropolis," 1955. Ink on board, 76.4 x 50.9. Lent by Reginald Malcolmson.

168. Reginald Malcolmson. Elevation study of the "Expanding Skyscraper," 1961. Charcoal on tracing paper, 143.2 x 107.5. Lent by Reginald Malcolmson.

169. Ludwig Karl Hilberseimer. Chicago Near North and West Loop study, c. 1960-65. Bird's-eye view to east. Ink and pencil on tracing paper. The Hilberseimer Collection, Gift of George Danforth.

170. Ludwig Mies van der Rohe, Architect. Helmut Jacoby, Delineator. Perspective rendering of One Charles Center, Baltimore, signed and dated 1961. Watercolor on illustration board, 61 x 48.3 (image). Lent by Metropolitan Structures.

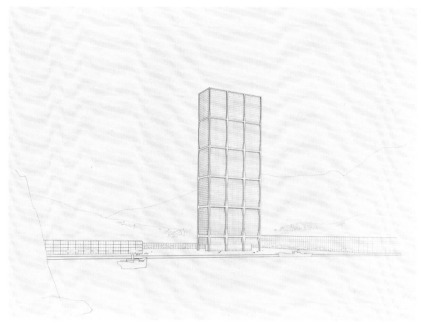

164.

167.

148

171. Ludwig Mies van der Rohe, Architect. Helmut Jacoby, Delineator. Perspective rendering of the Highfield House Apartments, Baltimore, signed and dated 1963. Watercolor on illustration board, 61 x 83 (image). Lent by Metropolitan Structures.

172. Ludwig Mies van der Rohe, Architect, with Schmidt, Garden and Erikson, C.F. Murphy Associates, and A. Epstein and Sons, Associate Architects. Everett Dirkson Federal Building, Chicago, 1969. Autographed (by Bruno P. Conterato, Sidney Epstein, and Alexander Bacci) photopanel, 72.2 x 101.7. Lent by Hedrich-Blessing, Photographers.

173. Jacques Brownson of C.F. Murphy Associates. Proposed Civic Center Plaza, c. 1964, rendered by Al Francik. Watercolor on illustration board, 104.2 x 211.3. Anonymous gift.

174. Jacques Brownson of C.F. Murphy Associates with Loebl, Schlossman and Bennett and Skidmore, Owings and Merrill, Associate Architects. Civic Center (now Richard J. Daley Center), Chicago, 1965. Autographed (by Jacques C. Brownson) photopanel, 101.7 x 76.2. Lent by Hedrich-Blessing, Photographers.

175. Ludwig Mies van der Rohe, with William Holford and Partners, Associate Architects, and Peter Carter, Project Architect. Proposed Mansion House Square, London, 1967. Three architectural models made between 1980 and 1985 by Presentation Unit, Ltd. Plexiglas, wood, and metal, 213.5 x 142.5 x 244; 91.5 x 152.5 x 122; 152.5 x 152.5 x 152.5. Lent by Peter Palumbo. (On display in Chicago only.)

173.

175.

176. Opinions in support of and in opposition to the Mansion House Square Project, 1982-84. Montage. Lent by Peter Palumbo.

177. Ludwig Mies van der Rohe, Architect, Joseph Fujikawa, Project Architect. Tan and Voss, Delineators. Perspective rendering of 111 East Wacker Drive, Chicago, 1968. Watercolor on illustration board, 80.5 x 51.8 (image). Lent by Metropolitan Structures.

178. The Office of Ludwig Mies van der Rohe, Architect, Joseph Fujikawa, Project Architect. Tan and Voss, Delineators. Perspective rendering of proposed plaza, Illinois Center, Chicago, 1970. Watercolor on illustration board, 64 x 63.5 (image). Lent by Metropolitan Structures.

178.

Appendix I: Disciples of Modernism
Biographical Sketches

1. Left to right: Edward Duckett, Alfred Caldwell, Walter Peterhans, Mies van der Rohe, Ludwig Hilberseimer, Daniel Brenner, A. James Speyer, Earl Bluestein, Jacques Brownson, James Hofgesang, c. 1948

The following biographical sketches of Mies van der Rohe's disciples and associates were written by Betty Blum, Victoria Lautman, Pauline Saliga, and John Zukowsky. Entries marked with an asterisk represent those whose oral histories are included in the project "Chicago Architects Speak: 1920-1970."

For information about this program and access to the transcripts of the oral histories, write the Department of Architecture, The Art Institute of Chicago, Michigan Avenue at Adams Street, Chicago, Illinois 60603.

Alfred S. Alschuler (1876-1940)

Alfred S. Alschuler earned his bachelor's degree and, in 1899, master's degree from the Armour Institute of Technology (later IIT). He was best known for his industrial architecture of the 1910s and 1920s, such as the Ilg Industries Building (1919). His masterpiece is the classical office building at 360 North Michigan Avenue built in 1923, originally the London Guarantee Building, and now the Stone Container Building. As a trustee of the Armour Institute, he was on the committee (with C. Herrick Hammond, Jerrold Loebl, and Alfred Shaw) headed by John A. Holabird which, with the advice of David Adler, chose Mies to be head of Armour's architecture school.

Just before his death, Alschuler prepared his own version of the campus of IIT (fig. 2), although his limestone-clad buildings indicate that his vision of modernism was more conservative than Mies's. The firm that succeeded Alschuler's – Friedman, Alschuler and Sincere – worked with Mies as associate architects on the Chemistry Building (Wishnick Hall, 1946) at IIT (see cat. nos. 89-91), and 900-910 Lake Shore Drive (1953-56) and Commonwealth Promenade Apartments (1953-56) in Chicago.

J.Z.

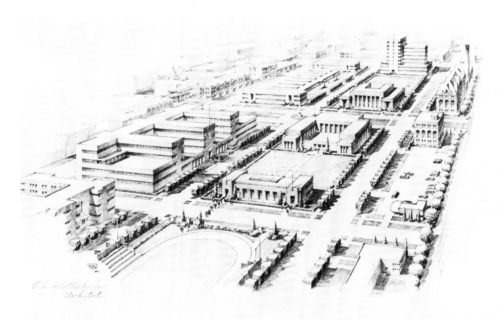

2. Alfred S. Alschuler, bird's-eye view of proposed campus at IIT, delineated by Frank O. Tupper-White, 1940

Daniel Brenner (1917-1977)

Daniel Brenner earned his Master of Architecture degree from IIT in 1949. While a student, along with A. James Speyer and James Prestini, Brenner designed a fiberglass chair for a Museum of Modern Art competition (fig. 3). He worked with Mies van der Rohe until the late 1950s, when he began an architectural practice with Dorothy Turck. It was then that he began to concentrate on historic buildings, an interest that resulted in the design of the 1957 exhibition "Louis Sullivan and the Architecture of Free Enterprise" at The Art Institute of Chicago (cat. no. 129). From 1961 until his death, Brenner was a partner

in the firm of Brenner, Danforth and Rockwell, and his work with them included renovations to the landmark Madlener House (1963) in Chicago for the Graham Foundation's headquarters, and alterations to the lobby of Adler and Sullivan's Chicago Stock Exchange Building (1965) before its demolition. One of his last works included a house and Miesian guest house (1974; figs. 4, 5; cat. no. 81) on his farm in Ellison Bay, Wisconsin.

J.Z.

3. A. James Speyer, Daniel Brenner, and James Prestini, fiberglass chair, Museum of Modern Art competition entry, 1947-48

4. Daniel Brenner, Guest House on the Brenner property with the main house (the Tower) in the background, Ellison Bay, Wisconsin, 1974

5. Daniel Brenner in the doorway of the Guest House, 1975

Jacques C. Brownson (born 1923)

Jacques Brownson was a student at IIT in the early 1940s, but he did not earn his degree until he returned from military service in World War II, when he was awarded a Bachelor of Architecture in 1948 and a master's in 1954. With his IIT colleagues Ludwig Hilberseimer, Alfred Caldwell, Earl Bluestein, and Reginald Malcolmson, Brownson prepared a plan for the South Side of Chicago in 1957 that was sponsored by the Southside Planning Board. Moreover, he was one of the very few IIT students to construct his master's thesis – a "Steel and Glass House" (figs. 6, 7) built in Geneva, Illinois, whose planning relates to Mies's Farnsworth House (1946-51) in Plano,

but whose roof is suspended from steel frames, much as the early studies for Mies's 50 by 50 House project (1950-51) and Crown Hall (1950-56) at IIT. But Brownson's most famous building is the 1965 Chicago Civic Center (now, the Richard J. Daley Center, fig. 8; cat. nos. 173, 174), which was a joint venture with C.F. Murphy Associates, Supervising Architects, Loebl, Schlossman and Bennett and Skidmore, Owings and Merrill, Associate Architects. Brownson presently lives and works in Denver.

J.Z.

6. Jacques Brownson, "Steel and Glass House," Geneva, Illinois, under construction, 1952

7. "Steel and Glass House," 1952-54

8. Jacques Brownson of C.F. Murphy Associates, Chicago Civic Center (now Richard J. Daley Center), 1965

Werner Buch (born 1917)*

After attending the Technische Hochschule in Berlin from 1936 to 1938, Werner Buch came to America, where he met Mies van der Rohe in 1939. He studied with Mies at the Armour Institute of Technology (later IIT) in the school year 1940-41, when the School of Architecture was housed at The Art Institute of Chicago. It was there that Buch once heard Mies admonish a student who asked "What is functionalism?" with the answer "Sweeping dirt is functionalism!" Unable to get his passport extended by the German Consulate, Buch returned to Berlin in 1941, via Tokyo and Moscow, provided by Ludwig Hilberseimer with introductions to Tetsuro Yoshida and El Lissitzky. He brought photographs of Mies's work to a surprisingly interested Heinrich Tessenow, Buch's former professor in Berlin, and the latest news of Mies in America to Mies's colleague and friend Lilly Reich. Buch maintained a friendship with her throughout the war until her death in 1947. Despite the official condemnation of Miesian modernism in Nazi Germany, Buch's training under Mies impressed the Austrian architect Lois Welzenbacher, who hired Buch to work on aircraft factories with him from 1941 through 1943, when Buch entered military service. After the war, Buch's fluency in English enabled him to work on the German radio news service, then being supported by American authorities. At the same time, he continued his architectural studies, mainly with Ernst Neufert, and graduated from the Technische Hochschule in Darmstadt in 1952. He received his doctorate there in 1961 and is currently professor honoris causa. Since 1955, in addition to his teaching, Buch has practiced architecture in Darmstadt, where he resides today.

J.Z.

155

Alfred Caldwell (born 1903)*

Alfred Caldwell was an assistant to the landscape architect Jens Jensen from 1926 to 1931, and practiced landscape architecture on his own in the early 1930s, as well as with park districts in Chicago and Dubuque, Iowa, during the mid- to late 1930s. During World War II he was a civil engineer with the War Department and, in 1944, he came to IIT to study with Mies van der Rohe and Ludwig Hilberseimer. After receiving his master's degree from IIT in 1948, he continued to teach there and work with Mies and Hilberseimer as a landscape architect and consultant on various projects such as IIT's campus and Lafayette Park (1955-56) in Detroit. He also taught at Virginia Polytechnic Institute and the University of Southern California (1965-73) and worked with the Chicago Planning Commission (1960-64). Since 1973 he has been in private practice in Bristol, Wisconsin.

J.Z.

Peter Carter (born 1927)

Peter Carter was born in London and he earned his diploma in architecture at the Northern Polytechnic, London. He worked for Maxwell Fry and Jane Drew's office in London, the Housing Division of the London County Council's Architects' Department, and Eero Saarinen in Bloomfield Hills, Michigan. He received his master's degree under Mies van der Rohe at IIT in 1958. He then joined Mies's office, became an associate of the firm, and was project architect for Toronto Dominion Centre (1963-69) and the Mansion House Square project (1967; cat. nos. 175, 176) in London. After practicing in Canada during the early 1970s, he returned to London in 1975 to set up his own office with Dennis Mannina, a former colleague from Mies's office. Peter Carter's office (in association with YRM) is responsible for the design of the Hambro Life Centre (1977-80; now Allied Dunbar Centre) in Swindon, England (fig. 9; see cat. no. 124). Other professional activities have included further buildings for Hambro Life, lectures at University College, Dublin, contributions to radio and television programs, and publications for various books and articles, including a book, *Mies van der Rohe at Work*, published in 1974.

J.Z.

9. Peter Carter, Architect, and YRM Architects, Hambro Life Centre (now Allied Dunbar Centre), Swindon, England, 1977-80

George Edson Danforth (born 1916)*

George Danforth had been studying architecture for two years at the Armour Institute of Technology (IIT after 1940) when Mies was appointed Director of the Department of Architecture in 1938. In 1939, while an undergraduate, Danforth became Mies's first draftsman and worked on the early planning stages and several buildings of Mies's first major American commission, the new campus for IIT. Danforth completed his Bachelor of Architecture degree under Mies in 1940 and subsequently did three years of graduate work and taught architecture classes at IIT (see fig. 10). After serving two years in the armed forces, he returned to teach at IIT in 1946. In 1953, Danforth was hired to establish a new school of architecture at Case Western Reserve University in Cleveland, and thereby was able to carry the influence of Mies and Hilberseimer as educators to another school of architecture. After Mies retired from teaching at IIT in 1958 and Reginald Malcolmson was named acting director for one year, Danforth returned to the school to head the Department of Architecture in 1959. In 1961, he joined Daniel Brenner and H.P. Davis Rockwell in an architectural partnership, succeeded in 1979 by the firm Danforth, Rockwell, Carow. Danforth retired as Dean of the College of Architecture at IIT in 1981.

P.S.

10. Left to right: A. James Speyer, Mies van der Rohe, and George Danforth, in a Fourth Year Studio Critique, 1939

Edward Austin Duckett (born 1920)

After attending Western Kentucky State Teacher's College and serving in the military, Edward Duckett came to IIT to study with Mies in 1944 as an undergraduate. He taught architectural courses at IIT beginning in 1945 while working in Mies's office. Duckett led Mies's furniture redevelopment program, worked as draftsman, delineator, and job captain, and he supervised the creation of study and presentation models for virtually all of Mies's projects from the mid-1940s to 1966 (see figs. 11-12), including several models for the IIT campus and buildings, Farnsworth House (1946-51), Promontory Apartments (1946-49), 860-880 Lake Shore Drive (1948-51), and the Seagram Building (1954-58) in New York. When Mies received the commission for the Seagram Building, Duckett opened Mies's New York office. Duckett worked in Mies's office until 1966 when Mies's health was failing and his influence on design projects was lessening. Duckett went with other Miesian architects to the largest architectural firm in Chicago, Skidmore, Owings and Merrill, where he was senior architect until his retirement in 1984. He now lives in Bowling Green, Kentucky, with his wife Blanche.

P.S.

11. Promontory Apartments, Chicago, 1946-49, model

12. Caine House project, Winnetka, Illinois, 1950, model

Joseph Fujikawa (born 1922)

Joseph Fujikawa began the study of architecture at the University of Southern California in 1940, and in 1943 he came to Chicago to complete his architectural work under Mies van der Rohe at IIT. When Mies's first draftsman, George Danforth, entered military service in 1944, Fujikawa joined Mies's office (see fig. 13), and he maintained a lasting association with the firm. Fujikawa was involved in the planning and design of thirteen educational, research, laboratory and housing facilities constructed on the campus of IIT. He participated in Mies's first executed highrise building, Promontory Apartments (1946-49) in Chicago, as well as other Chicago apartment buildings that followed, including 860-880 Lake Shore Drive (1948-51), and 900-910 Lake Shore Drive (1953-56). For the McCormick House in Elmhurst, Illinois (1951-52; fig. 14), Fujikawa served as project architect. He was also actively involved in all the developer-sponsored urban renewal projects undertaken during this period, including Lafayette Park (1955-63) in Detroit; Pavilion Apartments and Colonnade Apartments (1958-60) in Newark, New Jersey; One Charles Center (1960-63) and Highfield House (1962-65) in Baltimore; and Westmount Square (1964-68) and Nuns' Island (1966-69) in Montreal; as well as the master plan and first office tower for the Illinois Center development (see fig. 15; cat. nos. 177, 178) in Chicago, begun in 1967. In 1969, before Mies's death, Fujikawa became one of the partners in The Office of Mies van der Rohe, and, in 1975, he continued as a principal in the successor firm, Fujikawa, Conterato, Lohan and Associates. In 1982 Fujikawa formed his own firm with a long-time associate, Gerald L. Johnson.

P.S. (assisted by Claire Rose)

13. Joseph Fujikawa, c. 1950

14. Mies van der Rohe, assisted by Joseph Fujikawa, McCormick House, Elmhurst, Illinois, 1951-52

15. Mies van der Rohe, Architect, with Joseph Fujikawa, Project Architect, Illinois Center, Chicago (begun in 1967)

Charles Booher Genther (born 1907)

While he was studying architectural engineering at the University of Oklahoma, the effect of hearing Bertrand Goldberg speak on prefabricated housing and seeing a photograph of Mies van der Rohe's Barcelona Pavilion combined to inspire Charles Genther to join the modern architectural movement and study with Mies at the Armour Institute of Technology (later IIT). Genther's graduate study with Mies from 1939 to 1943 reinforced his long-standing interest in minimal building technique. After working at Skidmore, Owings and Merrill in 1942-43, and Holabird and Root in 1945, Genther organized Pace Associates in 1946 to collaborate with Mies, an association that continued for the next ten years. During that time some of Mies's most noted and innovative buildings, such as Crown Hall (1950-56) at IIT, Promontory Apartments (1946-49), Algonquin Apartments project (1948-51), and 860-880 Lake Shore Drive (1948-51) were built in Chicago (see fig. 16). Genther contributed working drawings, mechanical systems, and cavity wall construction to these projects and functioned as architect-in-charge at Promontory Apartments. Less well known is that he donated his fee for Crown Hall toward its construction. The influence of Genther's training with Mies continued throughout his career and is evident in projects by Pace Associates in the years following its collaboration with Mies, including some of the Illinois tollway restaurants and several towns Genther planned and built in Minnesota and Michigan. In 1966 Genther devoted himself to teaching architecture at the University of Illinois at Chicago, a post he held until his retirement in 1981.

B.B.

16. Left to right: Mies van der Rohe with Charles Genther and a contractor at 860-880 Lake Shore Drive, during construction

Myron Goldsmith (born 1918)*

Myron Goldsmith's dual role as architect and structural engineer was set early in his career. He was educated at the Armour Institute of Technology (later IIT) from 1935 to 1940, worked in the office of Prairie School architect William F. Deknatel in 1941, and worked as structural engineer for the Army Corps of Engineers and the Navy Bureau of Yards and Docks from 1942 to 1944. These experiences provided the background out of which emerged Goldsmith's strong commitment to a structural, rational approach to architecture. After Goldsmith had gained engineering experience in the Army Corps of Engineers, he joined Mies's office in 1946, where he worked for seven years (see fig. 17). During this time, Goldsmith completed his master's degree, his thesis project being "The Tall Building – Effects of Scale" (cat. no. 164). He also worked on important buildings on the IIT campus, and, in 1950-51, superintended construction at the Farnsworth House. In 1953 Goldsmith left Chicago to study in Rome with Pier Luigi Nervi, where he explored the possibilities of reinforced concrete in bridge and building construction. Goldsmith returned to the United States in 1955 and joined the San Francisco office of Skidmore, Owings and Merrill where he was chief structural engineer. In 1958 he moved from structural engineering to architecture when he joined the Chicago office. He was made a general partner in 1967, and retired in 1983. At Skidmore, Owings and Merrill, he was known as an advocate of a rational approach to building and was regarded as one of the major talents of the firm. Goldsmith's award-winning projects include: the Brunswick Office Building (1966) in Chicago; Solar Telescope (1962) in Kitt Peak, Arizona; Oakland Alemeda County Coliseum (1966) in Oakland, California; the *Republic* newspaper plant (1971; fig. 18) in Columbus, Indiana; United Airlines Executive Office Building (1962) in Elk Grove, Illinois. Goldsmith has been a professor at IIT since 1960, mainly advising graduate students on large-scale projects, and has been a visiting professor at Harvard University Graduate School of Design (1982-83) and at Huazhing University of Science and Technology in China (1985). He continues to teach and is currently working on a book about his architecture and ideas.

B.B.

17. Left to right: Ludwig Hilberseimer, Mies van der Rohe, and Myron Goldsmith in Mies's office, with model of Mannheim Theatre (cat. no. 130), c. 1953

18. Myron Goldsmith, the *Republic* newspaper plant, Columbus, Indiana, 1971

David Haid (born 1928)

David Haid left his native Canada specifically to study with Mies van der Rohe at IIT, where he received his Master of Science in Architecture in 1953. Shortly after entering the graduate program, Haid joined Mies's office staff and remained with the firm for nine years. During this period he contributed to a variety of Mies's most admired projects, and served as project architect for several IIT campus buildings between 1950 and 1956, the Chicago Convention Hall project (1953-54), and the Museum of Fine Arts (1954-58) in Houston (figs. 19, 20; cat. nos. 117, 118). Haid was also involved with other projects during his years with Mies, including the proposed National Theatre (1952-53) in Mannheim, West Germany, and the Seagram Building (1954-58) in New York. In 1960, he moved to Houston and established a partnership with the firm of Cowell-Neuhaus, producing such award-winning buildings as the McAllen State Bank (1961) in McAllen, Texas, and the Texas Gulf Oil Building (1962) in Midland. Returning to Chicago in 1963, Haid set up his own firm. His buildings include the Plastofilm Industries Factory (1964) in Wheaton, Illinois; the Abraham Lincoln Oasis (1965-67; cat. no. 119) in South Holland, Illinois; and the 1974 pavilion at the Rose Residence (fig. 21; cat. nos. 78-80) in Highland Park, Illinois. Haid currently lives in Evanston, Illinois, in an award-winning residence that he designed and built in 1968.

V.L.

19. Mies van der Rohe with David Haid at the opening of Cullinan Hall, October 1958

20. Mies van der Rohe, assisted by David Haid, Cullinan Hall, Museum of Fine Arts, Houston, Texas, 1954-58

21. David Haid, pavilion at the Rose Residence, Highland Park, Illinois, 1974 (cat. no. 78)

Ludwig Karl Hilberseimer (1885-1967)

Ludwig Hilberseimer studied architecture at the Technische Hochschule in Karlsruhe, Germany, and was active after World War I with the revolutionary Novembergruppe and the Berlin Movement. During the 1920s he was a prolific art and architectural critic, exhibition designer, and author of major works such as *Groszstadtarchitektur* and *Internationale Neue Baukunst* (both 1927). In 1927, he designed a house in Weissenhofsiedlung in Stuttgart, which was coordinated by Mies van der Rohe, and in 1928 he was appointed master of housing and city planning at the Bauhaus. He worked there until 1938 when he fled Nazi Germany for Chicago to teach with Mies van der Rohe at the Armour Institute of Technology (later IIT; fig. 22). In addition to teaching, Hilberseimer continued to theorize and publish such works as *The New City* (1944), *The New Regional Pattern* (1949), *The Nature of Cities* (1955), *Entfaltung einer Planungsidee* (1963), and *Contemporary Architecture: Its Roots and Trends* (1964). Hilberseimer also wrote a monograph on Mies van der Rohe in 1956 and worked with him on the planning of the housing at Lafayette Park in Detroit in 1955 (cat. no. 166).

J.Z.

22. Ludwig Hilberseimer with an unidentified student in a studio at IIT, c. 1953

Dirk Lohan (born 1938)

Dirk Lohan graduated from the Technische Hochschule in Munich in 1962 after starting his architectural education at IIT in 1957 under his grandfather, Mies van der Rohe. He returned to Chicago from Munich soon after graduation to work in Mies's office, where he assisted in the design of the Duquesne University Science Center (1962) in Pittsburgh and the University of Chicago's Social Service Administration Building (1964), and served as project architect for the New National Gallery (1962-67; fig. 23) in Berlin, and the unexecuted Mansion House Square and Office Tower project (1967) in London. The Office of Mies van der Rohe remained in operation for six years after Mies's death under the supervision of Lohan with Bruno Conterato and Joseph Fujikawa, until 1975. After that time, the three partners formed Fujikawa, Conterato, Lohan and Associates, which continued until 1982 when Fujikawa left the partnership. In 1977, the City of New York, under Mayor Abraham Beame, asked Lohan to adapt Mies's 1953-54 Chicago Convention Hall design to a specific site on the West Side of Manhattan (cat. no. 123). (Any plans the city may have had for using Mies's design for this project died when Beame lost his bid for reelection to the present mayor, Ed Koch.) Lohan's design work includes the McDonald's Headquarters begun in 1983 in Oak Brook, Illinois, and the TRW Headquarters (1982-85; fig. 24) in Lyndhurst, Ohio, neither of which is strictly Miesian in character. In 1986 Dirk Lohan changed the name of his firm to Lohan Associates, with offices in Chicago and Dallas.

J.Z.

23. Mies van der Rohe with Dirk Lohan (right) and Stephan Waetzoldt, General Director of the German Federal Museums in Berlin, 1967

24. Dirk Lohan, TRW Headquarters, Lyndhurst, Ohio, 1982-85

Reginald Francis Malcolmson (born 1912)*

Reginald Francis Malcolmson was born and educated in Dublin, and began the study of architecture in Belfast, Ireland, in the 1930s. He spent fourteen years practicing architecture in a traditional vein before photographs of Weissenhofsiedlung in Stuttgart, the published work of Erich Mendelsohn and Walter Gropius, and especially Mies van der Rohe's crystalline, precise Minerals and Metals Research Building (1942-43) so deeply impressed Malcolmson that he left a successful private practice in Dublin in 1947 to study with Mies. After earning a master's degree in 1949, Malcolmson worked on design projects with Mies, Hilberseimer, and Konrad Wachsmann. Malcolmson's most important contribution is as an architectural educator: first at IIT in the Department of Architecture and City Planning as a faculty member from 1949 to 1964, administrative assistant to Mies from 1953 to 1958, and acting director of the department in 1958-59; and then at the University of Michigan as Dean of the College of Architecture and Design from 1969 to 1974, and as a professor from 1974 to 1984. Equally important is Malcolmson's commitment to visionary architecture, an interest that dates from childhood when aviation and structural projects held endless fascination for him. His visionary projects, such as "Metro-Linear: the Regional Metropolis (fig. 25; cat no. 167); the Museum of Natural Sciences (cat. nos. 115, 116); and Hall of Sport and Culture (cat. no. 122) are unbuilt, but, according to Malcolmson, all have the potential to be realized. He compares these projects to Mies's glass skyscraper designs of 1921-22 and 860-880 Lake Shore Drive (1948-51), which drew upon those earlier designs.

B.B.

25. Reginald Malcolmson discussing details of the model "Metro-Linear: the Regional Metropolis" with an IIT student, shortly after its completion in Crown Hall, c. 1960. The model was included in the exhibition "Visionary Architecture" at the Museum of Modern Art.

Lilly Reich (1885-1947)

Lilly Reich studied with Josef Hoffmann in the Wiener Werkstätte in 1902. She is best remembered for her interior design activity with the Deutscher Werkbund, where she was named to its board in 1921 and where she designed a series of exhibits from 1924 to 1927. Reich was both personally and professionally involved with Mies van der Rohe. She was the only woman to have developed a close professional relationship with Mies. Under her influence, Mies's command of interior detail blossomed. Together they designed the Silk and Velvet Cafe at the Exposition de la Mode in Berlin in 1927, a project which evidences Mies's maturing concept of space. They also worked together on later projects such as the Berlin Building Exposition of 1931. When Mies moved to Chicago in 1938, Reich visited him once, but decided to return to Berlin, where she resided until her death.

J.Z.

A. James Speyer*

26. A. James Speyer, private residence in Pittsburgh, 1954

A. James Speyer was Mies's first graduate student at IIT and a long-time friend and colleague. Speyer received a Bachelor of Science degree from Carnegie Institute of Technology, studied at Chelsea Polytechnique in London and the Sorbonne in Paris, and came to IIT in 1939 specifically to study with Mies. After serving five years in the armed forces, Speyer returned to IIT in 1946 to teach architectural design and open a private architectural practice which concentrated primarily on residential projects. He designed elegantly detailed residences, such as parts of the Suzette and Victor Zurcher House (1950) in Lake Forest and their apartment in Chicago (1956); the Stanley Harris Residence (1953) in Winnetka and the Joel Sammet Residence of the same year in Highland Park; the Ben Rose Residence (1952; see cat. nos. 76, 77) in Highland Park; the project for the Solomon B. Smith Residence in Lake Forest (1953); a private residence in Pittsburgh (1954; fig. 26); the Herbert S. Greenwald penthouse (1959); and the residence of Mrs. Alexander Speyer in Pittsburgh (1960). These reflected the Miesian style while continually diverging from it into new expressions. Speyer ended his eleven-year Chicago architectural practice in 1957 when be became a visiting professor at the Polytechnic Institute of National University of Athens. When Mies retired from teaching in 1958, Speyer held his teaching position in the graduate school at IIT until he left the field of architectural education in 1961 to become Curator of Twentieth-Century Painting and Sculpture at The Art Institute of Chicago. Speyer continues to practice architectural design through his complex, architectonic exhibition installations at the Art Institute, one of the most important of which was a major retrospective of the career of his mentor, Mies van der Rohe, in 1968.

P.S.

Gene Summers (born 1928)*

Gene Summers came to IIT to do graduate work with Mies in 1949. Summers worked in The Office of Mies van der Rohe after 1950, a time when the office was very busy with some of Mies's most important commissions, including Crown Hall (1950-56) at IIT; Lafayette Park (1955-56) in Detroit; the Seagram Building (1954-58) in New York; the Bacardi Building (1957-61) in Mexico City; the proposed Krupp Building (1961-63) in Essen, West Germany; the New National Gallery (1962-67) in Berlin; and the Federal Center (1959-73) in Chicago. After some fifteen years in Mies's office, Summers resigned in 1965 and, for a short time, opened his own office and hired as his only draftsman a young architect, Helmut Jahn. Shortly thereafter, in 1967, Summers became a partner in charge of design at C.F. Murphy Associates, where he remained until 1973. Unlike many of Mies's disciples who went on principally to teach architecture, Summers concentrated primarily on design, and his Miesian training is evident in such beautifully detailed and structurally expressive buildings as the 1970 McCormick Place Convention Center (fig. 27; cat. nos. 120, 121) on Chicago's lakefront and the Kemper Arena (1973) in Kansas City, Missouri.

P.S.

27. Gene Summers of C. F. Murphy Associates, McCormick Place Convention Center, Chicago, 1970

Appendix II: Mies van der Rohe and the 1928 Stuttgart Competition

by John Zukowsky and Ines Dresel

Numerous books on Mies van der Rohe list his 1928 project for a bank and office building in Stuttgart, but few discuss it. Notable exceptions are the 1968 exhibition catalogue by A. James Speyer and Frederick Koeper, and, more recently, Franz Schulze's biography, which groups Mies's unsuccessful competition entry (see cat. no. 25) with three of his other commercial projects from this year, the most important being the proposed remodeling of the Alexanderplatz in Berlin. Both of these sources acknowledge that the projects prefigure later American work by the master in the use of a metal and glass curtain wall over concrete slab construction of a rectangular block. Schulze further observes that a photomontage of the Stuttgart project bears the name of the C & A Brenninkmeyer clothing store above that of the savings bank.[1] But the story of this competition has never been explored, and it awaits scholarly investigation and publication. For now, we publish, for the first time, some of the official report and visual documents related to the competition. These items were rescued from destruction some twenty-five years ago by Martin Werwigk, architect of the Württembergische Landesbank. They were located for this exhibition by Ines Dresel, and the excerpts from the official record of the competition have been translated by Ariane Nowak and Robert V. Sharp. Our intention is to summarize the circumstances of this competition in order to make others aware of the context of Mies's project and to encourage further investigation and analysis of the competition and its entries in relation to Mies van der Rohe's design. Ines Dresel is currently preparing such an investigation on the implications of the final award and the building actually constructed.

The competition itself was open to all architects in the province of Württemberg; a number of other individuals and firms were encouraged to compete as well. Entries for this proposed bank and office building, which was to replace tenement houses at the prominent intersection of Lautenschlager Street and Hindenburg Place, were received from August 21 through December 1, 1928. More than eighty entrants attempted to provide a solution to the problem addressed by the competition, often incorporating multiple uses within the project, such as apartments, restaurants, cafes, theaters, and stores. The jury, mostly bank and local officials with some architectural professors, met on December 20 and 21, 1928, and premiated two first prizes, one second, and three third prizes. In addition, they awarded the equivalent of honorable mention to three other competitors by purchasing their designs.

First prizes were awarded to G. Schleicher of Stuttgart with K. Gutschow of Hamburg (cat. no. 21), and to Ernst Stahl of Düsseldorf (cat. no. 23). Second prize was given to Heinz Wetzel and A. Schuhmacher (cat. no. 24), whereas third-prize citations went to Paul Bonatz and F. E. Scholer of Stuttgart (cat. no. 17), Carl Krayl of Magdeburg (cat. no. 20), and Richard Döcker of Stuttgart (cat. no. 18). Mies van der Rohe's entry (cat. no. 25) was among those that were considered to have merit, and, thus, was purchased for 1,500 M (the equivalent of $357 in 1928, or approximately $2,300 today.)[2] Unlike the prize-winning designs, Mies's proposal did not sufficiently take into account the site as regards building height and horizontality, and the judges criticized details of his plans and his glass and metal elevation. Yet, they awarded the first prize to the modernist designs by Schleicher and Gutschow and Stahl. The latter's "glass architecture" was considered quite elegant. These awards indicate that the jury was not prejudiced against contemporary design. On the surface, their criticisms of Mies seem rational and not politically motivated. After all, conservative architect Paul Bonatz, Mies's arch-enemy, also failed to gain first prize, placing third instead.[3] Nevertheless, we do not yet know enough about the career and interpersonal dynamics of the jurors in relation to the other premiated entrants, with possibly the exception of Bonatz, Krayl, and

Döcker.[4] There may well have been some bias against Mies's entry, since he was a prominent and controversial figure in Stuttgart's architectural community, following his coordination of the Weissenhofsiedlung complex in 1927.

A contemporary news article about the Hindenburgplatz competition noted that "the natural and beautiful background of the place, the hills in the distance, should not be hidden behind any kind of skyscraper," and, after commenting favorably on Bonatz's proposal, the writer suggested that Mies's entry marred the site because the "Dutchman Mies van der Rohe did not consider the already existing buildings at Hindenburgplatz sufficiently."[5] These buildings included the nearby neo-Romanesque railroad station by Bonatz and Scholer from 1911-28 and the adjacent Friedrichsbau, or Hindenburgbau, from about 1900, with its rounded entrance arches. Another reviewer of the competition stated that Mies "showed us his favorite idea of a glass building once more,"[6] thereby suggesting that Mies's proposal was easily recognizable and, perhaps, just as easily dismissed or premiated at a lower level. Were the winners also easily recognized? Again, not enough is known about the local situation and the principals involved. Despite local criticism of Mies's design, several avant-garde art and architecture periodicals published his competition entry and defended the boldness of his proposal in not being contextual.[7]

After the competition winners were announced, the entries were displayed in "the new exhibition building opposite the national theatre."[8] But the bank and office building itself was not constructed to any of the designs awarded first prizes. Instead, Bonatz and Scholer received the commission, and their project stands today as the Zeppelinbau, a structure that was added to in recent years by Martin Werwigk, Jürgen Ulmer, and Eberhard Ruff for the Landesbank, Stuttgart. The final awarding of the job to Bonatz and Scholer smacks of politicizing, but, again, the full story remains to be told.[9] Suffice it to say, then, that the publication of these entries in this volume will finally give scholars the opportunity to assess Mies's contribution accurately in relation to the other submissions and the executed building.

Notes

1. A. James Speyer and Frederick Koeper, *Mies van der Rohe* (Chicago, 1968), p. 20, and Franz Schulze, *Mies van der Rohe: A Critical Biography* (Chicago, 1985), pp. 146-148, fig. 94. For the development of photomontage presentation techniques and the worker-artist in the 1920s, see Schulze, p. 51, and Eleanor M. Hight, *Moholy-Nagy: Photography and Film in Weimar Germany* (Wellesley, Mass., 1985), pp. 106-114, esp. p. 106n.1, citing Hans Richter, *Dada: Art and Anti-Art* (London, 1978), pp. 114-118. According to A. James Speyer, in an interview conducted by Pauline Saliga as part of the Art Institute's Oral History Project (see Appendix I), the later presentation collages and photo-

montages served to document the more ephemeral models for Mies's various projects.

2. See *Deutsches Geld-und Bankwesen in Zahlen, 1876-1975* (Frankfurt, 1976) and *Statistisches Jahrbuch für die Bundesrepublik Deutschland* (Stuttgart, 1985).

3. See Schulze (note 1), pp. 132-134, regarding Mies's decision to drop Bonatz from the final list of architects chosen for the Weissenhofsiedlung and Bonatz's attacks in the press on Mies.

4. For Krayl, see G. E. Konrad, *Maximilian Worm und Carl Krayl, Architekten* (Vienna, 1928), and Leo Adler, "Neubau der Allgemeinen Orstkrankenkasse in Madgeburg," *Wasmuths Monatschefte für Baukunst* 12 (1928), pp. 103-110. For Döcker's work, see "Richard Döcker: Haus in einem Weinberggarten, Stuttgart," *Das Kunstblatt*, 12 (1928), pp. 274-276, and Muriel Emmaneul, ed., *Contemporary Architects* (New York, 1980), p. 208. See Emmaneul, pp. 110-111, for information on Bonatz.

5. "Der geplante Neubau am Hindenburgplatz," *Schwäbischer Merkur*, January 3, 1929, p. 1.

6. "Der Neubau der Girozentrale, Stuttgart, am Hindenburgplatz," *Illustierte Beilage der Süddeutschen Zeitung mit Südwestdeutschem Bautennachweis*, no. 1 (January 31, 1929), p. 1.

7. Wilhelm Lotz, "Wettbewerb für ein Bürohaus am Hindenburgplatz in Stuttgart," *Die Form* 4, no. 6 (March 15, 1929), pp. 151-153, and "Mies van der Rohe: Wettbewerbsentwurf für ein Verwaltungsgebäude in Stuttgart," *Das Kunstblatt* 13 (June 1929), pp. 190-191.

8. "Der geplante Neubau" (note 5).

9. Bonatz and Scholer had previously competed for a 1915 rearrangement of the Hindenburgplatz and the redesign of a number of facades there. See Stephan Waetzoldt, ed., *Bibliographie zur Architektur im 19 Jahrhundert*, 8 vols. (Nendeln, Liechtenstein, 1977), vol. 1, entries 7121-127.

Excerpts from the Official Report of the Competition

The jury met on December 20 and 21, 1928. Acting as judges were: Burgomaster Dr. Dollinger, Chief Burgomaster Dr. h.c. Lautenschlager, Chief Burgomaster Jaeckle, District President Richter, Director Oesterle, Government Architect Daiber, City Building Director Professor Elsässer, Professor Fahrenkamp, Professor Keuerleber, Site Manager Dr. Ing. Otto.

Jury's comments on the prize-winning entries

For the entry by architects G. Schleicher, Stuttgart, and K. Gutschow, Hamburg, awarded a first prize of 6,500 M

The design shows a clear and certain grouping of the building masses. Through the setting back of some parts of the building and the building height of approximately 28 m (91 feet 10 inches), Lautenschlager Street receives a strong, emphatic beginning, which simultaneously also gives the Hindenburg building a distinguished conclusion. The façades are well articulated and the author has arranged the advertising in a place where it will have an important effect. The ground plans are useful and well thought out. Fault is found with the areas in front of the elevators, for these spaces are too small. The cash-desk with its adjoining rooms is located on the first level. That is the right place and has sufficient lighting. The arrangement of a cinema and a cabaret on the first and second basement floors is very remarkable, in consideration of the bad building land and the especially deep foundation. The upper office levels are used well and sufficiently illuminated.

For the entry by government master builder E. Stahl, Düsseldorf, awarded a first prize of 6,500 M

This proposal betrays a sure hand and a purposeful sense of organization. The double horizontal emphasis, perpendicular to the railway station and the Hindenburg building, is correctly understood as regards urban development. The ground plan is clear and practical, it provides good economical use. For the development of the adjoining sites a neat and clear division can be seen. The architectonic creation, despite the considerable mass and height of the elevation, achieves through the glass architecture an attractive lightness and an effective relaxation, which leaves the monumental dominance with the railway station as well as it produces a welcome contrast to it. The design promises quiet yet surprisingly effective advertising at night.

For the entry by professor Heinz Wetzel and government master builder A. Schuhmacher, Stuttgart, awarded a second prize of 5,000 M

This design shows clear arrangements and natural solution for urban development: a clear and simple building perpendicular to the Hindenburg building towers over the openness of the railway station plaza at the right point. The ground plan with its two buildings running parallel offers a simple and logical solution. The accounts room with its different departments is easily accessible, sufficiently illuminated and clearly arranged. The first floor is mostly used for profitable rent. The back wing contains in the upper floors the clearing house offices, while the front part is reserved for other offices. The architectonic attitude is very agreeably reserved vis-a-vis the

railway building, good in its proportions and suitable for neon signs. Especially nice will be the shopping floor and the highest floor when they are illuminated at night.

For the entry by professor Paul Bonatz and architect F. E. Scholer, Stuttgart, awarded a third prize of 3,500 M

The advantage of this design is found in the ground plan. The clearing-house rooms are arranged in a very clear way around the accounts room. Ample light is provided to all the rooms on the first floor through the large glass-roofed court; no other design has this advantage. The technique of architecture in this design makes it possible to build a light-court this big. The advantages of this layout become apparent in the remaining upper floors, too. The stairs are arranged very thoughtfully, so that large office rooms emerge. There is plenty of rentable shop space. On the appearance of the exterior, we find fault with the treatment of the corner.

For the entry by architect Carl Krayl, Magdeburg, awarded a third prize of 3,500 M

With regards to town planning, it is correct to have the building diagonally opposite the railway station, except that the height of the elevation is unnecessarily large, with too much volume facing the railway station. The arrangements on the ground plan are clear and thought out: it takes advantage of the large first floor for shops arranged in arcades; garages are in the back. The clearing-house on the second floor is basically well arranged, but somewhat less well planned in access to it. Good economical use for office and business rooms. "Streamlined and sleek" design of the façades, with effective possibilities for advertising. Interesting suggestion for urban development for the relief of the site between the railway station and Schloss Place.

For the entry by government master builder Richard Döcker, Stuttgart, awarded a third prize of 3,500 M

In this proposal it is assumed that the site includes the land of the Wulle Brewery, but this is not yet certain. No allowance was made for the fact that the abandonment of the columned hall originally proposed in the city planning would require that the front of the building on Hindenburg Place be set back accordingly. There is sufficient room for the Württemberg Saving Bank and Clearing-House on the first and second floor. The few shops on the first floor are not large enough. A big hall with stairwell at the corner of Lautenschlager Street and

Hindenburg Place would take up too much valuable space. The proposed economical use of the building complex leaves a lot of possibilities open. The proposed architectural solution in combination with the advertising is very interesting and remarkable; it satisfies the requirements very well.

For the entry by professor Alfred Fischer, Essen, awarded one purchase of 1,500 M

Like the design [by Schleicher and Gutschow], this one marks the end of the Hindenburg building very nicely. The beginning of the Lautenschlager Street gets a good accentuation, because the building at the corner is moved back and pulled up. The front walls are ideally designed for a lot of advertising varieties. The glass building at the northern end would have to be moved forward because of the overlapping. The ground plan is clear and fulfills the needs concerning location and illumination of the rooms. The upper floors are planned effectively and the floors are suitable and bright.

For the entry by professor Adolf G. Schneck, Stuttgart, awarded one purchase of 1,500 M

The author intends to set opposite the lively façade of the railway station a more reserved building. The site is used effectively. The building is placed in a way to assure perfect illumination of the backfront rooms. At the Hindenburg Place the front with the shops would have to be moved back due to the traffic situation. The author proposes to use the room not required by the clearing-house as an apartment building.

For the entry by architect Mies van der Rohe, Berlin, awarded one purchase of 1,500 M

A single, cubical building is proposed for Lautenschlager Street and Hindenburg Place, which through the projecting bodies at the rear creates a strong vertical structure. The overall solution in glass walls is interesting but problematic. The height of the building is 28m (91 feet 10 inches) at the corner. Such a high elevation as this can only be justified if the height that is planned for the Hindenburg building is reduced. In this case urban development would gain a good spot at Hindenburg Place. The ground plan is not perfect. The banking hall is inadequately illuminated. The vault is placed too deep. The rest of the building contains shops at Lautenschlager Street and Hindenburg Place on the first floor and business rooms on the upper levels. The part of the building at Lautenschlager Street has floors beginning with the third level that are not deep enough. The superstructure does not extend over the back area after the third floor.

Statement by Mies van der Rohe submitted with his entry

The author is of the opinion that the banking house should be clearly separated from the business building. This conception is the basis for the whole project. The competition rules state that the bank should lie in the less valuable part of the site, and the author has, therefore, chosen the part at Hindenburg Place and Lautenschlager Street for business use, with the bank having but one entrance on Lautenschlager Street. The actual bank building lies parallel to Lautenschlager Street toward the courtyard. It contains all the space desired and is sufficient for its purposes.

The location of the bank buildings seems to the author no less critical that he intends to cover the whole structure, including the bank, with mirror-quality glass that has a mat finish. Thereby, a view of an unpleasant environment will be prevented, and all rooms in the complex will get excellent diffused light. Only the shops on the ground floor will have transparent glass windows. The bank as well as the business building will be skeleton constructions. There will not be any limit to the way of dividing the inner sections, and thus will guarantee the capability of transforming the divisions of the rooms for later uses.

The rules say further that the building must be suitable for the installation of advertisements. The author thinks that advertising will reach an extent that might seem unrealistic now, but that will be common within the next five years. He believes that advertising will become a factor more and more relevant in economy and that it will soon be the reason for changes in the arrangement of the façades of buildings. The author bases his arrangement of the building's exterior on this idea. He tries, as the model clearly shows, to keep the whole front empty for advertisements. Thus, he also tries to use the illumination of the interior for the effectiveness of the advertising. The building would glow at night. Any kind of advertisement could then be installed on these glowing glass walls.

Everything else becomes apparent through the plans, photographs, and model.

The following has to be said with regards to urban development: The railway station's strong grouped forecourt needs for artistic reasons an opponent that appears quiet and is made out of a seemingly monumental material that does not really compete with the sight of the railway station. The author chose glass and non-rusting steel as materials to create an impression of lightness for the building and to get a nice contrast to the fine construction of the railway station.

Photography Credits

Foreword
1. William Leftwick, gift of Edward Duckett; 2. The Art Institute of Chicago

Acknowledgments
Berko, courtesy of Dirk Lohan

Spaeth
1. Hedrich-Blessing, courtesy of David Spaeth; 2. The Hilberseimer Collection, gift of George Danforth; 3. Strähle Luftbild; 4. As published in *Das Kunstblatt*, 1927; 5. Berliner Bild-Bericht, the Hilberseimer Collection, gift of George Danforth; 6. Berliner Bild-Bericht, the Hilberseimer Collection, gift of George Danforth; 7. Curt Rehbein, the Hilberseimer Collection, gift of George Danforth; 8. Williams & Meyer, the Hilberseimer Collection, gift of George Danforth; 9. Hedrich-Blessing, the Hilberseimer Collection, gift of George Danforth; 10. Williams & Meyer, the Hilberseimer Collection, gift of George Danforth; 11. Gift of Edward Duckett; 12. Gift of Edward Duckett; 13. Gift of Edward Duckett; 14. George H. Steuer, gift of Edward Duckett; 15. Courtesy of Mrs. Herbert S. Greenwald; 16. Chicago Aerial Survey, courtesy of Mrs. Herbert S. Greenwald; 17. Balthazar Korab Ltd.; 18. Hedrich-Blessing, gift of Edward Duckett; 19. Hedrich-Blessing; 20. Gift of George Danforth; 21. Balthazar Korab Ltd.; 22. Ezra Stoller, Esto; 23. Jordan Joel Bernstein, gift of Edward Duckett; 24. Maurice Miller, courtesy of David Haid

Frampton
1. Hedrich-Blessing, courtesy of Edward Duckett and IIT; 2. Hedrich-Blessing, gift of George Danforth; 3. The Hilberseimer Collection, gift of George Danforth; 4. Hedrich-Blessing, gift of George Danforth; 5. Gift of George Danforth; 6. The Hilberseimer Collection, gift of George Danforth; 7. Courtesy of Kenneth Frampton; 8. Berliner Bild-Bericht, the Hilberseimer Collection, gift of George Danforth; 9. Michael Tropea, courtesy of IC Industries; 10. Berliner Bild-Bericht, the Hilberseimer Collection, gift of George Danforth; 11. Hedrich-Blessing, the Hilberseimer Collection, gift of George Danforth; 12. Hedrich-Blessing, the Hilberseimer Collection, gift of George Danforth; 13. Williams & Meyer, the Hilberseimer Collection, gift of George Danforth; 14. The Art Institute of Chicago, Ryerson Library; 15. Gift of George Danforth; 16. Williams & Meyer, gift of George Danforth; 17. Hedrich-Blessing, courtesy of David Spaeth; 18. Hedrich-Blessing; 19. Gift of George Danforth; 20. Hedrich-Blessing; 21. Gift of Edward Duckett; 22. Hedrich-Blessing; 23. Hedrich-Blessing, gift of George Danforth; 24. Hedrich-Blessing, gift of George Danforth; 25. Balthazar Korab Ltd.

Otto
1. Courtesy of Christian Otto; 2. Gift of George Danforth; 3. Gift of George Danforth; 4. The Hilberseimer Collection, gift of George Danforth; 5. Analysis and drawing by Mark Stankard, courtesy of Christian Otto; 6. The Hilberseimer Collection, gift of George Danforth; 7. Gift of Edward Duckett; 8. Gift of Edward Duckett; 9. Hedrich-Blessing, the Hilberseimer Collection, gift of George Danforth; 10. Hedrich-Blessing, the Hilberseimer Collection, gift of George Danforth; 11. Royal Institute of British Architects Drawings Collection; 12. Hedrich-Blessing, the Hilberseimer Collection, gift of George Danforth; 13. Balthazar Korab, Ltd.; 14. Hedrich-Blessing, the Hilberseimer Collection, gift of George Danforth; 15. As published in A. James Speyer and Frederick Koeper, *Mies van der Rohe* (Chicago, 1968); 16. Hedrich-Blessing; 17. Hedrich-Blessing, gift of Edward Duckett

Dal Co
1. Hedrich-Blessing, gift of George Danforth; 2. Gift of George Danforth; 3. Berliner Bild-Bericht, the Hilberseimer Collection, gift of George Danforth; 4. The Hilberseimer Collection, gift of George Danforth; 5. John T. Hill, Tigerhill Studio; 6. Balthazar Korab Ltd.; 7. John T. Hill, Tigerhill Studio; 8. Ezra Stoller, Esto; 9. The Art Institute of Chicago

Eisenman
1. Hedrich-Blessing; 2. Curt Rehbein, the Hilberseimer Collection, gift of George Danforth; 3. Collection of the Museum of Modern Art, New York, acquired through the Lillie P. Bliss bequest; 4. Hedrich-Blessing; 5. Berliner Bild-Bericht, the Hilberseimer Collection, gift of George Danforth; 6. Collection, Mies van der Rohe Archive, The Museum of Modern Art, New York, gift of the architect; 7. Collection, Mies van der Rohe Archive, The Museum of Modern Art, New York, gift of the architect; 8. Williams & Meyer, the Hilberseimer Collection, gift of George Danforth; 9. As published in Le Corbusier, *Early Buildings and Projects, 1912-1923* (New York and London, 1982); 10. Williams & Meyer, the Hilberseimer Collection, gift of George Danforth; 11. The Art Institute of Chicago, Ryerson Library; 12. The Art Institute of Chicago, Ryerson Library; 13. Williams & Meyer, the Hilberseimer Collection, gift of George Danforth; 14. Collection, Mies van der Rohe Archive, The Museum of Modern Art, New York, gift of the architect; 15. Hedrich-Blessing, the Hilberseimer Collection, gift of George Danforth; 16. As published in Ludwig Hilberseimer, *Mies van der Rohe* (Chicago, 1956); 17. Collection, Mies van der Rohe Archive, The Museum of Modern Art, New York, gift of the architect.

Tigerman
1. Hedrich-Blessing, courtesy of David Spaeth; 2. Library of Congress; 3. Library of Congress; 4. Hedrich-Blessing; 5. John T. Hill, Tigerhill Studio; 6. Peter Carter; 7. Courtesy of Metropolitan Structures

Catalogue
All photographs in this section are by the staff of The Art Institute of Chicago except for the following: p. 136, The University of Chicago; p. 144, Historical Archive Friedrich Krupp, GmbH, Essen; no. 11, Ute Nägele; nos. 72, 80, 130, Hedrich-Blessing; no. 175, John Donat, London; no. 178, Hedrich-Blessing

Appendix I
1. Hedrich-Blessing, gift of Edward Duckett; 2. Courtesy of IIT; 3. Courtesy of Rockwell Carow Architects; 4. George Danforth, courtesy of Rockwell Carow Architects; 5. George Danforth, courtesy of Rockwell Carow Architects; 6. Gift of Ed Duckett; 7. The Hilberseimer Collection, gift of George Danforth; 8. Hedrich-Blessing; 9. John Donat, London; 10. Courtesy of IIT; 11. Hedrich-Blessing, gift of Edward Duckett; 12. Gift of Edward Duckett; 13. Gift of Edward Duckett; 14. Hedrich-Blessing, the Hilberseimer Collection, gift of George Danforth; 15. Balthazar Korab Ltd.; 16. Gift of Edward Duckett; 17. Edward Duckett, the Hilberseimer Collection, gift of George Danforth; 18. Balthazar Korab Ltd.; 19. Maurice Miller, courtesy of David Haid; 20. Balthazar Korab Ltd.; 21. Hedrich-Blessing; 22. Gift of Edward Duckett; 23. Courtesy of Dirk Lohan; 24. Courtesy of Dirk Lohan; 25. Dan Ryan, courtesy of Reginald Malcolmson; 26. Courtesy of A. James Speyer; 27. Hedrich-Blessing

Raves for the First Edition

"This book will bring a smile to us all. We see that it is reaching out to so many people—to bring the understanding, solidity, and compassion so very needed in our society."
—Venerable Thich Nhat Hanh, Vietnamese Zen master; author of more than 50 books, including *Being Peace; The Heart of Buddha's Teaching; Living Buddha, Living Christ; The Miracle of Mindfulness*

"This book is not for idiots. It tells us what smart people want and need to know about Buddhist wisdom, history, theory, and its practice today. Gary Gach has done a fine job here, in lending a helping hand to lift ourselves toward the spiritual goal of awakened enlightenment."
—Lama Surya Das, author of *Awakening the Buddha Within; Awakening to the Sacred; Letting Go of the Person You Used to Be;* founder of the Dzogchen Center

"With great integrity and critical insight, Gary Gach immeasurably enhances authentic interfaith understanding and fellowship. *The Complete Idiot's Guide to Understanding Buddhism* is an exquisitely organized and comprehensive introduction to Buddhism that honors the intellect, illumines the spirit, and ennobles the human sojourn."
—Reverend Dorsey Blake, The Church for The Fellowship of All Peoples

"At last! *The Complete Idiot's Guide* makes Buddhism as accessible as Volkswagen repair. (Or is it the other way around?) It's so easy even a woman can do it. Not only that. Even a *man!*
—Susan Moon, author of *The Life and Letters of Tofu Roshi;* co-editor of *Being Bodies: Buddhist Women on the Paradox of Embodiment*

"If you meet the Buddha on the road—kill him! But if you meet the Buddha in the pages of Gary Gach's delightfully insightful new book, listen carefully to what he has to say. Gary is a clear voice articulating the history, culture, and universal appeal of the Dharma. This is a book for everyone: those who know a lot about Buddhism; those who know little; and those precious few who are blessed with knowing nothing at all."
—Rabbi Rami Shapiro, author of *Minyan: Ten Principles for Living a Life of Integrity; Proverbs: The Wisdom of Solomon; The Wisdom of the Jewish Sages: A Modern Reading of Pirke Avot*

"Gary Gach is like that teacher you always wanted—easygoing, full of information, able to communicate in humorous and meaningful ways, and a little bit wacky. So he's the perfect author for *The Complete Idiot's Guide to Understanding Buddhism* ... Gach brings it all together with a light touch and an enthusiasm that makes you want to get up and do something Buddhist."
—Brian Bruya, Eastern Religion Book Reviewer, Amazon.com; translator of a dozen Eastasian wisdom titles, including *Zen Speaks; The Tao Speaks; Confucius Speaks; Sunzi Speaks;* and *Words to Live By*

"What I liked best about this book is its ability to get across the incredible richness and diversity of the Buddhist experience without losing sight of the details. Expect the unexpected, expect the strangely familiar. *The Complete Idiot's Guide to Understanding Buddhism* is often illuminating, occasionally quirky, never dull. Enjoy!"
—Anthony Flanagan, Buddhism.About.com

"… Surprisingly enlightening and wonderfully accessible … this book truly shows how the complex ideas of one of the most ancient philosophies in the world can be adopted into anyone's life."
—Neela Banerjee, *AsianWeek*

"This new guide to Buddhism is lighthearted and entertaining, but also thorough, current, and very sincere. The author has brought together many aspects of Buddhist history and practice—from the precepts, and meditation, to Buddhism and science—in a very down-to-earth voice but without missing a beat."
—The Mountains and Rivers Zen Order

"… a creatively designed tour … organized in a playful yet highly efficient way … a simple yet profound mix of education and illustration along with exercises for integration … Pick a page and dive into any space …"
—Kennedy Hassett, *Creations*

"It is my belief that a book of this nature will be very helpful to people who find Buddhism complicated and confusing … You can be sure that this text will appear in my introductory class as a great and helpful aid in presenting Buddhism for beginners."
—Howard Gontovnick, Varnier College

"The best of its kind."
—Chevy Chase, comedian

"… fun, entertaining, and informative. Gary Gach hasn't dumbed down Buddhism here; he's jazzed it up. This *Idiot's Guide* covers the basic ground … doesn't lead us astray."
—*Shambhala Sun*

"It's like a college seminar on Buddhism distilled into Cliff's Notes. Before you know it, you'll be halfway through the book and down the path. It's essential reading … with incredible breadth and depth, *The Complete Idiot's Guide to Buddhism* makes Buddhism accessible, but it also makes it meaningful and fun. After reading it, you'll feel more like a genius than an idiot, but since you'll have attained a new sense of lightness and detachment, you'll realize how little either label really matters."
—Leza Lowitz, *The Japan Times*

"Gary Gach knows his stuff. Just as importantly for this book, he writes sharply, cleanly, and well. Gach's writing is elegant and sparse and the message is boiled down, never dumbed down and never, ever boring or dry."
—*January* magazine